Sexing the Trin

Sexing the Trinity

Gender, Culture and the Divine

Gavin D'Costa

scm press

0 334 02810 8

This edition first published 2000 by
SCM Press
9–17 St Albans Place London N1 0NX

SCM Press is a division of
SCM-Canterbury Press Ltd

Typeset by Rowland Phototypesetting Ltd,
Bury St Edmunds, Suffolk
Printed in Great Britain by
Biddles Ltd, Guildford and King's Lynn

for

Beryl,
Sachin and Roshan

Contents

Figures

Acknowledgments

Writing this book marks a shift in relation to my own previous theological position. Many people have helped me in the previous five years, and to them I am extremely grateful. Three institutional communities deserve special mention: Clifton Roman Catholic Cathedral, the Department of Theology and Religious Studies (Bristol University) and the Bristol Waldorf School. There are people in all three that have helped me more than they will realize. The conversations, writings and lives of the following friends have also been especially inspiring: Tina Beattie, Sarah Coakley, Sean Gill, Gerard Loughlin, Nicola Slee, Janet Martin Soskice, Brother Thomas CR and Graham Ward. Jill Rowe has been an inspired, supportive and questioning presence. My mother, father and sister have made me think about trinitarian relations in ways that they will never suspect. Thanks also to Gerard Loughlin for his inspiration for the title of this book. Without Alex Wright, the new Director of SCM Press, this book would not have been published. His support and encouragement are much valued, as is his friendship. Beryl, my wife, has been a patient and dear friend, and also severe critic, from whom I have learnt and continue to learn. Without her love and support, this book would not have been written. Sachin and Roshan, my children, have provided endless distractions from writing this book and helped me relate to my church in ways that I would never have imagined. I dedicate this book to Beryl, Sachin and Roshan, my earthly triunity.

I have tested out very slight versions of chapters 3 and 4 previously, and am grateful to the following for copyright permission: for part of Chapter 3, 'His Word or our Words?: Postmodernity's Angelic Predicament in *The Satanic Verses*', *English Literature, Theology and the Curriculum*, ed. Liam Gearon, London: Cassell 1999, pp. 265–85; for part of Chapter 4, 'The Christian Trinity: Paradigm for Pluralism', *Pluralism and the Religions: The Theological and Political Dimensions*, ed. John D'Arcy May, London: Cassell 1998, pp. 22–39. 'Rublev', quoted with kind permission from Rowan Williams, *After Silent Centuries*, Oxford: The Perpetua Press, 1994, p. 33.

Acknowledgments for copyright permission for figures 1–4:

Figure 1: Margaret Argyle, *Bosnia Christa* (copyright: Margaret Argyle, UK: 0161 225 6668)

Figure 2: Andrej Rublev, *The Trinity* (copyright: St Paul's Publications, Slough, UK)

Figure 3: Jyoti Sahi: *Abraham and Sarah Receiving the Three Angels* (copyright: Jyoti Sahi)

Figure 4: Jyoti Sahi: *The Word Made Flesh* (copyright: Jyoti Sahi)

Abbreviations

Beginning	Julia Kristeva, *In the Beginning Was Love: Faith and Psychoanalysis*
CDF	Congregation for the Doctrine of the Faith
DZ	Heinrich, *Enchiridion symbolorum*
Ethics	Luce Irigaray, *An Ethics of Sexual Difference*
EW	Luce Irigaray, 'Equal to Whom?', *The Postmodern God*, ed. Graham Ward
GCS	Die griechischen christlichen Schriftsteller
Je, Tu, Nous	Luce Irigaray, *Je, Tu, Nous – Towards a Culture of Difference*
Kristeva Reader	*The Kristeva Reader*, ed. Toril Moi
Marine	Luce Irigaray, *Marine Lover of Friedrich Nietzsche*
Moses	S. Freud, *Moses and Monotheism*
Reader	*The Irigaray Reader*, ed. Margaret Whitford
Sexes	Luce Irigaray, *Sexes and Genealogies*
Speculum	Luce Irigaray, *Speculum of the Other Women*
Thinking	Luce Irigaray, *Thinking the Difference*
This Sex	Luce Irigaray, *This Sex Which Is Not One*
Totem	S. Freud, *Totem and Taboo*

Preface

This book examines the Christian doctrine of the trinity as a cultural artefact. I assume that culture is the necessary medium for God's self-representation, and in this sense all representations of the trinity, be they in art, music, words or gesture, are susceptible to a form of theological-cultural analysis. In one sense, the very notion of theology might be understood in terms of an ecclesiological analysis of culture. But why bring together questions of gender and culture in focussing upon the trinity? The answer is simple: the church is made up of gendered persons. Furthermore, the church claims that these persons relate in particular ways that are a challenge to the world. If the church is shaped in the image of God, as are we, then the shape of God is all important. However, we cannot ignore the fact that the church's image of God has been for the most part publicly constructed by male celibate intellectuals. Hence, the way 'we' envisage the trinity is also a question about how 'we' see ourselves, which in turn is already a question about how 'we' view God. The process is inevitably circular, or, in its more constructive moments, open-ended, spiralling and dynamic, at least in so much as the least idolatrous images of God might actually refuse closure. God after all cannot be represented.

In the opening two chapters I attend to intra-trinitarian gender configurations. I do this in engagement with the French feminist psychoanalytical philosopher, Luce Irigaray. She, more than most contemporary philosophers, suggests that all language and culture is profoundly 'sexuate'. She also recognizes that the trinity is capable of providing the resources for allowing men and women to love each other, or for symbolic men to continue to murder women. This is put boldly, but I think Irigaray has a profound cultural-philosophical point. I develop her explorations by focussing on each of the persons of the trinity. In

Chapter 1 I start with the Holy Spirit. I suggest that Irigaray's approach throws light on the often bemoaned neglect of the Holy Spirit. Irigaray helps us see why this state of affairs has come about, and sends me back to the tradition to address the difficulties. Taking my cue from Irigaray, I suggest that this neglect, and the subsequent lack of 'subjectivity' of the Spirit is closely connected with the representation of women within early pagan and Enlightenment-modernist cultures. Christianity's succumbing to these modes of representation has too often meant that trinitarian theologies have helped to maintain patriarchy and idolatry. In contrast, the divine triune God might actually re-present the possibility of relations between gendered persons that are characterized by loving, forgiving, relational and redeeming indwelling – not occlusion, murder and male narcissism. In so much as the trinity is about the shape of human community, I turn to one major symbol for this community: Mary. Irigaray illuminates the vital link between the Holy Spirit and a Marian church.

I argue for the importance of Mary within the Roman Catholic tradition, and the significance of her disputed title 'Co-Redeemer'. What is true for Mary in her unique manner is also true and possible for all those who constitute the 'body of Christ': that they too are called to be co-redeemers. This is as near to divinization as Christianity can get. This Marian element is not of course exclusive to Roman Catholicism and many Christians might find hope from these traditions. I also focus on the cult of women saints within the Marian church as the 'body of Christ'. While this argument is negotiated on a field of eggshells, and advanced by a male theologian, I hope it will at least be considered. These Marian themes are an outgrowth of taking the Holy Spirit seriously. Unlike Irigaray and Christian theologians such as Leonardo Boff and Jürgen Moltmann, I resist either divinizing Mary or feminizing the Spirit. To develop this latter point, I end Chapter 1 by examining early Syrian Christianity with its alleged daring feminizing of the Spirit. Looking closely at the language of the hymns, I suggest that such images operate in complex ways. For instance, they refuse to fix gender within God, and, in practice, made very little difference to the life of women within the Syrian church. The second point reminds us that the relation between language and practice is a very fluid one!

In Chapter 2, after the Holy Spirit, I turn to Jesus and the Father. This achieves an appropriate reversal of traditional taxonomies whereby

Father and Son always come first and second, before the Spirit (who is always last). This reversal signifies a more important point in terms of my argument: the Spirit leads us into participation with Son and Father, and this participation is an ecclesial-forming event. Without the Spirit we never come to participate in the story of this Son and this Father, and never come to be children of this God. Regarding Jesus I respond to the question that Irigaray and others have posed: can a male redeemer save women? In responding to this, I first suggest that one of the primary weaknesses within Irigaray's questioning is to sometimes freeze the identification of 'gender' with 'body', so that male and female are essentialized. This 'moment' within Irigaray's work also conceals the 'phallic mother' within her texts and the problematics of her question. I then turn to the male body of Jesus and argue two things. First, that his male body was actually instrumental in bringing salvation into the world (as was Mary's female body); and secondly, the 'body of Christ' as the church is neither male nor female, but both. Jesus' gender cannot be fixed since it finds shape in 'his' body, the Marian church, which is constituted by men and women in very different roles.

In the final part of Chapter 2 I turn to the 'Father'. Following Ricoeur, I suggest that the biblical 'Father' is semantically transgressive and I develop the notion of the birth of the Father to ensure that trinitarian language about the 'Father' does not lapse into pagan trinitarian taxonomy – where father is viewed in terms of causality. In this argument I find a strong ally in Wolfhart Pannenberg, although I am critical of his resistance to alternative images and language for the person 'Father'. Pannenberg's struggle to maintain this word, and this one alone, seems to imply a univocal understanding of language which verges on idolatry.

The structure and strategy of these two chapters require some explanation. Three points are in order. First, critics may well find that my drawing from so many periods of church history, and from so many genres (theology, philosophy, liturgical texts, works of art) is prone to decontextualizing the materials and displaying a lack of specialist rigour. Regarding specialist training in all the periods covered, I plead guilty, but would ask fraternal correction. Regarding the variety, I have felt justified in moving between continents, genres and historical periods precisely to show the levels of continuity and discontinuity regarding the misogyny of the Christian tradition and to engage critically with Irigaray's wide-ranging thesis. I wanted to choose examples from different genres because my arguments concern culture in its widest sense, not just theological texts. In no sense have I sought to portray Christianity as a seamless and easy story to follow, nor that at this point in history do we have a superior vantage point to the rest of history. Critical conversation with our her-stories and histories is like all good conversation: unfinished.

Secondly, why have I allowed Irigaray to structure the questioning that is pursued? This question has ramifications for the entire book. The simple answer is that she poses very searching and difficult questions that Christianity must address. Her questions reflect three very important challenges that face western Christianity as it emerges into the twenty-first century: is Christianity irredeemably patriarchal; what is its relation to psychoanalysis; and can the churches be a location of an alternative culture in which the gospel is a light to the nations? If theologians do not address the best minds asking difficult questions, then the church has lost its salt.

The third and final question which relates to these two chapters as well as the rest of the book might be expressed: do I invoke an ideal church which does not exist? For example, when I suggest that Mary and the female saints are a resource for reconstructing female genealogies, do I fail to realize that these symbols are under the control of a powerful patriarchal institution that will not let them go? Irigaray seems to possess a profoundly Catholic sensibility when she recognizes that we can never simply create alternative cultures *ex nihilo*, but rather must work with what we have to hand, to deconstruct and question, and re-shape and re-present different possibilities. She, unlike me, has no commitment to working within the Roman Catholic tradition; but for all that, neither she nor I is in a more liberated culture. However, I do believe that the Catholic tradition has the resources to form an alternative culture, and that the church can never be defined exclusively by either the clerical hierarchy or the laity. Its mystery is precisely located in being defined and re-defined by its source: the triune God.

In Chapter 3 I remain with the questions of language, trinity, gender and psychoanalysis. However, in this and the next chapter I begin to engage with Islam, Hinduism and Judaism, both in terms of critical engagements with these traditions, but first and foremost in relation to the Christian representation of the trinity. It is not possible to deal with Christian doctrines and practices outside the context of Christianity's engagement with the cultures within which it finds itself. Hence, the movement out of traditional textbook theology in this and the next chapter. Furthermore, this chapter is an important exception within the book in that it apparently deals with a producer of culture who is manifestly not interested in Christian theology and the trinity. For reasons given below I would contest such a claim. Rushdie, like me, is concerned with language, gender and the divine and, as Augustine realized so early on in the tradition, vestiges of the trinity are to be found everywhere, even if they only become visible as such to the Christian eye.

After the focus on the three persons in chapters 1 and 2, in this chapter I implicitly turn now to questions of (subsistent) relations, mutual indwelling (perichoresis) and hypostatic identities. However, I do so without using such technical theological language, and in terms of looking at a celebrated postmodern novelist, Salman Rushdie. A curious choice? I choose his book, *The Satanic Verses*, because it allows me to look at Rushdie's fictitious investigation of Islam and male mono-theism versus trinitarian feminism. Here I explore three issues. First, Rushdie's novel shows how language itself is the source of our indwell-ing, because language is always open-ended, and can only exist in being shared. Hence, language as sign-symbol both facilitates and destroys our ability to love one another, and without language we can do neither. Outside bodily mediated language there is no salvation. Subsistent relations and perichoresis are concepts that are informed by what the ancients called 'vestiges' of the trinity, and these very concepts are found in bodily language, as Rushdie so brilliantly shows us.

Secondly, I argue that *The Satanic Verses* does for Islam what Irigaray tries to do for Christianity, and what Freud did for Judaism. I offer a close textual reading to suggest that *The Satanic Verses* is a critical re-rendering of Freud's *Moses and Monotheism*, whereby Rushdie shows that a single male God can only be 'established' at the cost of the murder of women. However, Rushdie avoids Irigaray's essentialism, and faces the phallic mother, recognizing that both women (and men) are capable of the most horrendous destructive forces. Rushdie reminds us that the repressed feminine trinity within fictitious Islam only over-throws patriarchy, but never establishes a golden age. Thirdly, I argue that in Rushdie's novel, as in the Christian narrative, the transformation of characters only happens through forgiveness and mutual love – which is always a cultural-linguistic exchange. Forgiveness is the precondition of peaceful mutual indwelling. This theme forms the bridge to the final chapter.

In Chapter 4 I turn to another cultural medium: the work of art. Most traditional philosophical theology, except for the Greek Orthodox tradition, pays little attention to the visual. In turning to three trinitarian representations in art, I pursue some of the themes I have examined so far regarding gender, occlusion, ecclesial community and the ambiguity of signs. I also introduce two more religious traditions: Judaism and Hinduism. I focus all these themes on a single narrative within Genesis 18 (a Jewish and Christian text), which is then taken up by subsequent narratives in words (the New Testament, St Augustine and the contemporary novelist, Sara Maitland), and also in art (in relation to Judaism and Hinduism). I look at two artistic depictions of this narrative, one Russian Orthodox and one Indian Roman Catholic, and show the polyvalent signification that arises in such trinitarian re-presentation. There are fragile parallels in the way that Judaism is sometimes repressed within Christianity and the way in which women have been occluded. This can be traced in the figure of Sarah within these narratives and depictions, and more so in terms of the way in which our Indian Christian artist (Jyoti Sahi) uses the iconographic traditions of Hinduism to highlight the forgotten significance of nature, and of women, within Christianity. In just such a strategy, however, Sahi also falls fowl of the danger of essentializing the feminine in the maternal and replicating Hindu symbolic patriarchy by drawing on Sāmkhya philosophy and Brāhminical iconographics. However, it is this same process of indigenization that also allows the artist to re-present an ascetic and erotic trinity which opens up new possibilities in Christian discourse and practice.

In the postscript, which is not a conclusion, I explore the notion of being sons and daughters of God, and fathers and mothers and lovers within the body of Christ, but a 'Christ' who is multi-gendered and corporate, not a singular historical person. I will develop a pneumatological vision of the church in which God's becoming incarnate in the world is always a gift and a birthing entrusted to the church. It will also be an ecclesiologically specific argument showing that such a church already exists, in fragments, as well as being profoundly perverted. The doctrine of the church as a church of saints and sinners is far too important to forget – as is the doctrine that God eludes our grasp and is pure gift.

Living in engagement with a trinitarian God within the Marian body of Christ makes for a very difficult and uncomfortable journey, but one in which Christians have no choice – unless they leave the church. Many are doing so – and for good reason. This book, written by a male Roman Catholic within the academy may not convince them otherwise, but it helped convince me that it is worthwhile remaining in such a disfigured body, for the Christian tradition also affirms that salvation comes into the world through disfigured bodies, that are glorified by God: in the unmarried pregnant Jewish girl Mary; in her son, hanging crucified on a cross; and in the lives of women and men who become co-redeemers with the triune God.

I

The Holy Spirit within a
hommosexuate trinity?

1. Irigaray's 'culture'

Luce Irigaray represents a unique confluence of different and influential contemporary cultural traditions: psychoanalysis, postmodernism, feminism and a persisting critical interest in Catholicism. I think her work helps to illuminate various crises in contemporary trinitarian re-presentation which are vital to the life of the church. I shall be focussing on two in particular: the significance of gender re-presentation regarding the persons of the trinity; and the reasons why the person of the Spirit has been shadowy and inchoate, and so shamefully neglected. Both, as we shall see, are profoundly linked.

Irigaray's project seeks to show how all language and signs have a sexual character (sexuate language). Her analysis of ancient and contemporary philosophy and the psychoanalytical tradition of Freud indicate the extent to which male representation (economies of signs) both occlude female forms of self-representation, and encode 'women' in terms of male desire, such that women can have no real subjectivity. This cultural semiotic process, according to Irigaray, is both testified to and kept in place by the lack of feminine divine representation, as seen in western Christianity. This holy triad (language, subjectivity and divinity) undergirds her entire critique of western culture. She argues that it is only possible to construct an alternative culture of sexual difference if we seek the repressed and murdered feminine that is glimpsed through the 'blanks, lacunae, overdeterminations, and persistent blindspots inherent in the patriarchal bias of history'.[1] She envisages the possibility of a culture characterized by the celebration of both women *and* men, the celebration of sexual difference, rather than (as is her contention) our present culture which is predicated upon the denial of women, and the representation of the feminine purely in terms of male desire and semiotics. Presently we live within a hom(m)osexuate imaginary such that our cultural world, inner and outer, bears the marks of only male desire and production. Hom(m)osexuate is spelt thus to equivocally refer to the French word for male (*homme*) as well as the Latin generic term for 'man' (*homo*) and the Greek word, *homo*, which means 'same'. Together they resonate to signify the linguistic exclusion of the female from representing the human. Irigaray's aim is to facilitate *parler-femme*, speaking (as) woman, such that signs will truly reflect, construct and facilitate difference, the difference between men and women. Irigaray's use of *parler-femme* evokes the embodiedness of the female speaker, and she often cleverly contrasts the symbolic elusive, fluid and plural form of the 'two lips' of the female body with that of the single phallus of the male.[2]

To see how Irigaray poses her trinitarian questions, her view of the relationship between language, subjectivity and the divine requires further brief exposition.[3] Sigmund Freud predicated the development of the infant via his or her negotiation of the Oedipal complex. The desire for the mother and the identification with the mother is weaned in the son by his fear of castration by the father, whose desired sexual object is also the mother. The male subsequently follows in the 'name of the father' as obedient son, repressing his murderous feelings towards the father and his incestuous feelings towards the mother, 'knowing' that he cannot compete and win. Later, Freud would posit this Oedipal configuration as the generative psycho-cultural source of Judaism and Christianity, recognizing the important ambivalence that is kept contained and repressed by the cosmic Father (God).[4] For Freud, negotiating the Oedipal crisis successfully will also mean that man comes of age and will no longer require religion, for religion's infantalizing function will be outlived. Freud realized that male and female separation from the mother took very different routes. The female infant's weaning from the maternal bond is established via her identification with the mother, so as to be a rival for the father's sexual attention. She, like the son, desires the phallus. However, her sexuality is defined by lack: she does not possess a penis herself, nor does she possess the father's penis. Hence, the father figure in this triangle, although in asymmetrical ways, is 'seminal' in the child's entry into the adult world. The son imitates and reproduces him; the daughter, in contrast, feels 'lack' in relation to him.

Jacques Lacan developed Freud's Oedipal staging in terms of structuralist semiotic mediation, and by his employment of the mirror theory.[5] According to Lacan, following Freud, entry into the symbolic order (which includes all culture which is constructed by signs) by both male and female child can only be under the semiotic 'name of the Father'. That is, the *desires* of both male and female child centre around phallic possession, such that these desires are constitutive of generating the symbolic processes that one calls 'culture'. However, the 'Father', who can never be attained within this symbolic order, is therefore productive of culture in generating the continuous and necessary separation from the mother, semiotically enacted. It is from this interval, the tension between two unattainable desires, that semiotic figuration is born.[6] Lacan is clear that the relation between the biological phallus and the symbolic phallus are arbitrary, and this allows him to posit the phallic mother, a concept resisted by Irigaray and some feminists. To the latter, the symbolic and morphological cannot be so easily disassociated.

Lacan's plotting of subjectivity as a dynamic process of relations, both ordered towards desiring love as well as containing within these relations that which will obstruct the attainment of love, poses a fundamental challenge to the understanding of the 'self', as a self-sufficient, rational being – of a self that could possibly exist apart from *relations*. Hence, those who follow on from Lacan are decidedly postmodern in their critique of the Enlightenment's notion of free, autonomous, rational selves; and are equally far more sensitive to the symbolic significance of religion in generating or hindering the process of maturation, a process that is always ongoing.[7] In this limited respect, there is a proper rejection of Freud's myth of scientific modernity as the apex of human development.

Irigaray, in *Speculum of the Other Woman* (1974), began her sexuate deconstruction of Freud and Lacan showing that their particular staging of the Oedipal struggle was a construction that occluded women from the economy of signs. The male is defined by the male and so is the fe/male. The 'father' is both the origin and goal of the Oedipal triangle – and therefore of semiotic desire within such an economy of signification.[8] Women can only appear as tokens of exchange within this masculine economy, but have no subjectivity of their own, for they are born into and constructed by semiotic systems that are predicated upon male desire. Their own re-presentation is by silence, absence, lack, or hysteria. Lacan's role in dismissing Irigaray from her post at the newly established University of Paris VIII at Vincennes after the publication of *Speculum of the Other Woman* curiously enacted the argument of her thesis.

Irigaray develops the process of 'sexual subversions' by attending to the 'blanks, lacunae, overdeterminations, and persistent blindspots' in the western philosophical and psychoanalytical tradition. There is nowhere else to begin, for one cannot escape the semiotic structures that shape us. For Irigaray, only the tactic of subversion is possible, hence the apparently 'oblique' style, pregnant with deconstructive psycho-analysis of sexuate discourse. The image of the speculum, a medical 'mirror' used especially for gynaecological investigation, for the seeing of women's hidden anatomy, becomes a strategic metaphor deployed by Irigaray. Lacan's mirror is only capable of reflecting the phallus, and when woman is mirrored in the Freudian-Lacan mirror there is only lack and deficiency. In the 'contoured' mirror of the speculum, female morphology, the hidden body of the murdered mother, begins to find form. Irigaray fluidly employs woman's anatomy to stage her questioning of phallic discourse (so called as it symbolizes male desire), and it is vital to Irigaray that this female morphology is not once more abducted and paraded within the economy of phallic desire. After *Speculum* she develops and returns to these themes, growing ever more nuanced about the relationship between morphology and symbols in her most recent work.

One of the western tradition's major semiotic resources are found within Christianity, and Irigaray frequently turns to Roman Catholicism, both to severely criticize its exclusion of the feminine from divine representation (God is Father, who has a Son, whose church is ordered and controlled by men, who represent Christ, and therefore God) and also to find within it possible resources for the subversion of such patriarchy. While both Irigaray and Julia Kristeva, another French psychoanalytical philosopher, tend to see the church (French Catholicism?) as on the verge of extinction, Irigaray speaks of her attendance at Christmas Day mass at Notre Dame Cathedral and at the pope's visit to Paris.[9] This possible source of Roman Catholic subversion is important, for no advances can be made outside semiotic configurations.

Irigaray, due to the necessity of object relations in psychoanalysis, argues that it is only in relationship to female sexuate signs and representations that women can reconstruct themselves and struggle towards real subjectivity. Christianity is usually complicit with matricide and the occlusion of the feminine in so much as the Father God of monotheism and the hom(m)osexuate trinitarian trio serve to affect the exclusive emergence of the male into semiotic representation and cultural production. It is only female divinity that can provide the imaginary, the symbolic order, whereby women can attain subjectivities, become persons, not 'equal' to men – but different from them, and therefore in real relation to them, and to each other. In this analysis of male-female relations within the phallic order a primary narcissism characterizes men's relationships to women. Women satisfy male desires, they are the incubators of the patrilineal order, and women are substitutes of the unacknowledged mother that has been buried, so as to attain male self-reproduction.

This effacement of women from the symbolic order, other than in terms of phallic desire (sex object, mother, carer to men and their children) requires that *parler-femme* give shape to *female genealogies*, so that the friendship and relations between women and women can be symbolized. This is especially true of the first relationship of a woman: the daughter–mother relation. Irigaray argues that not until women can relate symbolically to the same, to women, can they properly discover a female subjectivity and also relate to men, the other. She writes: 'no love of other without love of same'.[10] This is an important theme in Irigaray's writing.

To focus more closely on the trinitarian issue, we will turn to Irigaray's interesting review of Elizabeth Schüssler Fiorenza's *In Memory of Her: A Feminist Reconstruction of Christian Origins*.[11] Irigaray shows a real appreciation of Schüssler Fiorenza's book, speaking of the 'astonishment' and 'joy' at reading 'something new on Christianity!'.[12] However, Irigaray is finally dissatisfied, for Schüssler Fiorenza's ultimate goal is to promote women as 'equals' to men. This goal is unacceptable, even if Fiorenza brilliantly uncovers the way in which women have been occluded from view by patriarchally constructed texts and traditions. For Irigaray, to stop at Schüssler Fiorenza's goal is to capitulate

to the male economy of signs, locating woman as neuter and thus 'equal',
not different, and thereby failing entirely to dismantle and subvert the
semiotic system that keeps women still entrapped and enveloped in
positions that are constructed by (male) others.

Irigaray develops two basic criticisms of Schüssler Fiorenza which
take us to the heart of the trinitarian question. The first is at the level
of what Irigaray calls 'sociology', whereby Irigaray (in effect) questions
Schüssler Fiorenza's feminist theology's assimilation of liberation theology. Schüssler Fiorenza sees 'women' as one category among the more
basic category of the 'poor'. This explains women and the production
of culture in terms of capital alone (as did Marx), rather than unveiling
the vital role of sexuate language which itself, for Irigaray, is the more
primary cause of exploitation:

> Women aren't just poor among the poor. As half of the human race,
> it is their exploitation that makes it possible to exploit others. This
> exploitation is primarily cultural and only secondarily socio-
> economic.[13]

Irigaray notes that sexuate theological language is profoundly determi-
native of socio-semiotic orderings and power. For Irigaray, Schüssler
Fiorenza's failure to see this mirrors her failure to think sexual difference
at the heart of the matter: divine representation.

Irigaray's second criticism of Schüssler Fiorenza is that she does not
go far enough. The *male embodiment* of the divine still reigns supreme.
Irigaray writes:

> woman's role in the Gospels really isn't as 'central' as Schüssler
> Fiorenza would have us believe. It is Jesus himself who is at the
> center, surrounded by women . . . But it seems to me naive, dema-
> gogical (or maybe a mark of matriarchal acculturation) to say that
> women were 'at the center' of Jesus' life.[14]

The point she is making is that Jesus is finally male, and not until there
is female divine embodiment and representation can there be Good
News for women. This is why Schüssler Fiorenza's use of the feminine
Wisdom/Sophia tradition to speak of Jesus' divinity, rather than
employing the Logos conceptuality, simply 'doesn't suffice, or suffices

only to confirm the end of gynecocratic genealogy, the son descended from the mother–daughter line'.[15] But it is precisely in the depths of this crisis of representation that Irigaray turns, for a moment, *towards* Christ, rather than away from him – as have post-Christian feminists such as Daphne Hampson and Mary Daly.[16] It is precisely because Jesus' incarnation affirms *embodiment as divine gift* that it holds out the possibility for Irigaray of real redemption – but, at present, only for men as long as Jesus is proclaimed as *the* exclusive centre of redemption.

Irigaray, with unlikely allies such as Hans Urs von Balthasar and Pope John Paul II, recognizes the incarnation to be the Word *made flesh* which means *gendered bodies* count; even if her counting challenges their form of accounting, which tends to result in the rendering of the feminine in terms of 'passive receptivity which uncomfortably resembles the masculine encoding of the feminine within a phallic economy of representation.[17] Flesh only exists, for Irigaray, in two forms: male and female, not in an Enlightenment abstraction such as the 'human', which in history is only found in the form of male and female, not some genderless substratum. Hence, despite the many achievements of Schüssler Fiorenza's work, Irigaray succinctly judges her findings regarding social equality: 'sociology quickly bores me when I'm expecting the divine'.[18] For Irigaray, feminist theology must establish not only 'equal access to the priesthood, but rather an equal share in the divine. This means that what I see as a manifestation of sexual liberation is God made a couple: man and woman and not simply God made man'.[19] While Irigaray acknowledges that the Virgin Mary does have Aphroditic features in Schüssler Fiorenza's work – 'being pregnant outside of marriage and protected as such by the angels and birds of heaven'[20] – the fact that her special relationship to Jesus is subordinated to and undermined by Jesus' relations to his other women disciples,[21] and the fact that Mary is finally entrusted to John 'the beloved disciple' and not to a woman,[22] cumulatively show that Mary is relentlessly positioned within patriarchy. In other essays, however, Irigaray is slightly more hopeful regarding Mary's role – as we shall see below.

It is worth quoting in some detail Irigaray's main contention regarding the problem of male divine representation:

Monotheistic religions speak to us of God the Father and God made man; nothing is said of a God the Mother or of God made woman, or even of God as a couple or couples. Not all the transcendental fancies, or ecstasies of every type, not all the quibbling over maternity and the neutrality (neuterness) of God, can succeed in erasing this one reality that determines identities, rights, symbols, and discourse. It is for this reason that I've suggested that the divine incarnation of *Jesus Christ is a partial one*; a view which, in any event, is consistent with his own. 'If I am not gone, the Paraclete cannot come.' Why not? What coming of the Paraclete can be involved here, since Jesus is already the result of its work. We do not know the incarnation of the Spirit, but the notion of a Holy Spirit as the pure product of patriarchal culture seems erroneous in view of Jesus' personality.[23]

Irigaray offers, inadvertently, a high ecclesiological reading of John 16, such that the incarnation (in some way) continues in history. For the gospel writers, John and Paul, the body of Christ, the church, allows for this extension of the incarnation. For Irigaray, the focus is more on the Holy Spirit's work – both in making Jesus the Christ, and for continuing 'incarnations'. If Jesus' incarnation is the beginning and end of the story of divinization, then only men are offered the means of divinization, for God is represented in male, not female form. But when this happens, according to Irigaray, the very logic of the incarnation, the divine enfleshment of Jesus, is undermined, for the incarnation allows us to envisage 'the social outcome of the respect for the incarnation of all bodies (men's and women's) as potentially divine; nothing more nor less than each man and each woman being *virtually gods*'.[24] In one sense, and an important sense to which we will return, Irigaray seems to require that every woman and man be capable of being 'redeemer', if such is the quality of divine embodiment. If thinking through divine embodiment stops at Jesus, then, for Irigaray, Mary Daly is right: Christianity is irredeemably patriarchal.

Irigaray recognizes that the consolidation of patriarchy is attained in the symbolic representation of divinity, which in this case is trinitarian:

the appearance of the father's and the Father's power, the phenotype of a genotype glimpsed in the Word, since the father, unlike the mother, propagates outside himself and in a way that remains invisible. Thus, in order to affirm the reign of the father, it became necessary to eliminate the divine phenomenality of the daughter, of the mother–daughter couple, and lock it into the father–Father–son–Son genealogy and the triangle, father–son–Holy Spirit.[25]

('Phenotype' and 'genotype' represent the male sexuate phonetic form and the biological male genetic embodiment in 'the Word'.) For Irigaray this latter envisioning of trinity idolatrously reflects the male economy of production, thereby generating a patriarchal church that has no place for women, other than tokens of exchange within a male economy of desire. Irigaray is acutely aware how 'doctrinal metaphysics' translates into social configurations of power. For example, commenting on the exclusion of women from the priesthood, she tellingly notes of the male Catholic priest celebrating the 'sharing of food',

> which is our age-old rite, perhaps we might remind him that he would not be there if our body and our blood had not given him life, love and spirit. And that it is us, women–mothers, that he is giving to be eaten too. But no one must know that. That is why women cannot celebrate the eucharist ... Something of the truth that is hidden there might be brutally unmasked.[26]

Irigaray allusively suggests a reconfigured trinity, whereby what she calls the 'third age of the Spirit', the 'age of sexual difference', might usher in the parousia. We have already seen Irigaray's use of the Johannine quotation: 'If I am not gone, the Paraclete cannot come', and her questioning as to what this might possibly mean, especially as the Spirit has already been present and co-constitutive of Jesus' ministry. She hints that the feminization of the Spirit may provide just that divine embodiment, a female divinity embodied and celebrated, that could generate a feminine economy of signs such that an undreamed of fertility would result in a new creation.[27] Envisioning sexual difference within the Godhead would facilitate just that imaginary whereby female subjectivity could arise out of the cracks and fissures of the phallocratic economy of signs. She writes:

> Christianity tells us that God is in three persons, three manifestations, and that the third stage of the manifestation occurs as a wedding between the spirit and the bride. Is this supposed to inaugurate the divine for, in, with women? The female? Divinity is what we need

to become free, autonomous, sovereign. No human subjectivity, no human society has ever been established without the help of the divine . . . There is no *woman* God, no female trinity: mother, daughter, spirit.[28]

She utilizes, rather loosely, Joachim of Fiore's staging of the trinity to make her point when she speaks of the Old Testament as the reign of the Father, the New Testament as the reign of the Son, and this third era, which is both our horizon, and also the present time, as the age of the Spirit and the Bride.[29]

There are allusive and intermittent suggestions in Irigaray's writings that relate this third age, the marriage of the Spirit and Bride, to rediscovering the role of Mary. Like most feminists, she is well aware of the male economic rendering of Mary as pure 'mother', as mother to the Father's Son, so that Mary is rendered into a 'receptacle that, faithfully, welcomes and reproduces only the will of the Father'.[30] Irigaray is not arguing that motherhood is inimical to female subjectivity, but rather she resists the enthroning of this singular function, for if woman is only represented as 'mother', then she is in constant danger of being encoded within the taxonomy of male desire. Irigaray writes:

Our urgent task is to refuse to submit to a desubjectivized social role, the role of mother, which is dictated by an order subject to the division of labor – he produces, she reproduces – that walls us up in the ghetto of a single function. When did society ever ask fathers to choose between being men or citizens? We don't have to give up being women to be mothers.[31]

If one can avoid representing Mary within such a patriarchal economy of exchange, it may be that Jesus' sexually embodied incarnation 'nudges us towards the deciphering of the function of that virgin-mother'.[32] This comment might constitute an interesting angle on the debate as to whether the Roman Catholic Church should 'officially' pronounce Mary 'Co-Redeemer', along with the related titles, 'Mediator of All Graces' and 'Advocate of the People of God'. I will return to this shortly. For now, the above must suffice as an account of Irigaray's profound questioning of the hom(m)osexuate trinitarian economy.

There are points where I disagree with Irigaray, and I shall later question some of her fundamental presuppositions, but her critique of the trinity cannot be evaded.

I shall pursue Irigaray's questioning with a series of brief explorations, counter-questions and puzzlements. I have no desire to foreclose the productive interaction between her work and an embodied Christian theology. An engagement with Irigaray brings us headlong into the question: does trinitarian representation, by which Christians engage the world, itself require careful attention due to the church's constant tendency towards idolatry? I shall develop my trinitarian exploration by way of three interrelated sections, by means of asking about the representation of the Spirit, Son and Father. It should be clear that dividing the material into three sections is entirely artificial, for we cannot speak of one, without at the same time speaking of the others. The Son and Father will form the next chapter. However, in this following section, I shall deal with the traditionally third person first, the Holy Spirit.

2. The neglected Spirit: advocate, comforter, wind, fire, lover, 'he' or 'she'?

Starting with the Spirit is already implicated in Irigaray's taxonomy, and also fully justified on theological grounds that will be made clear soon. For Irigaray, this is the age in which we find ourselves, and it is especially telling that she empowers the Spirit and conceives of her in feminine terms. However, such a strategy is ironically ambiguous. The irony is found in the tendency within western trinitarian theology to subordinate the Spirit to the exclusive function of the relationship between Father and Son – the Spirit is third in order, as a result of the love the Father has for the Son, and the Son for the Father, and is therefore already positioned as woman within patriarchal discourse. Eastern theology's tendency to subordinate both Son and Spirit to the Father also retains male self-love as the central symbolics within the trinitarian Godhead. To see the Spirit as feminine therefore ironically highlights the patriarchal taxonomies of representation that have tended to exist in both east and west, and which have subjugated the Spirit in symbolically equivalent terms to the subjugation of women in western

culture. Hence, speaking of the Holy Spirit in feminine terms is quite
problematic, and Irigaray is not unaware of this.

When referring to women's representation under the control of the
phallic semiotic economy, Irigaray remarks that:

> its necessary *trinitarian* structuration included: subject, object, and
> the copula-instrument of their articulation. Father, Son, Holy Spirit.
> The bosom mother-nature permitting the conjunction of the (male)
> one and the (so-called) other in the matrix of discourse.[33]

The extent of hom(m)osexuate trinitarian representation requires theological exploration, and the clue which suggests that Irigaray's arguments may indeed be most timely is in the growing chorus of
contemporary theological voices concerned with the neglect of the Holy
Spirit in trinitarian theology.[34]

Given that the above characterizations are vast generalizations about
'east' and 'west', and both these traditions are extremely fluid and
complex, let me pursue my contention that Irigaray's identification of
a hom(m)osexuate trinity is extremely pertinent via a most important
recent trinitarian study that is entirely unconcerned with gender issues,
Thomas Weinandy's scholarly, well researched and creative study, *The
Father's Spirit of Sonship: Reconceiving the Trinity* (1995). Weinandy is
a Roman Catholic patristics scholar. His book is important to my purpose as he surveys both western and eastern trinitarian traditions and
finds them wanting precisely in their failure to provide adequate subjectivity to the person of the Spirit. What is particularly telling is that his
criticisms of the tendencies in western and eastern forms of trinitarian
representation bear an extremely close parallel to Irigaray's analysis of
the occlusion of feminine subjectivity within western semiotic forms.
What is also interesting is Weinandy's argument that the Spirit's lack
of subjectivity is a result of non-Christian (Greek) conceptualities being
uncritically utilized in Christian semiotic representation, what he calls
an 'unbaptized' use of Greek thought, that also runs against the biblical
witness.

In this section on the Spirit, I will first test whether Irigaray's argument is historically feasible in the light of Weinandy's study. I will argue
that Irigaray's critique is both historically sustainable and suggestive as
to where answers may be found. In pursuing such answers, I will turn

to another Roman Catholic theologian, Leonardo Boff, who divinizes Mary. Boff, a Brazilian, is a contemporary Latin American liberation theologian. I have chosen him because in his work we find a quite radical reading of the Spirit as hypostatistically incarnated in Mary. This seems to closely conform to just what Irigaray requires: feminine divine representation. But does it? In critically engaging with Boff's arguments, not only do I call into question whether Boff's project is successful, but I also ask whether various presuppositions of Irigaray are sustainable. On the constructive side I begin to develop a theology of the Spirit in terms of feminine representation, primarily with regard to Mary, but also through the female saints of the church. I shall be arguing that Mary should indeed be officially declared 'Co-redeemer', for this serves to highlight how the entire church, both women and men, are called to be co-redeemers. Irigaray's demand for feminine divine representation, it will be recalled, amounted to the requirement that women be capable of being redeemers.[35] Her desire can be met without feminine hypostatic incarnations. I will finally end these series of explorations by turning directly to the question: should we call the Spirit 'her'? To answer this I look at the early Syrian church where the feminization of the Spirit took place in liturgical prayer. In what follows I will be jumping between different historical periods and differing socio-political locations. In doing this I do not wish to create a universalizing discourse, which domesticates difference and particularity. I do this to give historical substantiation to some of Irigaray's claims and respond to some of her criticisms within the only arena possible: the history of signs.

Weinandy and Irigaray: the Spirit's diminished subjectivity

Weinandy argues that the tendencies to distort the trinity originate from the inclusion, in the west, of an unbaptized Aristotelian epistemology to structure our thinking the trinity: 'that is, something cannot be loved until it is known, and thus the Father logically begets the Son before he spirates the Spirit'.[36] This is a very important feature of Weinandy's criticism for it locates a pagan presupposition that generates the taxonomy of trinitarian relations. There is another feature of this presupposition that is worth noting briefly.

Weinandy sees clearly that this Aristotelian prioritizing of knowledge and consciousness, such that it foundationally becomes the precondition to love, serves to *conceal* the reciprocity between love and knowledge. Aquinas was to see this Aristotelian weakness and rectify it. However, also concealed, even buried, in this epistemology is a particularly female way of knowing and loving, or loving and knowing. In one sense, this Aristotelian epistemology is a very 'male' embodied rendering of the process of knowledge in omitting the vital experience of loving, prior to 'requisite' knowledge, such that takes place in Mary's love for her son prior to his birth.[37] Of course, Mary had 'knowledge' that she was pregnant, but no knowledge of her son as a concrete person, except that something quite extraordinary awaited both of them. However, the *relation* that exists between mother and unborn child is adequate to facilitate the bountiful love Mary has for the yet unborn Jesus. Many (but certainly not all) women testify to the love (or its often tragic lack or corruption) that they experience for their child *before* it is born and has an explicitly and socially recognized personality. Aristotelian epistemology occludes a very important experience particularly related to women's bodies. The premises of such an epistemology are also disturbed by psychoanalysis, where it is posited that our ability to love and the way we have been loved is not initially accessible to conscious knowledge and, therefore, certainly *not* dependent on knowledge as such.

The epistemological issues are of course very complex, but this pagan Aristotelian prioritization of the Father and Son within this 'divine' economy, according to Weinandy, leads to the deformed subjectivity of the Spirit, who is always subservient to Father and Son and thereby fails to attain 'his' own subjectivity. Let me cite Weinandy in full in his description of the dynamics of the western taxonomy, with my emphases added into the original text:

> Firstly, for the West, the Father and (*derivatively*) the Son play *active roles* within the Trinity. In contrast, the Holy Spirit assumes a rather *passive* function. The Spirit is merely the Love or Gift *shared* by the Father and the Son. It is therefore difficult to see why, in the Western conception of the Trinity, the Holy Spirit is a distinct person or subject – or who. The Father and Son *derive their subjective depth and personhood from their activity*. The Father is the Father because he *begets* the Son and loves the Son *he has begotten*. The Son is the

Son because he *loves the Father* as the *only-begotten*. But the Holy Spirit as the Love *between them does not play an active role*, and thus *appears less clearly* as an acting subject. He has no subjective depth because *he has no defining activity as a person*. Why then is the Holy Spirit a person, a subjective 'who', distinct from the Father and the Son?[38]

This configuration of the divine economy bears a remarkable and even idolatrous relationship to the economy of masculine desire, and Weinandy (unintentionally) discloses the hom(m)osexuate taxonomy in the passage just cited. Active roles are assumed by the symbolically male forms (Father and Son), and no mother or woman is required in this Father's begetting. The two active males generate the contrast of a third person with an essentially passive role that is there to serve their relationship and, more primarily, the Father's will. The Spirit's role is passive because the role is derived purely from the activity of the Father and Son, who share the Spirit between them. The Father and Son's clear active roles give them distinctiveness and relationality, but their relationality is achieved by the lack of distinctiveness and lack of role for the Holy Spirit, other than in facilitating their relationship. The Spirit has no clear subjectivity precisely because she is made the conduit of the semiotic and almost narcissistic love between Father and Son. If we rewrote Weinandy's passage replacing 'he' by 'she' and 'Spirit' by 'Spiritess' just to bring out the gendered sense in which 'Father' and 'Son' subliminally operate in gender terms, we see the economy of male desire and the inevitable subordination, neglect and resulting invisibility of the feminine analysed by Irigaray regarding western culture, and now represented within trinitarian theologizing:

Firstly, for the West, the Father and (derivatively) the Son play active roles within the Trinity. In contrast, the Holy Spiritess assumes a rather passive function. The Spiritess is merely the Love or Gift shared by the Father and the Son. It is therefore difficult to see why, in the Western conception of the Trinity, the Holy Spiritess is a distinct person or subject – or who. The Father and Son derive their subjective depth and personhood from their activity. The Father is the Father because he begets the Son and loves the Son he has begotten. The Son is the Son because he loves the Father as the only-begotten. But the Holy Spiritess as the Love between them does not play an active role, and thus appears less clearly as an acting subject. She has no subjective depth because she has no defining activity as a person. Why then is the Holy Spiritess a person, a subjective 'who', distinct from the Father and the Son?[39]

Why indeed? She seems to be not unlike women within Irigaray's analysis of patriarchal culture. It is perhaps no accident that some groups who place an extremely high emphasis on the Holy Spirit reflect 'hysterical' behaviour, and, in the case of the thirteenth-century Gugliel-mites, also posited a female incarnation and a female pope, which was considered not only hysterical but also heretical.[40] The Holy Spirit only operates as an adjunct of the Father–Son relation. In this taxonomy the Spirit confirms the Father and Son's mutual love for each other rather than displaying love's overflow, its orientation towards the other. This orientation towards the other is the shape of love disclosed in the story of Jesus who forges a relational link of love that includes, trans-forms and redeems all women and men in their bodily, gendered exist-ence. I shall return to this point below. In recognizing this 'fit' between Irigaray's critique of a hom(m)osexuate trinity and the actual western tradition of trinitarian representation as portrayed by Weinandy, Iriga-ray's critique seems to address precisely the problems diagnosed by theologians entirely unconcerned with gender. Admittedly, this argu-ment would need to be tested in more elaborate detail against the major trinitarian theologians of east and west, but my reliance on Weinandy will suffice to establish the apparent validity of Irigaray's critique.

So much for the trinitarian west. Now while a number of recent writers such as Colin Gunton, John Zizioulas and Catherine LaCugna have criticized the downplaying of pneumatology in the west and turned instead to the eastern tradition, in the form of the Cappodicians for reconceiving pneumatology within the trinity, Weinandy develops an equally incisive criticism against them.[41] This is because of the eastern infection by another unbaptized philosophy, this time in the form of middle and neo–Platonic emanationism. According to Weinandy this tradition renders the full subjectivity of the Spirit highly problematic because of its tendency to cast the trinitarian relations in a linear, sequential, emanationist form which leads to the sole mon-archy of the Father. The result of such a neo–Platonist staging is that:

The Godhead resides in the Father alone, and he shares his divinity with the Son and the Holy Spirit as they emanate out from him in a sequential pattern. This conception, while giving greater integrity to the distinct persons and priority to the unbegotten Father, jeopardizes Nicaea's *homoousion* doctrine that the one Godhead resides in and is the interrelationship among the persons, and not just in the Father alone.[42]

The male economy is exposed and laid bare: the Father has no equal, 'the Godhead resides in the Father alone'. He alone is active, and upon him all are dependent for he is their 'source' and 'origin'. The 'unbegotten' Father rightly indicates that God just *is*, is pure uncaused gift. However, it also metaphorically places a 'Father' as a figure who does *not* require a mother-woman, who once was a daughter, to 'beget' a 'Son'. The sole monarch is never co-dependent or co-related, until he chooses, such that there is a metaphoric moment in this staging where the Father is not unlike the Enlightenment man: self-sufficient, unrelated and utterly autonomous; a self who also bears resemblance to the neo-Platonic 'One'.[43]

This eastern monarchical tendency corresponds more closely to Freud's staging of the genesis of religion in the primal horde's hatred and envy of the Father's phallus, for the Father alone has the power that the sons are given derivatively (and jealously desire). In the western tradition, the Son seems to have attained equality with the Father without this struggle, but at the cost of denying representation to the feminine. Weinandy argues that this eastern sequential emanation tends towards either subordinationism (which means 'Father' must come first) or tritheism (which undermines the real *unity* of the *relations* between the persons – so that they eventually act autonomously of each other). The result once more is that the subjectivity of the person of the Spirit is compromised in two major ways. First, activity is once more the sole possession of one person (the Father) rather than two (the Father and Son, as in the west) – but certainly not metaphorically shared equally by the Spirit. Secondly, the linear sequence is incapable of facilitating co-equality with the Father, such that the patriarchal genealogy is the only manner in which there can be mention of a third, who is seen 'through' the relationship of Father and Son. I again cite Weinandy in full, with my Irigarian emphases:

while the East has emphasized the distinction of persons, in its legitimate desire to uphold the Father as the sole ungenerate source, it
has *diminished*, like the West, the *active roles* of the Son and *the Holy
Spirit* within the inner trinitarian life. In addition, the Eastern view
of the Trinity is quite linear – the Son is begotten from the Father,
and the Spirit proceeds from the Father *through the Son*. While some
positive noetic content can be perceived in the Son's being begotten,
the meaning of the Spirit's proceeding from the Father through the
Son is indeterminate. What distinguishes 'procession' from 'generation'? *What does proceeding 'through the Son' mean? How does this
proceeding 'through the Son' effect or determine the personhood of the
Holy Spirit?* Moreover, this linear view undermines the Orthodox
notion of *perichoresis* by which the persons are said to co-inhere in
one another. If the movement of the Son and the Holy Spirit is '*out
from*' the Father, how do they mutually interpenetrate each other?[44]

Weinandy's observations support my argument – and allow me to use
his survey of a wide group of eastern and western patristic authors on
which to base my argument. Weinandy's observations can also be seen
as extremely accurate in the context of one influential recent restatement
of the eastern account of the trinity. It is interesting that John Zizioulas,
so resolute and robust a defender of the eastern stress on 'persons' and
'relations' as constitutive of 'being' and 'substance', falls into precisely
the pattern that Weinandy has mapped out because Zizioulas retains
the Cappadocian notion of 'causality' within the Godhead. Admittedly,
he does this to safeguard the unity of the trinity, as had the Cappadocians. In so doing, however, Zizioulas succumbs to what Alan Torrance
appropriately calls a 'cosmological theology', that is a theology being
dictated by unbaptized philosophy, rather than developing, in Torrance's terms, a 'theological cosmology'.[45] In *Being as Communion*
Zizioulas defends the Cappadocians for they 'introduced the concept
of "cause" into the being of God' which was of 'incalculable importance', for in so doing it mitigated against the view that the ultimate
ontological category is a 'structure of communion existing by itself'.[46]
Alan Torrance, who thinks through the idolatry of causality more
thoroughly than Zizioulas (or Weinandy for that matter, who still retains
the notion of the 'Father as the sole ungenerate source'),[47] points out
against Zizioulas's argument:

Given that what is being referred to is not some contingent existent or mere 'structure' conceived as 'existing by itself', but nothing less than God, it seems to us that he [Zizioulas] fails to offer sufficiently compelling arguments as to why it should be of 'incalculable importance' that we do *not* conceive of the intra-divine communion of the Trinity as the ground of all that is, that is, as sufficient in itself and as indeed 'capable' of existing 'by itself'.[48]

The primacy of *relations* is oddly subordinated to the priority of the 'Father' in Zizioulas, thereby strongly endorsing Weinandy's comments – and Irigaray's – regarding masculine taxonomies and the prioritizing of the Father's phallus: his sole generative and creative power.

This is not to imply that the great trinitarian thinkers of east and west were unaware of the problem of introducing human metaphors to speak of God, and that of course they constantly qualified the terms they employed. The point that I am making is that all too often the semiotic economies of representation utilized by Christian theologians implicitly reproduce the male symbolics of desire. In a larger project one might extend Weinandy's argument to cover the western tradition's inclusion of an unbaptized Kant and Hegel to provide the conceptual resources by which revelation is unfolded.[49] Graham Ward locates Irigaray's project within these intersections: 'Irigaray is part of that anti-Hegelian trajectory' that 'wishes to move knowledge from the domain of the rapacious self-affirmation of the cogito, Hegel's *Geistessubjekt*' such that 'personhood is constituted only in the participation within an economy of desire for and by the other'.[50] Little wonder that the birth of the Spirit within eastern and western trinitarian economies has continued to be so troublesome – an almost endless labour.

Reading Weinandy through Irigarian lenses helps to locate a tenuous link between the inchoate subjectivity of the Holy Spirit, the undetermined subjectivity of 'women' and the lack of feminine divine representation. At first sight, the one person of the trinity who might bear feminine gendering is also the person who has the most diminished subjectivity and lack of personhood. The Holy Spirit has always been subordinate to either the Father alone, or the Father and the Son, or the Father through the Son. One might say that the Holy Spirit has always indeed been (implicitly) female in this male economy of representation. Hence, to call the Spirit feminine, *without problematization*, might simply legitimate the economy of male desire within this generative symbology rather than deconstruct it. This is precisely the problem, I shall argue, in Leonardo Boff's radical and creative feminization of the Holy Spirit.[51] However, what is important in Boff's work is his recognition that the role of the Father as 'sole', unoriginative source must be questioned if all three persons are to attain co-equality and full perichoretic unity. Boff takes up the challenge where Weinandy left off. But before turning to Boff, let us briefly look at Weinandy's own response to the trinitarian configuration and the Holy Spirit's status and his estimation of Boff which helps us focus on precisely what is at stake.

Weinandy's thesis is developed in the light of trinitarian problems of east and west, with an eye to overcoming the filioque impasse. It is grounded in some very fine biblical exegesis. His argument is that within the trinity the Father begets the Son *in or by* the Holy Spirit, who proceeds then from the Father as the one in whom the Son is begotten. In his own words:

> A proper understanding of the Trinity can only be obtained if all three persons, logically and ontologically, spring forth in one simultaneous, nonsequential, eternal act in which each person of the Trinity subsistently defines, and equally is subsistently defined by, the other persons.[52]

In so much as Weinandy is really refusing self-enclosed notions of person and being, and upholds the metaphoric co-constitutive, co-creative and co-generative reality of God who abides in loving difference, he moves some way towards overcoming the difficulties he located in eastern and western trinitarian taxonomies, and the resultant denigration of the Spirit.[53] However, Weinandy's failure to think fully through his important thesis is subliminally registered in two footnotes.

In the first footnote, Weinandy says, he will argue that while there is 'an order of origin and derivation among the persons of the Trinity, there is not an order of priority, precedence and sequence'.[54] The quoted sentence follows immediately with precisely the claim that should stop Weinandy trying to establish the notion of 'an order of origin and derivation' at all. He writes: 'The Trinity embodies or (better) is one simultaneous and harmonious act by which the persons are who they

are and they are who they are only in the one act of being interrelated.'
It is deeply problematic that Weinandy can then argue for an 'order of
origin and derivation', such as to affirm the 'Father as the sole ungenerate source'.[55] Weinandy is not simply contradicting himself, but is trying
to establish the distinctions between the persons in terms of their metaphoric constitutive origins – a procedure with a long tradition. However,
what I am calling into question is both the occlusion of feminine metaphors within the originative process, and more significantly the very
necessity of distinguishing the persons in terms of 'origins', for this
inevitably leads to subordinationism or Seballianism.

There are two further difficulties with Weinandy's claim here. First,
origins and derivations and orderings are not in themselves metaphorically inadmissible, even if they are not necessary for establishing distinctions. However, metaphors of origin often result in and arise out
of, as Irigaray points out, the murder of the mother and the feminine
divine, thus obscuring the redemption of women. Clearly, there is in
a proper sense neither male nor female genealogy within God, for there
is *no causality* within the Godhead; or, to put it another way, there is
absolutely no reason why God *is* love. Love is sheer gift, pure joy,
jouissance, without cause.[56] Hence, Weinandy's untroubled retention
of these generative metaphors (such as the 'Father is the sole ungenerate
source') is problematic for implying causality within the Godhead, and
thereby introducing idolatry. Within the intratrinitarian life there
simply can be no causality. The term 'origin' is unimaginable without
causality, and makes no sense (despite Weinandy's claim) without the
concepts of 'priority, precedence and sequence'. As Boff rather incisively, but rather loosely, points out regarding causality within the
Godhead:

> In the Trinity, the 'cause' (the Father) is not anterior to the 'effects'
> (the Son and Holy Spirit). The 'effects' possess the same eternity
> and dignity as the 'cause'. So what is the cause and what is effect
> here? In the same way, what does 'begotten Son' or 'procession of
> the Holy Spirit' mean? It is not surprising that the Fathers, particu-
> larly the Greeks, approached such questions with the greatest rever-
> ence and ended with an apophatic response (no longer using words,
> which are totally inadequate).[57]

Weinandy's second footnote leads us directly to Boff, for here Weinandy distinguishes his own position from that of Boff's who does not want to use causal language within the Godhead. After citing Boff at length, and saying that 'Boff argues for a view very similar to the one I have just expressed', Weinandy registers the following reservation regarding Boff:

> Boff, through his use of the phrases *Patreque, Filioque, Spirituque,* is striving to articulate that each person of the Trinity is constituted in a simultaneous and an active subsistent relationship with one another. While I endorse his understanding of *Filioque* and *Spirituque,* I find his use of *Patreque* ambiguous. The Father does not come forth from the Son and the Holy Spirit *similar as to the way* the Son and the Spirit come forth from him. However, if he is attempting to say what I have stated above, that is, that the *Spirit conforms the Father* to be the Father as the Father breathes forth the Spirit, and that the *Son helps establish the Father as Father* as he actively cries out 'Abba!' in his being begotten, then I would agree with his notion of *Patreque.*[58]

I think that Boff is ambiguous in his use of *Patreque.* Nevertheless, it is important to maintain distinct and reciprocal relations within the trinity to safeguard the distinctness of the persons. By my reading Weinandy could quite easily adopt *Patreque,* as he himself acknowledges, but he fails to realize that, in so doing, he must forego all language of 'origins'. While 'conforming' and 'establishing' are not employed to signify causation but to show the primary reality of *relationship* and that the relationships are *different,* which thereby maintains the difference of persons within the unity of love, these terms show that it is possible to conceptually establish difference without resorting to 'origin' and 'derivation', and 'founded upon the Father'. If Weinandy is rightly wanting to preserve the difference between the Father, the Spirit and Son, which is what I take his comment 'similar to the way' to mean, then that seems entirely correct. However, what cannot be appropriate is the use of the terms 'origin' and 'derivation' to signify the Father's difference, for such terms must imply both causality and priority which Weinandy earlier rejected for they lead to the denigration of the Spirit and the denigration of co-equal subsistent relations as constituting the very being of God. To reconceptualize the distinct *relations* which co-constitute the three persons is a constructive task that I have only just begun to address.

Given Weinandy's failure to think through the dynamic relationality of the trinity, even though only at the last moment of a book that achieves so much, it is worth turning to Boff to pursue the question of the Spirit for he seems to have freed himself from ascribing all 'origin' to a sole Father God, and in this sense *may* have escaped the semiotic taxonomy of male desire configuring the divine. Boff's is a very important study in this regard, because although he follows Jürgen Moltmann in his major doctrinal moves and strategies, as well as in his political theology, there is an important difference. Perhaps due to the Roman Catholic–evangelical Protestant difference between Boff and Moltmann, Boff, in his concern to overcome 'sexism', strongly associates the Holy Spirit with Mary. Moltmann fails to utilize such Mariological resources. Boff's is a daring move, and one worth examining in detail for it will begin to show both the problems within Irigaray's own work and the problems within Boff's position, and the promising avenues that Irigaray opens within trinitarian theology.

While Boff makes interesting moves regarding Son and Father, I will not deal with them in detail in this section, even if I cannot entirely avoid them. Boff has no familiarity with Irigaray but has read Mary Daly. In one sense she is close to Irigaray, but turns away from the incarnation into a definitive, rather than strategic, separatist position which is always therefore in danger of mimicking phallocentric exclusivism, even if it is precipitated by the violence of the phallic order. Nevertheless, whatever the genealogical stimulus for Boff's theology, let us turn to his identification of Mary with the Holy Spirit.

Mary: Co-Redeemer or Spirit incarnate?

Before turning to Boff, Mary and the Spirit, it is worth registering that although Boff does employ *Patreque* and criticizes the notion of attributing sole causality to the Father, he is not entirely consistent in carrying through this project and lingering traces of a patriarchal taxonomy still persist, even if ever so slightly.[59] Weinandy's biblical exegesis and Boff's own (as well as Moltmann's on whom Boff is so dependent) certainly mitigate against this taxonomy, but its marginal persistence foreshadows some of the difficulties in Boff's strategy to divinize Mary, and offer a feminine representation of the divine to affect women's subjectivity. Drawing on his two earlier studies of Mary, Boff's argument regarding Mary is significantly located in his chapter on the Holy Spirit.

Boff's argument for the divinization of Mary, driven by his feminist concerns, relies on two major hinges: biblical and conciliar (the documents of the Second Vatican Council: 1962–5). The first, and more important, is based on biblical exegesis, focussed on Luke 1.35. The second is based on *Lumen Gentium* (*Dogmatic Constitution on the Church*) 56b. Luke 1.35 reads: 'The Holy Spirit will come upon you . . . and the power of the Most High will cover you with its shadow'. Boff suggests that this is 'the first time in all the scriptures when the Spirit is said to have come down directly on to a woman'.[60] Then, using *Lumen Gentium* 56b, he attests Vatican II's confirmation that Mary was 'fashioned by the Holy Spirit into a kind of new substance and new creature' to suggest that Mary be seen in relation to the Holy Spirit, 'in the same way as the Son was incarnate in Jesus'.[61] Boff claims:

> I would say that the Holy Spirit, coming down on Mary, 'pneumatized' her, taking on human form in her, in the same manner as the Son who, in a personal and unmistakable manner, set up his tent amongst us in the figure of Jesus of Nazareth.[62]

In one sense this seemingly allows for precisely the divinization of the feminine that is urged by Irigaray. But does it? And is it faithful to the gospels and any of the traditions of the church?

The Lucan account certainly presents Mary as pre-eminent, but it would be difficult to argue for her unique and singular hypostatic divinization in the manner Boff suggests. Mary and Elizabeth set the stage for the parallel accounting of Jesus and John, and in this respect Elizabeth's angelically announced birth is clearly located to act as a counterpoint to the angelic announcement to Mary (not to her husband, as with Elizabeth). Furthermore, by Luke's placing of Elizabeth in this manner, he also highlights the *relational* nature of the story being told: it exists only because of a whole series of events which make it possible, not least the role of a series of women such as Mary's own mother, St Anne, who in the *Protoevangelium of James* is rendered in very similar terms to that of Hannah who bears Samuel in I Samuel 1. (Anne, Ann, Anna, derives from the same root as Hannah, which is the Hebrew for 'grace'). But the story of Hannah, who is 'barren' like Elizabeth and Mary (for different reasons), likewise also recalls the stories of Deborah, Ruth, Judith, Esther and, perhaps in this context, most especially Sarah.[63] Sarah is especially important in presenting a difficulty for Boff's claim that the Lucan account is unique in attesting to a woman upon whom the Spirit, the *shekinah*, comes down. The fact that these female genealogies have often been domesticated and assimilated within patriarchal orderings is an issue to which I will later return.

I do not think Boff's argument works, because Luke 1.35–8 evokes the *shekinah*, and with it, Sarah's account in Genesis 18. Luke 1.35 linguistically evokes a number of Old Testament passages, especially Genesis 1.2 and Genesis 18.9–15; and Boff rightly notes that verse 35 also recalls Exodus 40.34–5 and its 'theology of the *shekinah* (tent), the palpable presence of God which in Judaism represented an incarnational tendency'.[64] This tendency towards concrete creative form is well focussed in the creation account of Genesis 1.2 where the Spirit gives form, gives shape to creation. Keeping this utterly miraculous gift of creation in sight, we see God's creative power differently, but also relatedly, focussed through the account of God's bringing about another almost impossible creation: Isaac, through the figures of Abraham and Sarah. Here the 'presence of God', the *shekinah*, is seen in Sarah's miraculous fertility. And the theology of the *shekinah*, the tabernacled presence of God within 'the tent', is precisely evoked in Genesis 18.9–15, by placing Sarah within 'the tent' where she hears that she will have a son. Many of the early fathers noticed this detail which is omitted from a number of modern commentaries regarding the double significance of 'the tent'. (I shall return to the Sarah account in Chapter 4). Luke also explicitly alludes to Genesis 18.14 in his construction of the angel's closing words: 'For with God nothing will be impossible.' Genesis 18.14 contains a similar phrase uttered by the angelic, or divine presence, in rebuffing Sarah's disbelief: 'Is anything too hard for the Lord?' (Matt. 19.26; Mark 10.27 and Rom. 9.9 all also allude to Gen. 18.14 which was clearly an important text for the early church.)

This typological reading, such as I have advanced, involves a genealogical sense of the Spirit's presence in every creative act: be it in the creation of the world (Gen. 1.2) or, no less awesomely, in the creation of a child (Gen. 17–18). However, in the case of human persons, cooperation is also required (even when it is a very ambivalent act of cooperation), and this is especially true of Mary in Luke 1.35–8. Hence, I have no quarrel with Mary's special pre-eminence amongst all creation, nor with the later titles conferred upon her by the early church. Indeed, part of my argument below will be the urging of the official declaration of Mary's status as 'Co-Redeemer', both in terms of gender politics and in terms of properly representing the Spirit, as well as its intrinsic theological importance in underlying the significance of human cooperation, God's respect for our co-creative freedom.

I suggest that in Boff's biblical exegesis he is in danger of freezing the semiotic signification of the divine, in his divinization of Mary *alone* among women and in the *manner* of her divinization. Both are unwarranted within the biblical texts he examines. However, let me turn to the second hinge of his argument, *Lumen Gentium* 56b, to see whether the Vatican texts do really lend support to Boff's position, or to the alternative reading that I am suggesting and will now further develop. It is clear from the official commentary and subsequent commentaries that no one, apart from Boff, has read *Lumen Gentium* 56b's language of 'new substance and new creature' regarding Mary to intend another hypostatic unity of God and human flesh in the same manner as Jesus. In using these terms, however, the council fathers were clearly indicating that in Mary, quite uniquely, the *new redeemed creation* has begun.[65] She is a 'new creature', a second Eve, such that the process that sin had set in motion through Adam and Eve is now being deconstructed, by the second Eve and second Adam. She is also of a 'new substance' in being without sin, and her assumed body into heaven relates utterly to our own destinies as 'chosen' and 'redeemed'.

The *manner* of Mary's divinization suggested by Boff is problematic because by postulating a unique and singular hypostatization of the Spirit in Mary, such that it is 'in the same manner as the Son', Boff fails to allow for the 'divinization of all creation' (as the Eastern Orthodox tradition puts it) that *starts* in Mary's *active cooperation*, not *ends* in it. As the fathers of Vatican II put it in a later passage, in *Lumen Gentium* (65):

In the most holy Virgin the Church has already reached that perfection whereby she exists without spot or wrinkle (cf. Eph. 5.27). Yet the followers of Christ still strive to increase in holiness by conquering sin. And so they raise their eyes to Mary who shines forth to the whole community of the elect as a model of the virtues.[66]

Mary is *a* model, and the pre-eminent one *within* Christ's body, but not only within, for she herself also *forms* his body, the Marian church. However, she is not the *only* one.[67] In so much as Boff implies a unique hypostatic incarnation of the Spirit in Mary, like that of Jesus as Logos, he seems to defeat his own objectives. If Mary is a model and not the model, as affirmed in *Lumen Gentium* 65, there is no single static notion of the divinized feminine frozen alone in Mary, although in her giving birth, giving form and shape, mirroring that pre-eminent role of the Holy Spirit in creation, and in the many holy women and men of Israel, Mary is rightly held up as Mother of Christ and Mother of all Christians. Without her consent, without her active human cooperation, without her nurturing of Jesus and her abiding support and shaping of his ministry[68] – even unto death, and then after death, the story of Christianity could not be told. *Lumen Gentium* 56, makes the important contrast between Mary and Eve, such that:

just as a woman contributed to death, so also a woman should contribute to life. This contrast was verified in outstanding fashion by the Mother of Jesus. She gave to the world that very life which renews all things, and she was enriched by God with gifts befitting such a role.

In wanting to stress Mary as a model, not the model, her pre-eminent status is not under dispute, but the fact that Boff's hypostatic divinization of her threatens to destroy *her relationality* to all creation and with it, precisely, the possibility of multiple female 'divinizations', those women, sung and unsung, who have been active co-redeemers like Mary, traditionally termed the saints of the church.

Before proceeding, I need to address (for I cannot answer) one possible objection to the drift of my argument: why allow for the single hypostatization of Jesus and then claim, were Mary to be included in this divine economy, it would confuse matters? And does not my scenario, with a securely established male incarnation, utterly fail to address Irigaray's challenge regarding the feminine divine? My response to

Irigaray will be found more fully at the outset of Chapter 2. However, here I would at least stress that we cannot manipulate God's manner of revealing God's self in the economy of salvation. If the theological 'evidence' and 'arguments' point against Mary having the status that Boff desires, then we really cannot change and alter scripture to suit our desires. I realize that my exegesis of scripture and Vatican II are hardly 'definitive', but for the moment I ask the reader to grant the validity of my exegetical labours. At this juncture, some might well say with Daly that there is no redemption for women within Christianity, or that the recovery of a non-patriarchal trinitarian taxonomy is impossible. Leaving Christianity would be the only honest thing to do. I have tried to suggest, however, that there is an alternative reading that does not change the testimony of scripture regarding the scandal of particularly in Jesus Christ, but instead finds within it, and elements within the tradition, the possible resources to at least try and think through the unbaptized patriarchy that constantly threatens to strangle Christianity.

Regarding the maleness of Jesus, I will be arguing in the next chapter that while Jesus' embodiment (made flesh) is absolutely vital as Irigaray so relentlessly stresses, and that this flesh was undeniably male, *this* particular man and his life was not founded upon the murder of the mother, but a profound acknowledgment of her (sometimes rightly mirrored in the church – and sometimes grossly distorted); and, in *this* event, the creating of a new order is inaugurated, the age of the Spirit and the Bride. But the event of Jesus is itself utterly relational depending, as it does, on Mary. That, in turn, as I very briefly noted in my exegesis of Luke 1.35, is relatedly dependent on the holy women and men of Israel and finally relationally dependent upon the earth, just as we are told in Genesis 2.7, where man is created from the 'dust from the ground'.[69] Hence, the event of Jesus is itself *not* an isolated story of one man, his deeds, teachings, death and so on, but more specifically the entire story of Israel that is both concealed and told in the Old Testament, and, more widely, the entire story of all nations, eschatologically told in the book of Revelation. Hence, Jesus' relational significance excludes no one – and certainly not women, upon whom he acknowledges his dependence and relations. This should allow for a fuller recovery of the Marian church and the church of female saints such that an imaginary might be developed to facilitate both women and men's inter-subjectivities within the 'person' of Christ, and their full flourishing within the sharing of God's perichoretic love.

This would also suggest that a questioning of Irigaray's presuppositions is in order to show that, in this instance, Irigaray's specific demand for a female divinity which refuses the 'particularity' of the incarnation (which admittedly can be understood in a number of ways) perhaps highlights an underlying philosophy that is fundamentally inimical to Christianity. Perhaps the matter can be put tentatively for the moment. Because Irigaray portrays the male as phallic and presupposes a notion of feminine subjectivity, is she in danger of an essentializing 'male' and 'female'? And in so much as this essentializing then requires that there be male and female deities, a divine couple, might it be that carrying through her project in theological terms renders God not unlike Freud's 'Father' in the sky, but now we have 'father and mother' or, to use Irigaray's terms, 'a divine couple'? If female divinity is predicated upon the need for women's subjectivity, then it is very likely that divinity will be finally a projected desire for what women want to be – rather than a 'response' to a gift, that in its own story offers an alternative imaginary.[70] Admittedly, far too often, the church itself has failed to imagine, and continues to fail to imagine, its own alternative creation. For the moment, however, I will leave the question hanging and return to my argument as to how the figures of Mary and the many women saints could partially respond to Irigaray's challenge.

Let me tentatively develop my comments regarding Mary not being *the* model, but *a* model, and the special relationship to the Spirit that this claim does have. *Lumen Gentium* (62 and 66b) implicitly rules out Boff's elevation of Mary to a separate hypostatization, but only because through Christ *all* creation has been redeemed, and that all women and men can actively cooperate and participate in this redemption. This participation means a sharing in the divine life of love, not that we become Jesus, truly human and truly divine, but that through his representative humanity our humanity is transformed by participation in the divine life. We become 'adopted' daughters and sons. The Greek church daringly calls this our 'divinization', but never means by this that we are in hypostatic union with the Logos, as was Jesus Christ, nor in hypostatic union with the Spirit (as with Boff). Rather, through the Spirit we share the divine life that is made present in Jesus' 'person' and which resides sacramentally in his eucharistic communion within the church. Hence, Jesus' divinity means that all men and women are now capable of representing the divine in their participation with the risen Lord, through the power of the Spirit. And this process of virtual divinity, to echo Irigaray's phrase 'very nearly divine', is most clearly found in Mary, a woman, a mother, a virgin, a queen and a daughter.

In Mary's assumption into heaven we have prefigured our own resurrection; and in her immaculate conception, we have a reminder of our original becoming, more original than original sin, and prefiguring our final end. Her status as 'Co-Redeemer' mirrors our own invitation to be co-redeemers in our constantly flawed, but graced, attempts to be the body of Christ. *Lumen Gentium* 62 reads:

> For no creature could ever be classed with the incarnate Word and Redeemer. But, just as the priesthood of Christ is shared in various ways both by the sacred ministers and by the faithful, and as the one goodness of God is in reality communicated diversely to His creatures, so also the unique mediation of the Redeemer does not exclude but rather gives rise among creatures to a *manifold cooperation* which is but a *sharing in this unique source*. [my emphasis]

This passage opens up immensely fruitful avenues along which some of Irigaray's objections could perhaps be addressed, for it stresses that the embodiment of divinity in Jesus Christ does indeed open up a 'third age', that of the Spirit and the Bride, whereby female and male representations of the divine are facilitated in the power of the Holy Spirit. For the unique embodiment of divinity in *this* man Jesus Christ 'gives rise among creatures to a manifold *cooperation* which is but a *sharing* in this unique source' (my emphasis). The terms 'cooperation' and 'sharing' are neither purely 'active' nor 'passive' but reciprocal and, given Vatican II's grounding of the church in the trinitarian life of God, these terms are rather important for both reading *Lumen Gentium* as well as addressing our set of questions.

The *sharing* of this unique source requires a 'sharing' that is the nature of this unique source: the perichoretic reality of the divine persons. The history of 'perichoresis' is of course a complex one, but at least one function the term historically played was to avoid subordination and monarchy within the trinity by stressing the co-equal sharing between the three persons.[71] The two Latin terms used in translating the Greek word, *circuminsessio* and *circumincessio*, are telling in their different root metaphors. *Sessio*, being seated, brings out the sense that each is always seated by the other, for *circum* refers to 'side'. This sense of being seated by each other's side, so that one never sees one, without the other being seen, is beautifully expressed in Andrej Rublev's famous icon of *The Trinity* that is discussed in Chapter 4, where the three figures are seated together sharing in the eucharistic banquet, each gazing upon the other. *Circumincessio* conveys a more dynamic inner presence, related to the root *incedere*, meaning to permeate or interpenetrate. A good image for this might be the way in which psychoanalysis presupposes the presence of the father and mother within the patient in such ways that affect all object relations, often entirely unconsciously. One might say that the co-presence of the father and mother actually form whom we are. The analogy breaks down in so much as there is no equivalent 'unconscious' within the trinity. The conscious indwelling that does exist is often imaged with a nuptial metaphor. In Chapter 3, I will be exploring this sense of the term in relation to Rushdie's novel. For the moment, one might say that the broad sense of perichoresis as 'mutual indwelling' properly emphasizes the relational intimacy and unity that is both within the trinity and also characterizes God's relations with human persons, without the effacement or detraction from the distinctiveness of each and all persons, both human and divine. Similarly, in this co-redeeming cooperative function, enacted primarily in Mary, there is the greatest relational intimacy without confusion of natures, or erasure of the distinction and difference between creator and created order.

Paragraph 62 of *Lumen Gentium* occurs within its Marian-ecclesiological conclusion. Mary, like the church, is both active and passive – in this sense, reciprocating and sharing the gift of love. On the one hand, were she to be depicted as *primarily* passive, purely an instrument of a greater will and force, as is a tendency in von Balthasar and John Paul II, and not even absent from *Lumen Gentium*, there is a profound danger of her being incorporated into the representative semiotics of male desire. On the other hand, if she is represented as purely active, initiating salvation, she is in danger of being made into God, precisely the danger to which Boff does indeed succumb. Aquinas rightly notes that only God is pure activity, not a static being, a noun, but rather a verb.[72] We in contrast are both active and passive by virtue of being created dependent beings.

The debate in the late 1990s within the Roman Catholic Church as to whether there should be an official pronouncement of Mary as 'Co-Redeemer' could perhaps be seen as representing the force of Boff's suggestions without, like him, succumbing to divinizing Mary. And the very fact that a woman could be defined 'Co-Redeemer' (as she is already in terms of her liturgical role within the Roman and Orthodox communions) suggests that feminine divine representation is not only thinkable but, even more importantly, embodied and capable of pluriformity (as we shall see below).

To further elaborate on the significance of the title 'Co-Redeemer' as it develops a fruitful response to Irigaray's challenge, it is worth briefly analysing two interesting, although unconvincing, objections to the official definition of this title. The objections come from a Roman Catholic and a Greek Orthodox theologian. They both agree that Mary can be properly called 'Co-Redeemer', but argue that this should not be officially defined because of its ecumenical divisiveness. The reason for this brief exploration is to show how this rightful title for Mary actually highlights the legitimate point that Co-Redeemer is also a title that *all* Christians, women or men, share by virtue of Mary. Hence, the Marian church, the body of Christ, the people of God, are called to be co-redeemers, while always themselves in need of the redemption already attained by Israel, Mary and Jesus Christ.

Bishop Kallistos of Diokleia, our Orthodox theologian, warns that if 'Co-Redeemer' is understood apart from Christ or the rest of the church, then it becomes distorted. He takes up Paul's startling phrase in Colossians 1.24, 'I am now rejoicing in my sufferings for your sake, and in my flesh I am completing that which is lacking [hysterēma] in Christ's afflictions, for the sake of his Body, that is, the Church.' Paul's phrase about a deficiency in Christ startlingly alerts us that there could be something 'lacking' in Christ, and Paul's recognition that what is lacking is redeemed 'flesh', allows Paul to sacramentally relate 'Christ' to his 'church', the 'body of Christ'. Kallistos comments that Paul is not fundamentally calling into question the sacrifice of the Cross, but rather:

> at the same time through our own self-offering – through our own suffering and our martyrdom, inner or outward – we the baptised

make up 'that which is lacking' in Christ's suffering: we bear witness to his perfect sacrifice and we make it ever present in a bewildered and broken world. In this sense all the members of the Body are co-redeemers with Christ. Mary, however, is Co-Redeemer in a particular and outstanding way; for, as Mother of the Saviour, she is involved with a unique nearness in her son's work of salvation. There is, then, a special appropriateness in calling her the Co-Redeemer *par excellence*, so long as we never forget that she and we share the same vocation. We too are called, in union with her, to 'complete that which is lacking in Christ's afflictions'.[73]

Kallistos's point implicitly illustrates the startling possibilities of female 'divine representations', or rather 'virtually' divine, that begin with Eve. Without female genealogies, 'salvation history' simply does not exist. That redemption is carried within the transformed bodies of women in the church; and that this redemption is painfully borne 'from the beginning' via Eve, Sarah, Mary, Mary Magdala, Lady Godiva, Radegund, Mary Fisher, Margaret Clitherow, Perpetua and Felicity is the imaginary by which woman's salvation becomes representable.[74] Irigaray is utterly right in focussing on Christ's departure as heralding a new age, but to occlude the 'old age', as she does in her typology which tends to relegate the Old Testament to a frozen and irrelevant past, fails to realize that the very story of Jesus Christ is read both forwards and backwards, diachronically and synchronically, and is, at the same time, an unfinished story and unfinished reading. It is unfinished, precisely because all creation has not yet entered into and shared the redemption that has been attained and completed, precisely indicating the 'lack' in the Pauline sense. This unfinished incarnation, what Paul calls the lack within Christ's afflictions, is what checks against the incarnation being rendered into a static divinization of male flesh, but rather as the beginning of the transformation of all flesh, both female and male.

René Laurentin's objections, like that of Bishop Kallistos, concern ecumenical scandal. And he, like Kallistos, turns to Paul's ecclesiology to point out that the scandal of the term 'Co-Redeemer' is not because it is applied to Mary, but only scandalous when limited to her: 'For we are all "co-operators with God" in Jesus Christ (co-workers, St Paul says: the Greek word is *synergoi* in I Cor. 3.9).'[75] Laurentin argues, however, that there is a difference when the term 'Co-Redeemer' is applied to Mary as opposed to the rest of humanity. He comments on Cardinal Journet's attempt to placate critics of the Marian title when Journet argued, but 'we are all co-redeemer'. Laurentin remarks: 'This is an ingenious solution, but has nonetheless the disadvantage of making us overlook the fact that Mary's co-operation is the first, foundational and unique.' While Laurentin is right to suggest that the body of the mother is 'foundational', this metaphor has the danger of suggesting a foundationalism in the opposite direction that overcomes patriarchy – simply by replacing it with matriarchy. It is the relationship of love *between* father and mother, between two embodied persons, that is more foundational, and it is precisely the relationship between persons which reflects the trinitarian reality that constitutes the gift of being.

The point I am making is that Mary, along with women and men co-redeeming 'saints' of the church, provides the possibility for developing and employing an imaginary that includes rather than excludes women and the feminine within the divine economy. This is not unproblematic, for the process of creating saints and the values which they exemplify are often supportive of patriarchy. I will return to this in the final chapter. Nevertheless, while the exaltation of female virgins can easily become encoded within the economy of male desire, so too can they be utilized within an Irigarian outlook. Janette Gray (RSM), a Catholic nun, reflecting on celibacy incisively writes: 'Following Irigaray, woman's celibacy threatens the male *logos*, by subverting the male definition of woman as sexual object, through combining the feminist idea of non-mirrored woman with the male symbolic of female purity.'[76] This mimetic teasing, suggested by Gray, allows for the possibility of an imaginary in which women do not belong to the economy of male desire, but are, with men, caught up in the desire of God's love, the desire that will not efface, but bring forth further generative love. In this sense, women (with men) become co-redeemers and co-representers of a new order of creation. The concrete lives of so many women thereby constitute the 'tradition' and 'scriptures' by which the church is formed and guided, lives that more fully embody the 'sharing in this unique source', that make up 'that which is lacking' in Christ's afflictions. What I have been suggesting is that this Spirit-oriented ecclesiology, very akin to Irigaray's, pushes us to see that Christ is not a finished event, but a body coming into glory, a body that is a crucified body,[77] and a body in which male and female are co-constituted. This communal body is the site where *relations* between embodied persons analogically participate within the relations of God's trinity: *love as perichoretic relationship*, not *per se* in gendered bodies, but always *between* gendered bodies. I shall return to this theme throughout the book, and in the final chapter.

While the contemporary American Roman Catholic theologian Elizabeth Johnson's feminist constructivism is extremely illuminating and helpful, she perhaps minimizes the significance of the Spirit's co-constituting-subjectivities in the making of saints, in the empowering of persons to become more God-like, returning to the image in which they were created. She cites a Protestant student's complaint, with which she agrees, that:

> When I began the study of Catholic theology, every place I expected to find an exposition of the doctrine of the Holy Spirit, I found Mary. What Protestants universally attribute to the action of the Holy Spirit was attributed to Mary.[78]

This is not only a Protestant complaint, however, for the Catholic Johnson agrees with her student, and the French Dominican Yves Congar is also cited to support this concern.[79] In contrast, my argument has been that Mary and the church are precisely where one might expect to find a more developed doctrine of the Holy Spirit, for the Holy Spirit's reality is thoroughly ecclesial and community forming. The Holy Spirit does indeed create a new imaginary, a new counter-culture, in which women and men are redeemed from the name of the phallic Father, so that they might newly relate in forgiving and healing love. In some respects, Johnson's comment is uncharacteristic, given her later tentative suggestion that perhaps the neglect of the Spirit is because of the 'tradition's forgetfulness of the . . . alliance between the idea of Spirit and the roles and persons of actual women marginalized in church and society'.[80]

However, the entire strategy that I am proposing still falls short of Irigaray's demand for a strict female 'equal' to the male embodiment of the divine in Jesus. This demand for 'equal' representation is a demand ironically in danger of succumbing to just the logic that Irigaray criticizes in Schüssler Fiorenza: 'equal to whom'? It is also a demand that is a refusal to accept the scandal of the particularity of the incarnation, a scandal to Jew and Greek, male and female, and perhaps modernist and postmodernist too. Furthermore, a request for a divine feminine presupposes that God *per se* is gendered and the traditional doctrine of the incarnation refuses to allow maleness to *be* divine in its insistence that there is no co-mingling or heretical confusion between the human and divine. In this respect, predicating exclusive male priestly ordination on the grounds of Jesus being male is in grave danger of confusion between the natures.[81] I will return to these counter questions to Irigaray shortly.

Having shown briefly that an alternative trajectory to Boff's is preferable regarding the Spirit and the 'divinization' of women and men, rather than Mary alone, I want to return to Boff's argument regarding gender and divinization to focus on the way concrete lives within the church are far more illuminating in attending to questions of gender than are 'ideas' of what 'qualities' constitute 'masculine' and 'feminine'. Through the history of saints we see how women's lives within the church, as mothers, prophetesses, teachers, religious leaders, soldiers, martyrs, doctors and so on generate an imaginary that might facilitate 'feminine' subjectivities. However, Boff develops his definitions of masculine and feminine in what I take to be very problematic ways – especially as he then applies these terms to the divine. Boff regards not only Mary as feminine Spirit but also the 'Father' as 'motherly father' and the 'Son' as 'daughterly son'. While Boff opens very important doors, in other ways, I shall suggest, he succumbs to essentializing sexual difference within the divine, precisely because of his premature essentializing of sexual difference within the created order. This problematic within Boff is not unlike that found within some sections of Irigaray's corpus – which is why I want to stay with Boff for a little longer. I am not arguing against sexual difference, but rather suggesting that what such difference might mean is not all that clear in a fallen creation. This fallen creation is partly exposed in Irigaray's deconstruction of a phallic economy of signs, under which representing real difference remains a fragile utopian hope.[82]

Boff bi-sexualizes all three persons of the trinity and, despite his earlier arguments, he treats them in their traditional taxonomic ordering as Father, Son, Holy Spirit. In terms of the 'Fatherhood' of God Boff writes: 'Jesus' Father is a Father only through being also a Mother, uniting the strength of paternal love with the tenderness of maternal love.'[83] Regarding this characterization, David Cunningham criticizes Boff's redefining the word 'Father', while still retaining the term, despite Boff's acknowledgment of its inevitable patriarchal associations. Cunningham argues that Boff cannot simply *insist* that 'Father' should not be understood in single gender terms when its social reception is likely to be the reverse.[84] I think Cunningham's point is important. My further concern is the way 'tenderness' and 'strength' are polarized by Boff into feminine and masculine essences. When we turn to the Son, this suspicion is fuelled when Boff catalogues these gender essences in more detail. 'Femininity is a basic constituent of every human being, male or female. It involves a number of characteristics: tenderness, care, self-acceptance, mercy, sensitivity to the mystery of life and of God, cultivation of . . . interiority'.[85] While this catalogue may well have some truth in contemporary capitalist economies, it is surely odd to give it such ontological force. No wonder then, when it comes to the Spirit, Boff is inclined to elevate the embodiment of these 'feminine virtues' of tenderness, care and so on into a single hypostasis, enacting Irigaray's divine couple but only at the cost of ontologizing various virtues as masculine and feminine. This tension is seen in Boff in a sentence which seems to run against his Christological claim that Jesus embodies both the masculine and feminine aspects, where he suggests that if Mary is properly seen as the hypostatization of the Holy Spirit then 'Jesus and Mary would represent the whole of humanity'.[86] This binary divide eventually drives Boff to posit two paths of salvation, for sexual difference is now statically essentialized in God, leading to a heaven where sexual difference segregates the community of the blessed:

> Men will find themselves taken up, in the likeness of Jesus of Naza-reth, into the Person of the Son. Then they will everlastingly be adopted sons in the eternal Son, expressions of love, wisdom and life of the Father. Women will find themselves taken up, in the likeness of Mary of Nazareth, into the Holy Spirit, and will reveal the eternal Father-Mother and the only-begotten Son; they will be united to the divine Three in love and tenderness so as to be united in tenderness and love to all created beings.[87]

What is imagined in this description is a drastic falling short of precisely the key term that Boff has argued for throughout his book: perichoresis, the mutual indwelling of one in all, without the erasing of difference. Instead, Boff's beatific vision turns into a heavenly hostel with separate quarters for men after the order of the Son, where the residents there do not meet the feminine Spirit or the Father-Mother, but remain eternally adopted sons with the real Son experiencing the life of the Father. However, women enter after the order of the Mother, into the Holy Spirit, which also gives them access to the Father-Mother and daughterly-son, unlike the men. Women will have access to the men's dorms, but not the other way round! I do not want to trivialize Boff's very important achievements and concerns, but simply to recall a wiser statement he makes earlier in his book: 'It is difficult for us to identify what is feminine in the eternal sisterly Son or brotherly Daughter, without falling into cultural clichés or mere arbitrary statements.'[88] While recognizing the crisis of the phallocratic sexuate order, it is surely untimely to jump right over and out of this order with its still well-erected fences, in the guise of either 'new man' or 'liberated women'.

To summarize so far. First, I have tried to show that Irigaray's argument that the Christian trinity represents a hom(m)osexuate construction indeed highlights a most disturbing denigration of the Holy Spirit in both western and eastern trinitarian taxonomies. Secondly, I have suggested that the well-intentioned arguments advanced by Boff to rehabilitate the Spirit in feminine terms by divinizing Mary or by attributing to the Spirit a purely feminine identity might actually subvert his own intentions in essentializing sexual difference, either in terms of a premature list of characteristics or in terms of a reductionist biological morphology. Thirdly, in the process of carrying out this second task I have been suggesting in contrast to Irigaray and Boff that Mary should not be divinized, and in fact her very divinizing runs against the proper insight that *all* creation is divinized. This allows for multiple feminine divine representations, not just one as a mirror 'equal' to the one man Jesus – who is indeed not one, but is risen and now a community, called the 'body of Christ', which still remains a broken body until all creation is redeemed. It may be that Irigaray and Boff's goals might best be met by attention to the way in which the Holy Spirit is able to transform women (and men) into images of God, so that they may become co-redeemers, by loving and forgiving relationships, to each other. By arguing that the official declaration of Mary as co-redeemer may properly highlight her pre-eminence as the first redeemed

Co-Redeemer, the cult of female saints and co-redeemers might also provide just that imaginary whereby women's subjectivities may be attained in multiple forms.

My proposal is advanced with a clear recognition that the politics of saintly representation require much further investigation, and that many women were burnt, tortured and killed rather than being allowed appropriate power within the church. Joan of Arc is one of the few to be recovered from the fire. However, my argument is that despite these serious problems, quite uniquely within western culture, the Catholic tradition provides a symbolic order which does not feature women entirely in terms of male desire. That this symbolic order is multiple and complex has also meant that it has been and continues to be utilized to justify the worst excesses of phallocratic domination. Nevertheless, I want to suggest that the Roman Catholic Church, not without significant ambiguities, is capable of responding to the crisis of feminine representation so disturbingly raised in Irigaray's work. Were it even more fully to respond to some of the alternative patterns generated from its own symbolic world, the Guglielmites might not seem so heretical and some of the accounts of women saints in Sarah Maitland's *Angel and Me* might be incorporated into the *Divine Office*.

I now turn to the final section of this chapter in which I want to ask: should we call the Spirit 'she'?

Is the Spirit a 'she' or 'he' or 'it'?

To examine this question I will turn to a Christian community who prayed with ease to the Holy Spirit, whom they addressed in feminine terms. Before doing this, however, I also want to point out that the relations between feminine divine representation and social order and structuring are extremely complex, such that there is no straightforward causal trajectory: feminine divine representation equals socially liberated feminine subjectivities and redeemed relations. When Irigaray valorizes aspects of Greek and eastern cultures where divine matriarchies and divine triads have flourished, I would want to ask whether her theorizings paid adequate attention to the practices within those cultures?[89] Such research as there is problematizes clear causal connections whereby it can be said that female divine imaginaries necessarily lead to unimagined social orders of women flourishing. This is not to question the psychoanalytic point regarding object relations and representation but simply to suggest that specific semiotic configurations do not inevitably generate identical social configurations of practice. The transparent causality of signs is likewise assumed by Boff (and Moltmann) when they ahistorically predicate that politically correct doctrinal representation would result in politically correct societies. Boff repeats Moltmann's uncritical adoption of Pesch's famous thesis regarding monotheism as political monarchy. The Jewish biblical prophetic tradition is an obvious counter-example, and Moltmann and Boff never really address the serious criticisms of Pesch's thesis.

To repeat, I am not suggesting that doctrine has nothing to do with practice. On the contrary, practice is impossible to conceive without semiotic representation. What I question is whether such causalities are easily transparent or always homo-logic, always operating in terms of equivalence. Caroline Walker Bynum nicely expresses the complexity of the situation:

> Neo-confucian theories, which may be understood as feminizing the cosmos, were produced by men. Male mystics in medieval Europe venerated the Virgin Mary and wrote of Jesus as mother. Mormon theologians (all male by theological prescription) prohibit the priesthood to women because fatherhood means leadership. But what is the significance of Chinese men elaborating the idea of wholeness as feminine? Do female mystics in Christian Europe see God as mother and mean by *mother* what their male counterparts mean?[90]

To pursue my remaining question regarding the Spirit I will briefly turn to the feminization of the Holy Spirit within Syrian Christianity prior to the fourth century. I shall pursue my question primarily in relation to the important work of Susan Ashbrook Harvey on early Syrian prayers.[91] Harvey, closely using Sebastian Brock, offers an interesting analysis of two primary sets of texts in early Syrian Christianity where the Spirit is represented as feminine. There is little difference between Harvey and Brock on most technical points that follow, except that Harvey thinks the demise of the feminine Spirit was not, as Brock has it, exclusively due to translation techniques following Greek forms of discourse. Harvey suggests that it also occurred 'in concert with other changes to bring the Syrian churches into closer conformity with those of the Graeco-Latin west'.[92] The texts examined are the second-century hymns the *Odes of Solomon* and the fourth-century hymns of Ephrem Syrus. Ashbrook is well aware of the positioning of the genre she has chosen: hymns are not rational speculation, but form the praise offered by the body of the church. Before turning to the results of her close linguistic analysis of the materials, which focus my question well, it is worth citing in full *Ode* 19 of the *Odes of Solomon*, to get a taste of one of the most daring hymns (at least to modern sensibilities), showing that this feminization of the divine did not stop with the Spirit (*ruha'* is feminine in Syriac as is the Hebrew *ruah*) but was also employed of the Father and, as we will shall see later, also the Son.

A cup of milk was offered to me
And I drank it with the sweetness of the Lord's kindness.
The Son is the cup,
And He who was milked is the Father.
And She who milked Him is the Holy Spirit.
Because His breasts were full,
And it was not necessary for His milk to be poured out without
   cause.
The Holy Spirit opened her womb,
and mixed the milk of the two breasts of the Father.
And she gave the mixture to the world without their knowing,
And those who received it are in the perfection of the right hand.
The womb of the Virgin caught it,
and She received conception and gave birth.
And the virgin became a mother with many mercies.
And she labored and bore a son and there was no pain for her.
Because it was not without cause.
And she did not need a midwife
Because he [God] delivered her.
Like a man she gave birth by will.
And she bore with manifestation
And she acquired with much power.
And she loved with redemption,
And she guarded with kindness
And she manifested with greatness.
Hallelujah.[93]

In this hymn we see daring metaphoric applications, which are highly anatomically specific, and as such have evoked revulsion in some.[94] The Father has breasts and lactates, and the Holy Spirit milks the father and conceives the Son within her womb. Note also the overthrow of traditional sequential taxonomies. The Virgin, while having a womb, gives birth like a man! The question: what if the Holy Spirit was feminine? seems to be capable of being answered here.[95] But does it? And what kind of church did it produce?

One of the many interesting observations that Harvey makes is that the feminine images of the Spirit in the literature she examines, in *strong contrast* to the traditional pagan religions of the Syrian Orient and certain contemporary Gnostic speculative cosmologies, do 'not indicate either an understanding of [God as] a female being *per se*, or of a feminine Spirit like that of gnostic cosmology'.[96] Rather than feminizing the Spirit, which would be to anatomically fix various human sexual characteristics within the divine, Harvey charts a much more subversive and interesting use of language in the two sets of hymns of which *Ode* 19 is just one within a set. Harvey notes that the Holy Spirit is not exclusively feminine, that feminine gender words are also applied to the Father (womb – giving birth; breasts – feeding) and Son (womb – from which the world arises), and that gender metaphors are never used to identify divine being *per se*. Instead, she suggests that these metaphors are generated from an 'intense physicality' found in the *Odes*, which arise from both the human embodied experience of God, and in God's manifestation through bodies: Jesus, Mary and the saints.[97] Harvey locates this connection between bodies and language in the incarnation of the Son: 'Two patterns of images predominate beyond all others in this collection of hymns: that of the body's complete participation in the action of worship and that of speech, of declaring God's praise.'[98] This is developed by Ephrem Syrus' stressing that God becomes *flesh and language* in the person of Jesus Christ.

What is so interesting in Harvey's analysis, which raises counter-questions to Irigaray's project, is the feature that while fluid feminine imagery is employed, with sometimes amazing effect (although it would be imprudent to suggest that second-century hearers would respond like us), there is, according to Harvey, a relentless refusal to attribute gender to the divine *per se*. Such attribution is always in danger of idolatry, of univocally attributing to God what we find in the created world, for analogy reminds us that any likeness that indeed exists always does so within a greater unlikeness and difference. To forget this is to be idolatrous and anthropomorphic. However, without metaphorical and analogical attribution the glory of God's redemption of *all* creation is deeply neglected. Let me quote Harvey's extremely nuanced conclusion regarding the *Odes*:

> In the *Odes of Solomon*, gender imagery for the divine declares that the whole of the human person is created in God's image – including the body, including gender; the imagery also declares that gender, like any other part of human identity, barely reflects a reality that contains all things, transcends all things, and is greater than any language can convey. Thus the imagery tells both who humanity is (male and female, in the image of God), and who God is (more than gender can convey). At the same time, it bears witness to the notion that gender – but not one gender only – is somehow fundamental to both human and divine identity, albeit in ways that do not fit the human social conception (or construction) thereof. Gendered imagery here has its basis in the Godhead, not in the human biological and social order.[99]

Harvey's conclusion underscores the suspicion I have tentatively voiced at some trajectories within Irigaray's project: that the divine becomes a projection of a desired social order. Apart from Harvey's last sentence, which may seem to presuppose a rather untroubled acultural positivism in God's revelation, Harvey seems to capture well the way in which God's incarnation in human flesh has the capacity to destabilize all our forms of discourse: an unmarried man (Jesus) can have a womb from which all creation is born – including himself. Ephrem's *Hymns on Nativity* contain just such startling imagery:

> He was lofty but he sucked Mary's milk,
> and from His blessings all creation sucks.
> He is the Living Breast of living breath;
> by his life the dead were suckled, and they revived.
> Without the breath of air no one can live;
> Without the power of the Son no one can rise . . .
> As indeed He sucked Mary's milk,

He had given suck – life to the universe,
As again He dwelt in His mother's womb,
in His womb dwells all creation.[100]

Or, to recall another destabilization: the 'father' in heaven can have lactating breasts, for it is only a nourishing breast that can warmly and securely suckle new-born life. However, these images are not themselves unproblematic. Indeed they may well perpetuate patriarchy in unilaterally colonizing female metaphors for male figures (with the exception of Mary giving birth like a man?). This danger seems very real indeed, and we shall see it later in a more blatant form in Moltmann's work. The church structures and the place of women within them at the time suggest that it is not so straightforward to read these as subversive images. These images, however, avoid attributing gender to God *per se*. In contrast, Boff like Irigaray (in places) is drawn by the *temptation* to hypostatize sexual difference within the Godhead *per se*, which is always then a danger of reading off our socio-biological self-renderings on to our representation of God. At least in the *Odes of Solomon* there is a refusal against the idolizing of social configurations, be it the social family triunities of neighbouring pagan communities of 'Father, Mother and Son', or 'Mother, Father and Daughter', or the Gnostic male–female polarizations that were hypostatized within the divine.[101]

This subversion of gendered imagery is already found within the Bible, a point that is sometimes overlooked by Boff. Take for example the following comment by Boff:

> the Old Testament portrays the love of God for God's people through the figure of a mother in several places: 'Does a woman forget her baby at the breast, or fail to cherish the son of her womb?' (Isa. 49.15). Tenderness and comfort are expressions of motherly love.[102]

But the cited text from Isaiah is far more subversive, for it suggests that while we may in fact expect our human mothers to behave like this – and sometimes they do not, God is in one sense therefore like, but also very unlike, our human mothers. The full context of the quotation renders it quite differently compared to what Boff has retained by citing verse 15a alone and not 15b. 15a: 'But Zion said, "The Lord has forsaken me, my Lord has forgotten me." "Can a woman forget her sucking child, that she should have no compassion on the son of her womb?"' 15b continues: 'Even these may forget, yet I will not forget you.' Hence, in Isaiah there is a clear refusal to essentialize these gender traits within the divine. Equally, God's fatherhood is likewise not to be hypostatized according to the best expectations of human 'fathers' that we have (or the worst), which also means that there is no reason *per se* why the word 'Father' must be retained for God, even though I think it should be retained – but only along with other terms – because of its biblical resonances. However, there is no justification in treating Father as a proper name, as some theologians are inclined to do.[103]

Finally, it is also worth reiterating that the causality between divine female imaginary and social practices is far from clear. Harvey's analysis admittedly shows that the deity was not given essentialized gender attributes, even if analogically represented as feminine, and in this may differ from Irigaray's idealized (?) 'great Oriental traditions' where male and female deities 'exist alongside' each other and 'in their movements and their stability, neither one exists without the other'.[104] But Harvey's important study *Asceticism and Society in Crisis: John of Ephesus and the 'The Lives of the Eastern Saints'* shows clearly that the kind of imaginary generated within these hymns did not in itself result in any radical social re-ordering within an essentially patriarchal Christian community. In her study *Holy Women*, she writes of the depicters (the hagiographers) and depictions (the lives of the saints) that:

> in hagiography women often represent the extremes of sinfulness and sanctity. Above all, because they are women, not men, they reveal what our writers see as the astounding greatness of the Lord's grace and mercy. Deserving these gifts less than men by virtue of their gender, they thus display them all the more . . . The paradox is that in the society from which our hagiographers came, not different from others of its time, women were not valued as women. Yet some people of value were women.[105]

The upheavals of the sixth century did perpetuate change in women's roles but they were short lived, such that even 'during the period of crisis, women's roles, although expanded, were still at the periphery of church activities. They might head communities or dispense charity, but they did not become institutionalized leaders or gain any positions in the church hierarchy.'[106]

In the course of this chapter I hope to have carried out three related tasks in close engagement with Luce Irigaray. First, I tried to show that Irigaray's critique of a hom(m)osexuate trinity throws radical light on the denigration of the Holy Spirit within eastern and western trinitarian taxonomies. This is in large measure due to unbaptized Aristotelian and Platonic philosophies determining Christian theology. It need not be this way. I then explored Leonardo Boff's attempt to rectify some of the gender problems within the trinity in terms of his divinizing of Mary as an incarnation of the Spirit. This move would also seem to address Irigaray's difficulties. However, I argued that the biblical and conciliar tradition did not support Boff's proposals. Instead, they undermined the basis of Boff and Irigaray's questions in so much as there was a fundamental refusal by Boff and Irigaray to accept the particularity of the incarnation. Rather than the particularity of the incarnation promoting a hommosexuate imaginary, I tried to show how Jesus' particular incarnation brings into view the role of Mary and women saints as co-redeemers. Such an understanding of the Christian tradition may help to generate an imaginary whereby female subjectivity could be defined apart from the economy of male desire, and one in which both male and female together might find new life. I also noted that recovering these traditions from their often patriarchal control within Catholicism is an extremely difficult task. Furthermore, were such a recovery possible, it would not necessarily guarantee different practices within the community of the church, for there are complex causal relations between the imaginary and practices. I sought to illustrate this in the third section where I examined the question of whether it is right to speak of the Spirit as feminine in relation to the concrete practices of the early Syrian church. Following Harvey, I suggested that it was entirely legitimate to employ female metaphors of the Spirit, but interestingly the texts of the Syrian church also show that gender attribution to the very being of God is inappropriate, for God *per se* is neither male nor female. Analogical attribution to God must retain the sense that analogical likeness, and therefore representation of the divine, always operates within a greater dissimilarity and unlikeness, such that to retain either exclusively male or female metaphors for the Spirit is idolatrous, and not unlike Feuerbachian projectionism.

I do not imagine that the above has done anything other than raise further questions that require more clarification and response. My major concern was to show that trinitarian theology is itself faced with the question of its own authentic articulation in the face of the disturbing questions raised by Luce Irigaray. However, I have also tried to show the way in which the pluriform Roman Catholic tradition offers resources with which to respond to the difficulties and questions in a creative and interesting manner, and, to begin a series of counter-questions – which we will see in the next chapter. There, I continue this complex engagement in terms of the person of the 'Son' and the 'Father'.

2

Jesus' womb and the birth of the Father

1. The mother's son: Jesus

In this section, I will first turn to Irigaray's interpretation of the incarnation and one possible sense in which she understands divinity. This is a sense found in her by Grace Jantzen. If Jantzen is correct, I suggest that Irigaray's staging of the divine is finally guilty of Feuerbachian projectionism and of primary oral narcissism. If this is Irigaray's understanding, then the scandal of the incarnation of God made 'man' might not mitigate against feminist concerns. To then pursue this latter question, I will turn to a feminist Roman Catholic theologian, Tina Beattie, who engages with Irigaray on the question of the incarnation of a man. Beattie's essay indicates one important theme that I had begun to develop in the previous chapter. That is, the story of salvation requires a larger story to be told, which *relates* Jesus Christ most primarily to Mary and thus, by relating their story to that of Adam and Eve, another man and woman. This chain of relations is incomplete, and only comes to completion in the eschaton. Here genealogies run wild, and embrace all creation. Hence, Jesus' salvation is *only* understood in terms of co-redeemers, both women (primarily Mary) and men. I then further explore the relationship between the 'anatomical' and 'gender' in Jesus by asking whether Jesus' anatomical maleness means that the questions of gender difference are so easily settled either in terms of God being 'male' if the saviour is male or in terms of defining human sexual difference. The way I deal with this anatomical issue is to look at it – in art. First, I do this through an examination of a controversial Christa (the portrayal of a feminine Christ). Secondly, I look at the portrayal of Christ's penis in Renaissance art and in the cross-gendered image of Jesus in later medieval art, whereby the wound in Christ's side is transformed into both a 'vagina' and 'womb', out of which are born the church. In the light of these anatomical examinations, I end the Christological section returning to Colossians 1.24, to suggest that Irigaray is prophetic in one of her startling claims: the incarnation is partial. It is partial in so much as Christ's body, the church, lives between the Cross and final resurrection, between the now and the parousia. Christ's body is coming to completion primarily in those who eat his body and drink his blood, in the bodies of women and men, by the power of the Spirit. But first, let me problematize the terms of Irigaray's challenge, a questioning that I have alluded to throughout the previous chapter.

2. The phallic mother

If there is only male divine representation, then only men can be redeemed. Such is the claim made by Irigaray. Speaking of Jesus' incarnation in terms of the enfleshing of the feminine Sophia/Lady Wisdom, as Schüssler Fiorenza, Johnson, Ruether and other Christian feminists have suggested, fails in Irigarian terms to think through sexual difference. If the incarnation is unique, 'Jesus truly does represent the realization of the Patriarchy, the appearance of the father's and the Father's power' and thus eliminates 'the divine phenomenality of the daughter, of the mother–daughter couple' so as to 'lock it into the father–Father–son–Son genealogy and the triangle, father–son–Holy Spirit'.[1]

You will recall that Irigaray cites the Johannine passage (16.7) to imply that Jesus himself saw his incarnation as a partial one, thereby ushering in the age of the Spirit and Bride, whereby feminine divine representation may become part of the western imaginary. In the previous chapter, I have suggested one very fruitful avenue in which female representation can be facilitated: the retrieval of the Marian Co-Redeemer and the cult of female saints (sung and unsung). However, Irigaray's extremely allusive style suggests a number of possible interpretations of her project. Clearly, given her criticism of Schüssler Fiorenza, it is most likely that she is challenging Christian theology in a manner not unlike that of Mary Daly. This is certainly the way in which Grace Jantzen reads her. But how unlike Daly is Irigaray?

Jantzen's reading of Irigaray seems to me to replicate a *possible* idolatrous trajectory within Irigaray's work, which itself is in danger of failing to think sexual difference amidst human and divine difference. I would not want to press this criticism of Irigaray too far, but it remains spectral in her earlier work. It is worth raising simply to note a possible trajectory within her corpus. Her allusive style and shifting foci make it difficult to suggest a definitive reading. Jantzen commenting on 'Equal to Whom?' writes, that if Jesus' incarnation is partial:

> then his incarnation leaves room for other incarnations, other trinities, other sexualities. The masculinist symbolic is subverted, and the door is open for women to develop a new religious imaginary which will enable our sexuate becoming.
>
> Irigaray suggests that Jesus himself saw his incarnation as a partial one, as he indicated in his promise of the Paraclete. I am not clear whether or not she means this as a sober historical claim (which I suspect would be difficult to substantiate). What is more important is that she sees Jesus as a bridge: a bridge between men and God the Father, but also a bridge in the recognition that incarnation, divine flesh, must also be female, that each of us is (and is to become) divine. Women are not called upon to be equal to men: Are we not rather called upon to be equal to God – God the mother, the daughter, and the sister?[2]

There are some interesting questions generated by Jantzen's prose which further focus issues raised by Irigaray. The idea of Jesus' incarnation being partial and therefore facilitating 'other incarnations' requires some unpacking, as does the idea that we are called to be divine, 'equal to whom'? – equal to God? I have tried to show that precisely such a manoeuvre, in regard to Boff's divinizing Mary as 'equal' to Jesus eventually frustrates his intended outcome: that there be both male and female divine re-presentations. I suggested that a more sacramental understanding of the church as the Marian body of Christ opened the way to appreciate the potentiality of such symbolic representation within Roman Catholic ecclesiology – even if this church has a painful and long history, still vividly present today, of encoding its traditions within a patriarchal economy of signs. While such a strategic engagement with the sexually differentiated symbolic economy of Roman Catholic practice is fraught, it perhaps indicates a body within which such a new creation, as is desired by Irigaray, might arise – and has already perhaps risen with its Lord. It may well be that Irigaray's comment that the incarnation requires that each woman and man be 'virtually gods' actually suggests that we should not read her in the manner of Jantzen, even though one can hardly blame Jantzen's reading given the allusiveness of Irigaray's text and the possible logic of some of Irigaray's arguments.

There is a further difficult phrase in Jantzen's commentary. It evokes a disquiet that I have regarding Irigaray. While women are not called to be equal to men, surely the idea that they are called 'upon to be *equal* to God' is very curious. Such a claim is in real danger of simply generating God according to our own image (confirming Freud and Feuerbach), but now in the image of postmodern French feminist philosophy. This is not to question Irigaray's arguments regarding female representation and female genealogies, which I take with full seriousness in my ecclesiological proposals regarding Mary and the female saints. Rather, it is to question the kind of ' "equal" to whom' that is presupposed in her dis-ease with Jesus as male. Here there is an unresolved, and perhaps unresolvable, ambiguity within Irigaray's question: can a male redeemer save women?

Part of the difficulty is in knowing what constitutes male and female, other than purely anatomical difference. To make a point, one could reverse the question: if Jesus had been a woman with a vagina, then would only women be saved – and not men? I think this question fruitless because it detracts from the way in which God's self-revelation has taken place, but it is fruitful in focussing the question as to whether Irigaray has rendered gender difference inadequately by resorting to female morphology as the manner of establishing difference – and women's identity. While Irigaray's strategy has a proper concern to preserve sexual difference, and is required to subvert Lacan and Freud's phallocratic mirrors of representation, is there a possibility that Irigaray's speculum may also obscure the complexity of sexual difference, while at the same time essentializing it within both the human and divine imaginary? Some feminists have criticized Irigaray for essentializing woman in terms of women's anatomical taxonomy and, in so doing, succumbing entirely to the phallocratic discourse she has identified so effectively, a discourse that objectivizes and fixes woman in the gaze of the male in terms of her anatomical distribution. It has even led one feminist critic, Monique Wittig, to deny that she has a vagina in protest at Irigaray's 'anatomical specificity' which 'is itself an uncritical replication of a reproductive discourse that marks and carves up the female body into artificial "parts"'.[3]

I would like for a moment to develop a *very tentative* set of questions to Irigaray's feminine morphology, arising in part from Ana-Maria Rizzuto's groundbreaking study: *The Birth of the Living God: A Psychoanalytic Study*. Rizzuto is critical of Freud's rendering of religion as 'wishful childish illusion' and, following Winnicott, grants religion a necessary and important space in the imaginative symbolic that is required for human maturation and healthy object relations. Since this process is never completed, religion can play an important part in healthy human development throughout life. In the light of her clinical research Rizzuto, drawing on Erikson, also posits a plotting of transitional stages within religious maturation and the type of object relations related to those levels, and the corresponding representations of God related to each stage.[4] It is here that one of my questions to Irigaray becomes focussed.

Rizzuto claims that, at the oral stage of development, there is primary focus on bodily sensations with narcissism constituting identity, and at this stage there is no clear differentiation from the mother. God, within this oral stage, is experienced through the senses and mirrors the narcissistic child – which is a necessary moment in the child's development if the child is to develop object relations successfully. Fixation within this oral stage can be represented symbolically in the patient, who, while masturbating, says: 'My penis is my God.'[5] This intense sense experience provides gratification and positively reaffirms the primary narcissism that is required by the 'infant'. And 'unbelief' at this stage is the cry to God: 'You are not making me.'[6] Rizzuto is describing typical symptoms of fixation at the oral stage. I do not want to press Rizzuto's detailed Ericksonian taxonomy, but simply to use it to ask whether Irigaray is in danger of regressing into an enlightenment self, a female self-constituted and self-sufficient subjectivity, which in psychoanalytic terms constitutes oral fixation.

The reason why I have focussed on this fixation with the oral stage is because of Irigaray's strategic employment of the autoerotic metaphor of woman's identity *being constituted* by their own two lips which generate sexual pleasure. Irigaray's morphological argument is in danger of failing to affirm that *relationship* is central to self-constitution – and the trinity shows that the two are indivisible. In this respect, within Irigaray's work there is the possibility of seeing the emergence of an enlightenment self (and a pagan god), who is self-generating and self-constituting. Irigaray's autoerotic metaphor is of course strategically important in deflating the phallocentric economy of male desire, where woman never knows her own desire and is rendered purely an object of male desire (his wife, his lover, his mother, his sister). Nevertheless, Irigaray's employment of such morphological deconstruction comes close to simply counter-mirroring the male phallic deity, such that woman's authentic pleasure now symbolically generates the divine, rather than male autoerotic pleasure emblematically represented in a hommosexuate trinity. Irigaray sometimes seems to perpetuate the violence of the phallocratic economy in failing to think *relationality*, which is more primary and even constitutive of difference. Let me cite one of her most famous and representative passages:

> woman's autoeroticism is very different from man's. In order to touch himself, man needs an instrument: his hand, a woman's body, language . . . And this self-caressing requires at least a minimum of activity. As for woman, she touches herself in and of herself without any need for mediation, and before there is any way to distinguish activity from passivity. Woman 'touches herself' all the time, and moreover no one can forbid her to do so, for her genitals are formed of two lips in continuous contact. Thus, within herself, she is already two – but not divisible into one(s) – that caress each other.
>
> This autoeroticism is disrupted by a violent break-in: the brutal separation of the two lips by a violating penis, an instrument that distracts and deflects the woman from this 'self-caressing' she needs if she is not to incur the disappearance of her own pleasure in sexual relations.[7]

In this metaphor woman must construct her own identity, her own pleasure, but primarily *out of relationship* to either *other* women or men. This amounts to an almost pure oral narcissism. If the male phallocratic order mistakes the erect penis as God, as Rizzuto's study suggests, and as many feminist theologians maintain,[8] then curiously Irigaray's discourse on clitoral masturbation replicates this idolatrous taxonomy of the divine. Curiously, this establishes women as 'equal' to men in terms that mirror male phallic power (seeking its own pleasure and gratification) and find an 'equal' God to men's God, such that the anatomically specific body is distended and catharechted into symbolizing the divine. While the penis necessarily signifies 'violent break-in' within Irigaray's morphological staging, she fails to see, as Kristeva does, that love could mean that *relation* to *other* more fruitfully constitutes 'self'.

My concern is reinforced by Jane Gallop's employment of Kristeva to question Irigaray's autoerotic staging of female subjectivity. Gallop treats Irigaray's remarks addressed 'to Mother': 'Mother, I prefer a woman to you.' Gallop cites a passage in which the struggle for separation from the mother seems to overcome the authorial voice. Here is the cited Irigaray passage:

> You put yourself in my mouth, and I suffocate . . . Continue to be also outside. Keep yourself/me also outside. Don't be engulfed, don't engulf me, in what passes from you to me. I would like so much that we both be here. That the one does not disappear into the other into the one.[9]

Gallop asks whether Irigaray's statement and the syntactical paralysis of the text 'Is naively to believe one could ever totally separate the woman from the mother'.[10] Gallop, like Irigaray, refuses to identify femininity with maternity, but asks whether Irigaray's fear of the mother is her refusal of the 'phallic mother'. As noted in Chapter 1, the concept of the phallic mother was central to Lacan in his refusal to equate and identify morphology and the order of symbols. Gallop writes, in defending herself from an obvious feminist objection in employing the phrase 'phallic mother':

> A feminist protest might be lodged that to speak of a 'phallic mother' is to subsume female experience into male categories. Kristeva, however, hangs on to the phallic categories. Perhaps it is this insistence on the seemingly paradoxical term 'phallic mother' which can most work to undo the supposedly natural logic of the ideological solidarity between phallus, father, power and man. The Phallic Mother is

undeniably a fraud, yet one to which we are infantilely susceptible. If the phallus were understood as the veiled attribute of the Mother, then perhaps this logical scandal could expose the joint imposture of both Phallus and Mother.[11]

That Irigaray's morphology can sometimes lend itself to essentializing underscores one trajectory of her autoerotic metaphor: infantile narcissism. It seeks to make a space which is non-phallic, but makes instead a space which excludes all conflict, all danger, all risk and relationship, for even the women who inhabit this space are 'idyllic' rather than real in failing to confront the possibility of 'egotism' in their own drives.[12] Gallop makes this same point, pursuing the Kristeva–Irigaray engagement:

> The idyllic space of women together is supposed to exclude the phallus. The assumption that the 'phallus' is male expects that the exclusion of males be sufficient to make a non-phallic space. The threat represented by the mother to this feminine idyll might be understood through the notion that Mother, though female, is not the less phallic. So, as an afterthought, not only men, but Mother must be expelled from the innocent, non-phallic paradise. The inability to separate the daughter, the woman, from the mother then becomes the structural impossibility of evading the Phallus.[13]

It is precisely this 'structural impossibility' that might make it impossible to evoke pure feminine representations (or pure male representations) which really save women (or men). Or to put it in theological terms, sin affects both women and men, even if differently. In Irigaray's undisturbed space of autoeroticism, there is no question of disruption, which might indicate there is also no question of real relations and the difficulties of negotiating them.

I am sure that Irigaray as a psychoanalyst is well aware of such difficulties, but my comments relate to the level of her discourse and its hidden manifestations, not her biographical space or her explicit text.[14] Even if my criticisms have some grounding, they do not discredit Irigaray's work, nor do they call into question the strategic importance of single sex caucuses, be they women's groups, schools, or convents – in terms of women finding sites whereby women can begin to develop and generate different and multiple representations that work against phallocentricism.

The point I have been labouring is that trinitarian theology, at least of the type reconfigured in contrast to a hom(m)osexuate trinitarian economy, suggests that *relations* are fundamental, and relations of per-ichoretic reciprocity and love generate the creativity that bears analogical resemblance to God's creativity and God's love – which in fact we, as embodied persons, represent. Hence, loving, redeeming *mediated* object relations are an essential precondition for love to flourish. However, trinitarian relationality also serves to question an assumption that oper-ates possibly within Irigaray, and certainly within Jantzen and Daly: if maleness equals one sex, and Jesus was male, then only one sex is saved. What women need is a female saviour. What remains problematic within this equation is the assumption that men could possibly be saved *apart* from women, or women apart from men, given that God created human persons 'male and female' (Gen. 1.27), in relation, and in God's own image. While the creation stories in Genesis are certainly problematic and capable of patriarchal interpretations (as the history of Christianity shows), I am wanting to question the dualistic idea in Jantzen and to some extent Irigaray that one gender could actually be redeemed without that being a sense of related events which require the redemption of all persons, of whatever gender, for any redemption to be possible. Otherwise, what seems to be envisaged is a 'maleness' that exists within some hermetically sealed autonomy, apart from relations to women and men and vice versa. Redeemed female subjectivity is not possible out of relationship to redeemed male subjectivity; and neither male nor female redemption is possible under the sign of the phallus, or within hommosexuate language. Without God's trinity, thinking difference is in danger of running into thinking duality, for without *relationships of love* difference has no chance of being celebrated, let alone established.

If, as I indicated earlier, unbaptized Aristotelian epistemology and middle neo-Platonist emanationism were and are in danger of restricting trinitarian thinking, while nevertheless being central in trinitarian theol-ogy's development, might there be an analogy with unbaptized feminist psychoanalytical philosophy shaping trinitarian theology? On the one hand, unbaptized feminist psychoanalytical philosophy so positively contributes to rescuing the subordination of the Spirit in both eastern and western taxonomies, precisely by pointing to male economies of desire encoding trinitarian figuration such that the Spirit plays the role of women: lacking subjectivity and personhood. On the other hand, when this is driven too far in the other direction, in divinizing female gender in the person of the Spirit, or in the person of Mary, or in divinizing male gender in the person of Jesus and the Father, there is set in train the dangers of anthropomorphism such that 'god' reflects our gender stereotypes or social patterns. Hence, we have cosmological anthropomorphisms (Torrance's criticisms of Zizioulas) where 'god' reflects the idea of good human heterosexual couples – Irigaray's divine 'couple', or the nuclear family with the tritheistic family trinities of paganism, or, as we have seen in the counter-tendency, a binatarian male couple that excludes women in the reign of father and son. If sexual difference is projected into the divine reality, then it begins to dominate the divine universe such that sexual difference is predicated as a dual salvation process in Boff's two ways of the Son and Mary, or in Irigaray's assumption that only a female god could save women just as only a man can save men. In contrast, I want to return to the argument begun in the previous chapter, that redemption consists in the transforming of *relations between* men *and* women, and between each other. Let me return to this via an essay by a contemporary Catholic feminist, Tina Beattie.

3. Why Jesus was male

Beattie addresses Irigaray's challenge concerning the maleness of Jesus, but from within the context of Roman Catholic symbolics. Beattie responds to the Irigarian critique that Christ as man could not be redeemer of both male and female. In reply, Beattie simultaneously retells the Christian story from the middle (the story of Jesus Christ), the end (that of the resurrected communion with a trinitarian God), and the beginning (the creation story). This retelling has the effect of showing that God's perichoretic love transforms both our conception of time and of relations. Commenting on Genesis 3.12–13 where Adam blames Eve, Eve blames the serpent, and both experience alienation from themselves and God, Beattie argues that the creation narratives show that: 'After the fall, difference represents not the diverse goodness of creation but otherness and alienation marked by guilt and blame.'[15]

Commenting then on Genesis 3.17–19 she argues that in the fall Adam is alienated from his own body and from nature. To Adam it is said: 'Accursed be the soil because of you. With suffering shall you get your food from it every day of your life.' Adam's predicament generates the phallic order: 'The phallus symbolizes Adam's need to achieve domination over the body of Eve and over the body of the earth in order to survive'.[16] The phallic order of power and domination characterize his false search to overcome the alienation between man and woman and between persons and nature. Eve, meanwhile, remains in contact with nature through her fertility, but now this relationship with nature is under the mark of domination and pain. To Eve it is said: 'I will multiply your pains in childbearing, you shall give birth to your children in pain. Your yearning shall be for your husband, yet he will lord it over you' (Gen. 3.16). While I have one reservation about Beattie's exegesis and a possible trajectory within her argument, let me continue with my exposition.[17] Note how the positioning of Christ is *relatedly dependent* on a story about a man and woman, and then further *relatedly dependent* on the story of Mary's cooperation. Beattie now goes on to suggest how it is that the man Jesus redeems both men and women without erasing sexual difference.

I cite her at length at this important juncture of her argument:

Why does the Word become male flesh? Is it because Eve, paradoxically cursed and blessed in childbirth, offers no symbol of femininity akin to the masculine phallus that represents the severance between word and flesh? It is Adam who experiences alienation from the earth and enters into battle with the material world, while Eve remains bound in her fertile but suffering body to the cycles and rhythms of nature. When the Word becomes flesh, Adam is reunited with the body he has denied, but in that reunification the power of the disembodied phallic symbol is disabled by the reality of the body's suffering, its softness and vulnerability. Christ took on the phallus in order to expose the 'big, hard, up' lie which sanctions male power and brutalizes the male body.[18] 'God dealt with sin by sending his own Son in a body as physical as any sinful body, and in that body God condemned sin' (Rom. 8.3). If the social order is governed by the phallus, then women as well as men sin by their association with the phallic order, whether through aggressive participation or through passive collusion. When Christ became the sinful male body, he liberates women as well as men from the domination of the phallus.[19]

Beattie begins to address the nub of Irigaray's and Jantzen's objection, and in the process shows that if a focus is placed on male gender without considering the *actual particular male* that is being redescribed, and the significations that are generated by that particular body, then to argue that only a man can save men amounts to redemption via anatomical identification – and, in my terms, a narcissistically projected divine. Furthermore, Beattie's strategy further allows for the unmasking of patriarchal 'Fatherhood' in so much as this 'Son' points to a different sort of 'Father':

> Every religion and culture has its law and its God which control our fallen desires by rewarding conformity and punishing difference. Until one day, a man comes claiming to be the Son of a different God, a God who puts love before the Law, who touches and heals, who communes with women and children, with lepers and outcasts, a God who seeks to topple the Freudian [phallic] world from within.[20]

With her emphasis on Mary's necessary part in the drama of redemption, her necessary cooperation, Beattie utilizes this typological pattern to show how the Marian dimension is vital to the proper telling of the Christian story, both in maintaining the female genealogies within the story – Eve and then the second Eve – and to show that the story is untellable without the *relation* between Adam and Eve, both first and second. In this way, just as the fall is untellable without both Adam and Eve so is the particular incarnation of God untellable without Mary and Jesus. Beattie also notes that the Marian dimension makes it possible to read Roman Catholic symbolic culture such that 'Mary's spirituality has the power to subvert sexual hierarchies that associate men with spirituality and women with carnality'.[21] Mary is after all the spiritual mother of the church and of all Christians. Hence, without having to resort to Boff's deification of Mary, Beattie develops an already extant tradition to provide the near-divine feminine representation(s) that Irigaray rightly demands and which might facilitate women's subjectivity within a new creation:

In the Catholic tradition, the resurrection and acension of Christ
finds its sexual complement in the assumption of Mary, declared as
a dogma in 1950. Mary, assumed into heaven body and soul at the
end of her life, is the heavenly bride, queen, mother, daughter and
virgin, loving transgressor of all the kinship systems that keep the
Freudian [phallic] world in place.[22]

Beattie shows how Christ's redemption cannot be spoken of without
speaking of all creation, both men and women, and also shows that the
event of redemption also requires and enlists a co-redeemer, first and
foremost, Mary. Mary is shown to be bride, queen, mother, daughter
and virgin, which is quite a typological triumph. This does not exclude,
however, but rather generates the possibility of other female divine
representations in the established and unwritten calender of female
saints, further co-redeemers: intellectuals, aunts, sisters, economists,
grandmothers, artists, goddaughters and teachers – to name a few.[23]

The argument of my previous section on the Holy Spirit indicates
how pneumatology and trinitarian theology cannot be disassociated from
Christology, Mary and human persons, both men and women, reflecting
God's glory. Here, via Beattie, I have also tried to suggest that the
reverse is also true. Christology cannot be dissociated from the Spirit
and Father, but, because Jesus is truly divine and truly human, neither
can he be disassociated from all human persons. It may well be that
'subsistent relations' is appropriately used not only in speaking of the
divine reality but also of the now transfigured human reality in the
light of Jesus Christ. Hence, subsistent relations are not only analogically
applicable but are also characterized by perichoresis which is important.
Relations and perichoresis together mean that Jesus' story cannot be
told out of its relationship to a series of stories and lives that interpenetrate each other and are formed precisely through these complex
relations of love and forgiveness, sin and violence, that together form
the creation that groans for a redemption that has already been attained.
In so much as creation is permeated by this redeeming love, seen first
and preeminently in Mary, then in the women and men who become
co-redeemers in the fecund diversity that constitutes becoming Christ-
like, we see an alternative form of life to that characterized by death,
narcissism and self-deception. In the next chapter, I will further explore
the notion of relations and perichoresis in terms of indwelling.

Before proceeding with my Christological argument, let me summarize this section so far. First, I have explored more closely Irigaray's allusive Christological challenge, showing that Irigaray may be in profound danger of simply generating a binary opposite to the phallic economy that she rightly opposes. In part, this may stem from her Freudian psychoanalytical background which (despite Winnicott and some others) tends to position God purely in terms of projected object relations. Hence, the need for a female god to equal the male god, Jesus, by which female and male subjectivity may be freely formed. However, I have suggested that it is in the relationship between gendered difference, not in gender itself, that we find the analogical bridge to the trinitarian God. Secondly, I then briefly outlined Beattie's defence of Jesus as male, as in fact 'necessary' for the redemption of the phallic order, a defence which also shows that the Roman Catholic symbolic tradition of Mary (and the female saints as argued earlier) is capable of providing the imaginary to sustain sexual difference and generate further patterns of redeeming life between women and men, patterns that challenge hommosexuate signification. I will now further explore the implications of the fact that Jesus had male genitals and what this might imply about the question of 'gender' in both human and divine persons.

4. Jesus' vaginal wound-womb

To proceed to examine the significance of Jesus' anatomy and whether 'Son' may be subsequently ontologically reified into male deity, I pick up on an aside made in Beattie's essay. Regarding the portrayal of the Christa figure, that of a female body on the cross, used by some feminists to challenge patriarchal representation, Beattie says:

> While there is a certain iconoclastic value in such tactics, I think they are fraught with risk. The crucified woman's body affirms rather than subverts the social order, holding up an image that does not call into question the values of patriarchy but affirms those values in their most violent aspects. Christa perpetuates the violence done to women by eternally inscribing the female body with the marks of her suffering.[24]

Beattie's objection to the Christa figure is not that Jesus was a man
per se and that he should not be represented otherwise, but to the way
in which such a representation risks affirming the phallic destruction
of women rather than subverting it. While I find this objection convincing, for it may further perpetuate the sadomasochism that is always
potentially positioned within patriarchal eroticism,[25] it raises two further
questions which I wish to examine. The first regards hypostatically
identifying phallocratic power with genital men. While Beattie at one
level steers clear of this identification, at another, this subliminal identification is present in her argument as I noted in an earlier endnote, and
likewise present subliminally in Irigaray.[26] While this kind of identification makes metaphorical and strategic sense, there is always a danger
of the metaphor turning literal. Is Beattie's criticism of the Christa
figure an example of this?

Take for instance Margaret Argyle's controversial and disturbing
woven tapestry: *Bosnia Christa* (see Figure 1).[27] It was completed in
1993 and was Argyle's response to hearing of the rape and brutal
denigration of women in Bosnia. The mixed textile work depicts a
Christa, the naked body of a woman on a grainy cross, against a deep
but translucent red vaginally shaped background, which has two lips/
curtains on either side both framing and containing the Christa. While
the tapestry could be interpreted as reinforcing the problems Beattie
identifies with Christa figures, it strikingly and metaphorically relates
the phallic violence upon Jesus' body on the Cross with that of the
violence against women, specifically the systematic raping of women in
Bosnia. By placing the cross within the bleeding vaginally shaped red-
form, there is also a metaphoric exchange of the blood associated with
the wounds of Christ, the thrusting of the spear into his side tearing
open his skin and breaking his life, with that of the literal phallus that
destroyed and deformed the lives of so many Bosnian women. The
'lack' in Christ's suffering is curiously woven into the fabric of this
image. Furthermore, by placing the symbol of death at the entrance to
a woman's vagina, Argyle's representation dramatically evokes Irigaray's
insight concerning the murder of 'woman' and the mother as the hidden
secret of western culture. The vagina, as entrance to the womb, is
battered with the violence of the spear in Christ's side. The unspoken
unshaped ecclesiology implicit in Argyle's representation, and it must
be unrepresented, is that not until such women as the Bosnian rape

Figure 1: Margaret Argyle, *Bosnia Christa* (1993) (Mixed textile)

victims have experienced healing can the church dare to call itself the
risen and glorified body of Christ. These women's bodies, as well as
the male rapists' bodies, belong in different ways to the body of Christ
– and without their redemption, without addressing their sufferings,
which form the 'lack' in Christ's afflictions, all flesh is not yet redeemed.
The church, with all creation, still resides within the tomb of Holy
Saturday, living between the crucifixion and the full resurrection.[28]

Irigaray seems to develop a not dissimilar meditation upon the
wounds of Jesus, which negotiate a delicate path between valorizing
abjection or glorifying violence against the innocent. Instead, Irigaray
sees in the wounds of Jesus the sharing of a wound that women bear
and, in this very act, the affirmation of women's subjectivity in naked
and vulnerable love. The passage is haunting and I cite it fully:

> And if 'God' who thus re-proved the fact of her non-value still loves
> her, this means that she exists all the same, beyond what anyone
> may think of her. It means that love conquers everything that has
> already been said. And that one man, at least, has understood her so
> well that he died in the most awful suffering. That most female of
> men, the Son.
>
> And she never ceases to look upon his nakedness, open for all to
> see, upon the gashes in his virgin flesh, at the wounds from the nails
> that pierce his body as he hangs there, in his passion and abandon-
> ment. And she is overwhelmed with love of him/herself. In his
> crucifixion he opens up a path of redemption to her in her fallen
> state.[29]

Clearly, this passage is evidence that my earlier criticisms of Irigaray
should not be pressed too far. It is a sublime insight into the trans-
signification that is generated in the Cross, such that a male at the very
point of death, can represent redemption for both men and women.
Argyle's Christa is a disturbing representation of an ecclesiology that
remains fragmentarily present in the life of the church, that of a church
that lives with the abject.

Argyle's Christa depiction (and many other contemporary Christas)
suggests further questions, only one of which I will here address. The
Christa is a modern semiotic representation, which perhaps betokens
women's more recent access to public modes of cultural production.

That the male figure of Christ allows some women the representational symbolic resources by which to depict themselves, without self-hatred and without denying sexual differences, is telling, for, perhaps as they are victims of phallic power, the 'identification' with Jesus is the source of their being able to represent a *response* which resists complicity or counter-phallic violence, but instead looks to love and forgiveness as the only way of disclosing the hollow sham of such 'power', and opening up the possibility of another way of life. But endorsing a female Christa also therefore raises the question of Irigaray's essentialist sexual morphology and her possible biological essentialism. Graham Ward makes this point well while discussing Irigaray and Christology:

> Those feminist theologians who opt out of Christianity because Jesus is male are in fact locking themselves into a biological essentialism that forgets, as Michel Foucault has pointed out, the historical mediation of sex and the biological. I am not wishing to deny that Jesus had the genitalia of a male . . . but the social construction and representation of his sexual identity (gender) and the orientation of his sexual desire (his sexuality) are not so easily determined. These forces complicate the representation and manifestation of his maleness.[30]

Hence, it may be that Christa representations produced by women might signify the generative birth of female representations of the divine within Christianity. Beattie's reservations remind us, however, that the reception of such cultural artefacts encounter altogether different risks, but 'risk' can signify a possible re-encoding that beckons women and men towards a new creation. For just as Beattie argues that female representations of Jesus (on the Cross) are fraught with risk, perhaps the same might be said of exclusively male representations of Jesus. Do they not perpetuate a fixed sense of what constitutes gender, for in the history of Christianity Jesus' gendered representation has been far from straightforward – and perhaps necessarily so, in so much as Jesus becomes a representative of all of us, women and men, Jew and Chinese, slave and industrialist. Whether such representations are possible without effacing sexual difference is complicated by the social imbalances of power and access to cultural modes of production. While sexual difference is irreducibly important, how these differences are to be represented cannot be statically and ontologically defined. To be sure, no anatomical erasure is possible, and the desire for such erasure is profoundly regressive (in penis envy, castration complex, rape and transsexual medical surgery). It is regressive for it signifies a rejection of God's created goodness. What I now want to focus on a little more is the complex sets of relationship between anatomy and gender, what Ward calls 'the social construction' of gender and sexuality.

To explore the symbolic terrain between anatomy, gender and sexuality both as it applies to humans and, analogically, to the divine life, I want to turn to two remarkable books about Jesus in art: Leo Steinberg, *The Sexuality of Christ in Renaissance Art and in Modern Oblivion* (1983), and Caroline Walker Bynum's *Fragmentation and Redemption: Essays on Gender and the Human Body in Medieval Religion* (1992) in which she discusses Steinberg's interpretations and assumptions. My discussion is not intended to resolve any difficulties, but rather highlight the complexity and the extent of the difficulties in addressing Irigaray's questions about the male, Jesus Christ, within the context of Catholic symbolics. Steinberg argues that a number of late medieval and Renaissance artists made Christ's penis the focus of their artistic representation. The 'Oblivion' in Steinberg's title indicates the modern refusal to notice this phenomenon, which is not surprising given modernity's staging of the neutral, rational, detached disembodied subject. However, Steinberg's actual analysis of the paintings and the texts of the period suggest that the representations of Jesus' penis were not to show Jesus' divinity as male *per se*, but rather to address the docetic tendencies which deny his full humanity, his full embodiedness.[31] Hence, events such as involuntary erections, and the interest in the infant's penis by both male and female onlookers, are linked by Steinberg to the flourishing of devotion to the holy foreskin and the feast of the circumcision in the fifteenth and sixteenth centuries, which focussed on the *full taking on of flesh*, indeed to the very last detail. Equally tellingly, Guilbert of Nogent was most unhappy about the cult of the holy foreskin as it risked denying the full resurrection of Christ, foreskin and all.[32]

Bynum joins in this argument to suggest also that the modern association of foreskin with penis and therefore eroticism is entirely misplaced and anachronistic. Rather, the foreskin in this instance suggests that salvation is not gnostic, but the redemption of real bodies in all their specific particularity. Provocatively, Bynum cites one nuptial image and one eucharistic image related to the foreskin to make her point. Catherine of Siena herself claimed that she married Christ with a ring made from Jesus' circumcised flesh, despite her hagiographer Raymond of Capua changing this detail, and the subsequent artistic depiction of this scene displays a gold wedding ring. Catherine was emphasizing the physical union in her marriage to Christ, despite her biographer. Furthermore, what might be seen as somewhat 'odd' today is curiously transformed when 'the Viennese beguine Agnes Blannbekin received the foreskin in her mouth [eucharistically] in a vision and found it to taste as sweet as honey'.[33]

Steinberg's book raises two questions germane to my exploration. Is attention to male morphology in these artistic depictions related to perpetuating a social order in which the male is divinized and given power over those who do not share the phallus? Alternatively, is Jesus' penis in fact tacitly part of a new order inaugurated in Christ whereby the phallus can represent other than control over the feminine? In one sense the answer to the first question is clearly no, for even the erections of Jesus' penis according to Steinberg are related to Jesus' vulnerability as a body that is like 'ours' in all things, even unto death.[34] The semiotic phallus, contrary to the violating depiction in Irigaray's *This Sex which Is Not One*, does not univocally lend itself to violent interruption of the self-caressing two lips that is woman. Here, the erect penis signifies its place within an alternative, redeeming economy of signs. Of course, Irigaray is not closed to equivocal significations, for she suggests, in keeping with my reading here and even developing it, that if the erect phallus was not predicated upon the murder of the mother and the subsequent identification with the power of the father it could resignify relatedness and vulnerability – precisely Steinberg's point. Her imagery in speaking of this reconfigured phallus interestingly evokes the ever-open wounds of Christ, that suffering which is still his lack, until all creation is healed:

No longer omnipotent, the phallic erection could, then, be a masculine version of the umbilical bond. It would, if it respected the life of the mother – of the mother in all women, of the woman in all mothers – reproduce the living bond with her. Where once was the cord, then the breast, there shall come in its time, for man, the penis which binds, gives life to, nourishes and recentres bodies, recalling in penetration, in touching beyond the skin and the will, in the outpouring, something of intra-uterine life, with detumescence evoking the end, mourning, the ever-open wound. This would be a preliminary gesture of repetition on man's part, a rebirth allowing him to become a sexuate adult capable of erotism and reciprocity in the flesh.[35]

Hence, Steinberg's location of the erect penis of Jesus within representations of his passion and death actually take on a significance that Steinberg is not concerned to explore: that these erections are not encoded within the phallocratic order; rather, they take place in a story of the phallocratic order's un-doing, such that there is now a new order of signification that generates and facilitates the coming together of the different sexes in bodily mutuality which need not be sadomasochistic.[36] Within this new order, the living bond to the mother, and therefore feminine representation, need not be repressed or denied. This is seen at the end of John's Gospel. John uniquely has the last conversation between Jesus and his mother take place while Jesus is actually dying on the cross (John 19.26–8). Jesus' relationship to Mary and the church is encoded within this critical transaction. It is particularly worth attending to this passage for a number of reasons. First, because Irigaray criticizes the details of the Johannine account in her review of Schüssler Fiorenza, seeing it as confirming patriarchal control in so much as Mary is 'given' into the care of the beloved disciple rather than into the care of women. Secondly, because in seeing why Irigaray's disquiet is misplaced, we further uncover the Marian church which responds to so many of Irigaray's criticisms, and which unveils a new order of creation. Thirdly, the birth of the church from the dying wounds of Jesus will help us better appreciate the biblical background to the pictures that we will later explore with Bynum.

In John's account, after the soldiers have cast lots for Jesus' clothes, such that we have the scene of Jesus naked upon the cross, 19.25b–7 takes up the story:

But standing by the cross of Jesus were his mother, and his mother's sister, Mary, and the wife of Clopas, and Mary Magdalene. When Jesus saw his mother, and the disciple whom he loved standing near, he said to his mother, 'Woman, behold, your son!' Then he said to the disciple, 'Behold, your mother!' And from that hour the disciple took her to his own home.

Since the fourth century, this passage was typologically interpreted such that Mary was seen to represent the mother of the church, and the beloved disciple to represent the community of those who follow Jesus faithfully, and who now have Mary as their mother, as did the wounded Jesus upon the cross. A long tradition of exegesis focussed on this particular passage for the establishment of a number of Mariological titles, well until the time of the scholastics.[37] If we turn to some of the details of this Johannine passage, it may be possible to recover it from the obsessions of some historical-critics who fail to see the representative and typological nature of 'characters' within the narrative.

Irigaray objects to Jesus' giving of his mother to a man, not to a woman, which enacts the end of 'gynecocratic genealogy'.[38] But in fact neither of these events that Irigaray describes takes place. Let us look at the giving of Mary to a man. The RSV (which I have used above) mistranslates *lambanō* into 'the disciple *took her* to his own home', but when John uses this Greek term in a number of other places (for example, John 1.12, 16; 3.11; 14.17) it signifies the *receipt* of a gift that will change the receiver, not their possession of the gift. Hence, in 1.12, we have 'But to all who received [*lambanō*] him, who believed in his name, he gave power to become children of God'. Here, the gift is not within the control of the receivers, but rather changes them and their relationship to the gift. Later in verse 16, likewise, 'And from his fullness have we all received [*lambanō*], grace upon grace.' Hence, in this linguistic context, Mary might be better understood as 'gift', like the gift of grace, which is not under our control, or the beloved disciple's, but rather transforms and changes us and him in our reception of the gift. It is to her, as mother, that we are indebted for the graced life that she brings us and for her nurturing within this life.

This reading is further supported when we see that the 'beloved disciple' can be interpreted as a type, not a man as such. Raymond Brown, even though spending much time discussing the historical candidate who might be the 'beloved disciple', freely acknowledges that there 'is little doubt that in Johannine thought the Beloved Disciple can symbolise the Christian'.[39] But he symbolizes the Christian in his faithful following of Jesus, not in his specific gender *per se*, which might well be why his person is not concretized and named. Furthermore, recall that in John's account we have a full complement of women who are with Jesus at the crucial hour when most of his male disciples have deserted him. Hence, Origen makes the Pauline connection in interpreting the Beloved Disciple in terms of Christ's body, not as a male body or a male person as such: 'Every man who becomes perfect no longer lives his own life, but Christ lives in him. And because Christ lives in him, it was said to Mary concerning him, "Here is your son, Christ".'[40]

Two other major clues support and develop this reading. The first lies in Jesus' address to Mary. He addresses her: 'Woman, behold your son!' Why speak to your own mother, at the hour of death, in such terms as 'Woman'? A possible answer to this might follow from our attention to a further clue: this event is framed in a symbolic time–space moment for John, the 'hour': 'And from that hour the disciple took her to his own home.' The use of 'Woman' in Jesus' addressing of his mother refers us back and forward to three other crucial biblical texts. The first is John 2.1–11, where Jesus's ministry begins with his turning of the water into wine at the wedding in Cana. Mary inaugurates and starts Jesus' ministry, despite the reading that Jesus responds to her request: 'O woman, what have you to do with me? My hour has not yet come.' The fact that Mary inaugurates the ministry is rejected by Raymond Brown, even though Mary's very request structurally parallels Eve's request of Adam to carry out an action, and Adam's response inaugurates the fall.[41] Here, Jesus' response, despite his apparent verbal refusal, is to enact the first of the signs of redemption that will lead to the final transforming sign: the Cross and Resurrection.

The fact that John is indeed referring Mary's action to that of Eve's is also clear from John's use of 'woman' in addressing Mary, for this is the address given to Eve in Genesis 3.15, 2.23 and 3.20. The typology that Beattie has already alerted us to earlier is particularly vital in this passage. But the reference to Genesis and the first Eve, who is now replaced by the second Eve, is also referred forward to the eschatological Eve in Revelation 12, where we find another 'woman', who is 'clothed with the sun, with the moon under her feet, and on her head a crown of twelve stars' (Rev. 12.1). Brown's resistance to seeing Mary as inaugurating Jesus' ministry means that a tradition from Justin onwards, who reads Mary as the new Eve, is entirely obscured, as well as the fact that Brown is unable to explain why on earth Jesus does what he is bidden to by his mother, despite his apparent resistance to it, saying that it is not the appropriate 'hour'. Is it that Brown's resistance is because any *dependence* on Mary and on others by Jesus, other than his dependence on his heavenly Father, seems to weaken the high Christology of John? However, if my reading is correct, then John's high Christology only works through the network of subsistent relations that exist between Jesus and human persons, which actually reflects the perichoretic subsistent relations that exist between the three divine persons.

A further exegetical point is worth noting which relates to the transformation of signs, such that we might envisage that a phallus will not represent the economy of male desire. In Genesis 3.15 there is enmity between Eve's seed and the serpent; in John, Jesus transforms this enmity into reconciliation. He does this with superb pictorial skill, in drawing on Numbers 21.9, where the serpent is held aloft in the desert by Moses to save those who are bitten by serpents, so that the holding high above the people that which might kill them (sin, the serpent) now redeems them (Jesus taking upon himself the sin of the world, and in his murder redemption is brought about). Hence, the Cross and the serpent are fused together by John, to signify that no sign is beyond Jesus' transforming power. The drama of Revelation 12 reflects the fact that the battle with the serpent, although won, is still one that continues. The 'woman' battles with a dragon, who in Revelation 12.9 is identified with the serpent of Genesis 3.15, thereby portraying the Marian church as both giving birth to a new creation (the final scenes after the battle) and its continual struggle with sin, darkness and death that are part of the church's vocation, as it was their Lord's.

Finally, if we attend to the 'hour' in which John frames his action, we see that the Cana incident is the 'first of his signs' (John 2.11), and in this sense is the hour, not of his final transformation but of the intimation and inauguration of that transformation, symbolized by the changing of the water into wine, a transformation that also intimates that transubstantiation which takes place in every eucharistic meal.[42] If the figure of the new Eve, like that of the old, inaugurates the change that is to take place within all creation, John further intensifies this theme by placing Mary and the new church at the foot of the Cross in this final 'hour' of the drama. From the wounds of Christ, the church is born. Rudolf Bultmann rejects the identification of Mary and the church on the grounds that Mary cannot be the church, for the church is portrayed as the Bride to Christ in the book of Revelation. Mary cannot be both a mother and wife to the same person. However, such a literal and rigid reading of symbols fails to recognize that 'Symbolism is very plastic, especially in different contexts: in Hos ii 18(16) Israel is the wife of Yahweh while in xi 1 Israel is the son of Yahweh.'[43] If Israel can be both wife and son, then Mary can be both mother and bride. It should be noted that, while this type of typological reading is still supported by mainly Catholic and Orthodox exegetes, they are not entirely alone.[44]

Hence, John 19.26–7 indicates that if anything happens in the trans-actions at the foot of the Cross, rather than woman being encoded within a male economy, Jesus' 'hour' reverses Eve's predicament, as well as Adam's, so that Mary now sets in train, *with* Jesus, a new possible semiotic order. Mary is not 'given' into the possession of a man, nor is there an ending to gynaecologic genealogy as Irigaray claims.[45] Both women and men are required for the drama of redemption to be enacted. The church's too frequent incorporation of this story into the order of the phallus is of course testimony to the church's need of redemption. But equally, that the story is still told within the church is testimony to the possibility of the church's being Co-Redeemer. Let us revisit this incident in its pictorial form in now turning to Bynum to pursue the issue of the significance of Jesus ana-tomical representation. Steinberg's study showed that the penis, erect or flaccid, represented a new type of humanity in Jesus. His pictorial argument compliments Beattie's theological argument. This still means that the divine representation is not female, and this cannot be denied, but most interestingly in terms of the art of the late middle ages neither can it be affirmed. Bynum's essay 'The Body of Christ in the Later Middle Ages: A Reply to Leo Steinberg' helps to explore this interesting ambivalence in regard to gender and anatomical representation.[46]

By my reading, Bynum's criticisms of Steinberg are misplaced, which does not affect my own approach, nor the value of Bynum's study.[47] She uses Steinberg as a foil to criticize a prevalent assumption in analysing religious culture of the high middle ages: that genitality is associated with sexuality.[48] She then shows that bodily focus in the later middle ages signified preoccupation with the body as the site of vulnerability and suffering; and that feeding, suffering and salvation were far more important to these religious cultures than genital sexuality.[49] What is most significant for my concern is her claim, also developed in her book *Jesus as Mother: Studies in the Spirituality of the High Middle Ages* (1982)[50] that 'late medieval people saw the body of Christ as female. There is thus better evidence for the assertion that the late Middle Ages found gender reversal at the heart of Christian art and worship'.[51] Modern interpreters are far more literal minded about these features than the audiences of the fifteenth and sixteenth centuries.

Bynum elegantly illustrates her case and I will focus on just one feature of her discussion of anatomical interpretation, whereby the wounds of Jesus are reconfigured and represented as lactating breast, vagina and open womb. The fifteenth-century painting *The Saviour* by Quirizio of Murano[52] evokes the theme of Jesus as mother and woman in showing a sweet-faced Christ sitting clothed on a throne, but offering his naked wound (through a split in the cloak), with the lifting gesture and fingers around this wound positioned in a manner that recalls Mary's offering her breast to the infant Jesus. In the background angels carry banners bearing phrases from the Song of Songs that were traditionally interpreted as referring to the eucharist. A Poor Clare nun kneels in the left side foreground to receive the host. Most moderns might find this painting a little gruesome and even repulsive, but Bynum shows how this depiction ties in with gender reversals, closely connected with Mary, such that Christ becomes feeding mother, for he feeds the church from his body, just as he was fed by Mary's. But now, Jesus' breast is the wound, and the blood that spills forth is like the milk of salvation to those who drink of it. These fluid connections between different types of bodily fluids are reinforced by medieval physiognomy that presumed that all bodily fluids were primarily derived from the blood.

Breast feeding is not, however, the only metaphoric transformation of the wound of Jesus. If the wound of Jesus can be reconfigured into a breast that lactates life-giving food, as in the eucharist, so too can the wound become transformed into the parted lips of the vagina leading to the womb that gives birth. Bynum shows how the wound becomes the vagina/womb when she comments on a depiction from the thirteenth-century French Moralized Bible (at the Bodleian, Oxford) where a small baby is being born from the wound in Christ's side while Jesus is still on the cross.[53] Mary acts as midwife, and above this scene is depicted the birth of Eve from Adam's side. The church emerges from the wounds of Christ, with Mary as midwife. This action reverses the birth of death that is generated in the Adam and Eve account. The gender reversals and confusion might recall the *Odes of Solomon*, and with it the sense that all genders find analogical affirmation in the life of God, while God's life itself is not gendered.

These depictions are also capable of a different reading, however, such that they might simply reinforce the generative power of God in the patriarchal line to the exclusion of women, for they draw on the Genesis account which derives Eve from Adam, and Mary here is midwife rather than the mother of the church. This ambiguity shows just how delicately balanced is the possible encodings of these figurative representations. Bynum charts the complex and multiple ways in which images actually did work differently for men and for women in the late middle ages and how in one sense gender reversals both allowed for a critical commentary on society, while at times simply duplicating the misogynist taxonomies of just those societies.[54] Such complexity also shows how the resources for the salvation of all women and men, indeed all creation, are actually relentlessly enacted within the constant re-presentation of this particular narrative, even if constantly thwarted by patriarchy.

This excursion into artistic representation (and biblical exegesis) at least lets us see how figuration of the male Jesus is not necessarily encoded in exclusively male representative imagery. Indeed, what the late medieval church was able to see, as was the fourth-century Syrian church and various groups within the church throughout history, is that while Jesus was anatomically male, the representation of the gendering of Jesus is never a straightforward matter. It is capable of numerous configurations. I have been exploring one type of gender interpretation as in keeping with my wider trinitarian argument. In bringing together such gender differences, without erasing them, Jesus inaugurates our sharing in that 'source' in which all differences, created and uncreated, are harmoniously and subsistently related, such that a transforming perichoresis of love might take place.

To summarize: I have tried to argue that the scandal of particularity, the stumbling block of the incarnation, cannot be bypassed. Rather than

trying to divinize a woman 'equal to Jesus', I have tried to show that
Mary is Co-Redeemer, both before and after Jesus, and with him. She
is only the first of many that form the corporate 'body of Christ', and
in this communion both female and male genealogies count. There is
therefore a real sense in which the incarnation continues after the
resurrection, and to this extent Irigaray points to something so often
forgotten within the Christian tradition. I realize that my argument
always sails perilously close to those who would want to re-establish
the significance of Mary and the saints within the church, but in terms
of patriarchy. Furthermore, I have tried to show that the particularity
of the incarnation, the particularity of Jesus as a male, an owner of a
penis, might be interpreted as the overcoming of patriarchy. But I
also tried to show that this morphological specificity does not make
transparent the significance of gender, nor of personal identity. Jesus
can be properly viewed as mother, or as a corporate personality coming
into being (the church). This delightful transgression will also be present
in the naming of the father. It also confounds those who want to control
symbols. Let me turn to Bynum to summarize the argument of my
own Christological reflections in engagement with Irigaray:

> If we want to express the significance of Jesus in both male and
> female images, if we want to turn from seeing body as sexual to
> seeing body as generative, if we want to find symbols that give dignity
> and meaning to the suffering we cannot eliminate and yet fear so
> acutely, we can find support for doing so in the art and theology of
> the later Middle Ages.[55]

5. In the name of whose 'Father'?

Irigaray poses some difficult questions regarding the hom(m)osexuate
nature of the trinity, and perhaps no more so when we come to the
'Father'. She argues that by stressing the father's originative power at
the cost of the mother's the woman becomes receptacle to the patriarchal
line and, in this, eventually becomes invisible for she is simply a token
of exchange in the male economy of desire and self-reproduction. In
an essay on Freud, and just before discussing Marx and Engels regarding
the 'means of production', Irigaray notices how the womb is often

construed as the passive receptacle, whereby the woman has no claims on its workings, but only acts as container to the product made in the father's name such that it is 'possessed as a means of (re)production'.[56] Elsewhere, Irigaray writes:

> The problem is that, by denying the mother her generative power and by wanting to be the sole creator, the Father, according to our culture, superimposes upon the archaic world of the flesh a universe of language and symbols which cannot take root in it except as in the form of that which makes a hole in the bellies of women and in the site of their identity.[57]

This is seen in the eradication of female genealogies and female representation. A heavenly father begetting his Son (even if an eternal act) still employs the metaphor of begetting without a woman in sight. While this of course helps the conceptual de-anthropomorphizing of the 'father', it nevertheless begs the question of the metaphorical 'fall out' whereby male generative power 'alone' is employed to envisage the divine. Although quoted at the opening of the previous chapter, it is worth citing Irigaray's poignant critique of this logic:

> the appearance of the father's and the Father's power, the phenotype of a genotype glimpsed in the Word, since the father, unlike the mother, propagates outside himself and in a way that remains invisible. Thus, in order to affirm the reign of the father, it becomes necessary to eliminate the divine phenomenality of the daughter, of the mother–daughter couple, and lock it into the father–Father– son–Son genealogy and the triangle, father–son–Holy Spirit.[58]

As we shall see, the pagan cosmological picture of a father with originative powers, causally begetting a Son, is still all too present within Christian metaphysics, such that Irigaray's criticisms are well directed. That such gross anthropomorphism prevails is not simply a matter of forgetfulness on the part of otherwise diligently analogical theologians. It is indicative of the serious intrusion of unbaptized pagan cosmological thought determining Christian theology. A typical example of this is found in a review of Weinandy's book, where the Thomist reviewer, Timothy L. Smith, writes (in criticizing Weinandy's thesis): 'the traditional reading must posit a logical "moment" when the Father was alone'.[59] This lone self-sufficient origin of all creation, the Father, is a curious pagan deity. How could a Thomist posit such a 'father' when *relations* is so fundamental a Thomist trinitarian category?[60] And what does such a claim imply about the two other persons of the Godhead? Surely patriarchal subordinationism follows, on the model of a 'Father' who is able to generate a Son without relationship to a 'Mother'?

My limited concern in this section will be to argue that 'father' is only acceptable for the name of the 'first' person, when it is rid of this causally generative association regarding 'origins'. Indeed, in the Bible, we find numerous checks against such anthropomorphism, which have often failed to surface in metaphysical discussions of the intratrinitarian life. If the language of origins is not removed from relations, then Irigaray's incisive criticism that Christianity perpetuates neo-pagan cosmological patriarchy is surely correct.

To develop my argument I will first briefly examine some of the biblical materials related to the use of 'father', drawing heavily upon Paul Ricoeur to establish various conclusions regarding biblical trajectories. With these in mind, I will then examine the pervasiveness of cosmological metaphysics in which trinitarian re-presentation looses its moorings from the biblical God, and instead dangerously re-presents an alien god under the guise of Christian triunity. I will also be showing that an uncritical inclusion of maternal imagery regarding the 'first' person can be equally problematic. But this latter claim also occurs in the context of my argument that to exclude feminine metaphorical language of the 'first' person is to fail to properly re-present the triune God.

6. The biblically transgressive 'father'

When we turn to the Old and New Testaments, we find some very curious features regarding the use of 'father'.[61] Furthermore, if we turn to this material in the company of Paul Ricoeur's essay 'Fatherhood: From Phantasm to Symbol' where he addresses the meaning of 'father' in the thought of Freud, Hegel and the biblical materials, the argument becomes all the more interesting.[62] This is so for two reasons. First, because Ricoeur challenges the notion that the meaning of father is 'invariable' but, rather, father is a

> problematic figure, incomplete and in suspense. It is a *designation* that is susceptible of traversing a diversity of semantic levels, from the phantasm of the father as castrater, who must be killed, to the symbol of the father who dies of compassion.[63]

Hence, while the image of father is often initially restricted, based on a literal originative function, its symbolic use in the biblical texts begins to 'crack the shell of literalness of the father figure and liberate the symbol'.[64] Ricoeur is well aware that even when this shell of literalness is cracked, the primitive figure always returns, 'to the degree that it is susceptible to several actualizations, [and] opens the field to several interpretations which belong in their turn to the designation of the father'.[65] This is a salutary criticism of those who insist that 'father' in the Bible has got nothing to do with the 'father' of our cultures and varied experiences, for Ricoeur's point is that there is a constant meeting of these different semantic fields in which the transformations, the 'several actualizations' and 'interpretations' that are possible, cannot be entirely predicted. If Ricoeur has a thesis about the biblical father it is this: that one needs to see 'fatherhood as a *process* rather than a *structure*, and it [the Bible] proposes a dynamic and dialectical constitution of it'.[66] In an important sense, we might then see that the unoriginative God the Father is actually co-constituted by Son and Spirit (as Weinandy already began to argue) such as to be 'born' into re-presentation.

Secondly, Ricoeur, in a different manner, shares a suspicion that I have voiced regarding the metaphysics of 'father' in systematic theology. The biblical-narrative linguistic contexts of father can easily be forgotten by the systematic philosopher. Ricoeur says that he prefers the company of exegetes rather than theologians, for:

> Exegesis has the advantage of remaining on the level of representation and of delivering up the very process of representation, its progressive constitution. In deconstructing theology right to its original representative elements, exegesis plunges us directly into the interplay of the designations of God, it ventures to deliver up to us their originary intention and proper dynamics ... Another reason for having

resource to exegesis rather than theology is that it invites us not to separate the figure of God from the forms of discourse in which these figures occur.[67]

Let me very briefly and schematically outline the biblical findings of Ricoeur. First, in the earliest strands of the historical tradition 'father' as a designation for God is non-existent. Instead, Exodus 3.13–15, with its disclosure of the name 'I am that I am' suggests that God's proper name is:

> the dissolution of all anthropomorphisms, of all figures and figurations, including that of the father. The name against the idol. All nonmetaphoric sonship, all literal descent, is thus reduced.[68]

Ricoeur shows the significance of this control against anthropomorphic idolatry via the creation accounts in Genesis. Here, in comparison to the Semitic myths surrounding the Israelites of a father god originating or begetting creation, 'God is not designated as father and that a specific verb – *bara* – is used to tell about the creative act; any trace of begetting is thus eliminated'.[69] Ricoeur sees this process of eliminating paternal fatherhood as paradoxical, for it is the condition by which 'father' can later emerge within the tradition, shorn of patriarchy.

He argues that its symbolic return is predicated upon the key notion of Israel's election and covenant, and Yahweh's faithfulness to Israel. 'This election is equivalent to adoption; thus Israel is a son, but it is a son only by a word of designation. By the same stroke, fatherhood itself is entirely dissociated from begetting.'[70] It is true that Ricoeur is nowhere sensitive to the question of why Israel becomes 'son' rather than 'daughter', and does not explain why other metaphors of God as maternal are not considered, and whether this predication of Israel as 'Son', that does not arise from a reproductive generative analogy, is either fixed or need be fixed. Biblically, it need not be, for after all Israel is described in feminine terms, as daughter (Ps. 45.10; Matt. 21.5; John 12.15; and Ps. 137.8 which includes reference to Babylon under this metaphor), as loving wife (Rev. 21.9), as unfaithful wife (Hos. 1.2; Jer. 3.19–20) and in one verse as both 'widow' and 'princess', now turned 'vassal' (Lam. 1.1).[71] Later, within the New Testament, the New Israel will indeed be represented in the figure of Mary: as 'heavenly bride, queen, mother, daughter and virgin, loving transgressor of all the kinship systems', as Beattie incisively puts it.[72] But let me return to Ricoeur's accounting.

Ricoeur notes the emergence of the 'father' in the works of the prophets Hosea, Jeremiah and Trito-Isaiah. He sees the prophetic books working within an eschatological context, such that 'father' is not so much connected with a figure of origins, although he is that within the terms of the community of Israel (the God of *their* fathers); rather, 'father' is a figure of the future, of the 'new creation'. However, this 'father' certainly traverses literality, as is seen for example in Jeremiah 3.19b–20. Jeremiah says: 'and I said, Thou shalt call me, My father; and shalt not turn away from me. Surely as a wife treacherously departeth from her husband, so have ye dealt treacherously with me, O house of Israel'. Commenting on this verse, Ricoeur notes that by means of this:

> strange mutual contamination of two kinship figures, the shell of literality of the image is broken and the symbol is liberated. A father who is a spouse is no longer a progenitor (begetter), nor is he any more an enemy to his sons; love, solicitude, and pity can carry him beyond domination and severity.[73]

Compared to the sparse use of 'father' in the Old Testament (roughly twenty clear instances), the New Testament abounds with the term. John uses it more than a hundred times, Mark four, Luke fifteen, and Matthew forty-two times. Ricoeur links this usage to the centrality of the preaching by Jesus concerning the kingdom, and the eschatological orientation of the kingdom. I want to quote his summary of the New Testament evidence because it also so clearly brings out the ecclesiological-trinitarian dimensions which I have been urging throughout. Ricoeur speaks of the culmination of the 'father' image in Jesus' use of Abba, which is 'a movement from designation to invocation'.[74] He then concludes:

> Far, therefore, from the addressing of God as father being easy, along the lines of a relapse into archaism, it is rare, difficult, and audacious, because it is prophetic, directed toward fulfillment rather than toward origins. It does not look backward, toward a great ancestor, but

forward, in the direction of a new intimacy on the model of the knowledge of the son. In the exegesis of Paul, it is because the Spirit witnesses our sonship (Romans 8:16) that we can cry *Abba*, Father. Far, therefore, from the religion of the father being that of a distant and hostile transcendence, there is fatherhood because there is sonship, and there is sonship because there is community of spirit.[75]

I have already noted Ricoeur's occlusion of daughters and mothers in his focus on son and father imagery, but the point he is making is still germane to my broader argument in so much as 'father' does not operate in terms of origins, begetting and generation, but in terms of election, intimacy and the inauguration of an eschatologically new creation of the kingdom, a relationality that is open to the women and men who imitate Jesus through the power of the Spirit.

There is one final point that Ricoeur makes in his study that is important to my argument. This is that the figure of the 'father' is further complicated within specifically trinitarian representation. In the New Testament we do not have just any son or any father, but two specifically narrated and interrelated figures. This is a Son who is in communion with his Father, not as a rival, but in relation. The Oedipal configuration is overthrown. Ricoeur criticizes punitive or penal theories of the cross as sacrifice, precisely because these stagings of events fail to break free of the Oedipal configuration, for in Jesus we find 'completed the conversion of death as murder into death as offering'.[76] Hence, the very notion of 'father' here is actually related and dependent on that of this 'son', such that the prioritizing or separation of one from the other becomes impossible. Ricoeur writes: 'Is it not then this death of the son which can furnish us the final schema of fatherhood, to the degree that the son is also the father?'[77] Ricoeur notes that this question belongs to the domain of the 'great trinitarian and theological interpretations',[78] and my argument in this and the previous chapter has raised a question as to whether trinitarian re-presentation has gone seriously astray in making the 'father' a cosmological causal originative term within the Godhead, rather than a relational figure to the Son and Spirit.

Before exploring this crisis in metaphysical representation further, I would like to examine one issue regarding the biblical evidence that Ricoeur has advanced. Many of those defending the usage of 'father' either against 'Mother' or against non-personal terms such as 'Creator' and 'Sustainer' insist that this naming of the 'father' derives not from human culture but is a challenge to the various human conceptions of fatherhood.[79] To capitulate to the renaming of God is to begin to shift the axis of revelation from the biblical narratives, that is 'who is the "Father" that Jesus names?', to that of the narratives of multiple cultures where 'father' is understood polysemantically: 'father' stages infantile regression; 'father' stages violence or sexual abuse; 'father' stages remoteness, playfulness and absence; 'father' stages love, support and joy; 'father' stages honour, integrity and love of mother; or 'father' stages pure absence. Defenders of the use of 'father' certainly have a point and the biblical 'Father' challenges various human conceptions of 'fatherhood' as we have seen with Ricoeur's help. However, I have two difficulties with the position as stated above.

First, there is no reason why other metaphorical terms should not be employed, with due care, of the 'first' person – either biblically based, or from the tradition, or from Christian communities reflecting upon their experience of God. There is no good argument for the sole and exclusive retention of the term 'father' alone, even though there are very good arguments that it cannot be jettisoned because of its biblical context. Secondly, the fact that some people associate God the 'father' with their own 'father' indicates the extent to which our culture has become so secularized, and the need for Christians to relearn the proper use of their own Christian language. Having said this, there is an important pastoral situation in which, for all sorts of good reasons, 'father' God is difficult to bear. One only has to read the accounts of those who have been seriously sexually or emotionally abused by their 'fathers', and who subsequently find the worship of a God termed 'father' so difficult, to realize the profound pastoral damage done by the uncomplicated retention of this term.[80] I am not suggesting that liturgically abandoning 'father' solves the problems of relationship with our earthly fathers. What I am questioning is the refusal to acknowledge that the sole use of father re-enforces, rather than undermines, a univocal association with social linguistic usage. We do not usually call our earthly fathers 'mother'. Hence, in calling the 'first' person mother (and father), we can more easily question and undermine the potential anthropocentricism in exclusive usage of father. As I shall be arguing below, the use of 'mother' is entirely appropriate to name

God, but like 'father' is equally problematic and prone to all sorts of idolatry.

The fixation on a single manner of naming, 'father' and nothing else, moves close to a phallocratic epistemology of representation which Irigaray has so artfully unveiled. Language within the phallic economy of desire is univocal and fixed: only 'father' will do, for it operates, quite idolatrously, like a 'proper name' rather than, as Aquinas so well recognized, as a name that relates to an *action* which has no proper name.[81] Hence, I agree with Colin Gunton's critique of Sally MacFague's exclusive usage of non-personal forms of addressing the 'first' person of the trinity. MacFague's use of 'Creator' and 'Sustainer' eventually obscures attention to the personal relations of love within the Godhead and in God's relation to us.[82] Gunton seems to use this argument to also resist 'mother', however, and the alternative terms MacFague employs for the naming of God. MacFague's strategy, exclusively employed, is problematic. But Gunton gives no reasons why we should not include the full range of biblical metaphors for the first person, each coexisting with others, as indeed they do within the prayers of the church. Psalm 18, for instance, takes a whole series of inanimate objects, as well as militaristic constructions, to daringly speak of God: 'I love thee, O Lord, my strength. The Lord is my rock, and my fortress, and my deliverer, my God, my rock, in whom I take refuge, my shield, and the horn of my salvation, my stronghold' (Ps. 18.1–2). The Psalmist shows that nothing within creation, even inanimate and seemingly violent constructions, can be excluded from re-presenting God's redemptive relation to us.

If we have seen that the biblical 'father' need not be a father of genealogical patriarchy, a father of origins, but rather challenges such cosmological anthropomorphism, the subsequent question is whether this transgressive father is improperly re-presented in trinitarian meta physics. The biblical father is concerned with election, relationship, intimacy, judgment and forgiveness, and is 'generated', made known to us, by our participation in Christ's life, through the gift of the Holy Spirit. The fundamentally relational nature of this 'father' has been obscured in certain traditions of metaphysical representation: primarily, those concerned to affirm the Father as 'sole originative cause' of Son, Spirit and all creation. Let me now turn to the birth of a non-patriarchal father.

7. The birth of the father

My main concern in this section is to investigate the pervasiveness of
a pagan father within metaphysical speculation, a figure of originative
causality within the Godhead. In the section on the Holy Spirit in
Chapter 1, we saw how Weinandy had traced the denigration of the
Spirit to the prioritizing of the Father and Son in the west and the
sole monarchy of the Father in the east. We also saw that his own
creative and exegetically substantiated solution begins to take us along
the right path. He argued that within the trinity the Father begets the
Son in or by the Holy Spirit, who proceeds then from the Father as
the one in whom the Son is begotten. In his own words:

> A proper understanding of the Trinity can only be obtained if all three
> persons, logically and ontologically, spring forth in one simultaneous,
> nonsequential, eternal act in which each person of the Trinity subsist-
> ently defines, and equally is subsistently defined by, the other
> persons.[83]

This is a much required move for proper trinitarian re-presentation.
However, I have tried to show that Weinandy fails to think through
this utterly 'orthodox' and very important proposal, in so much as he
rejected Boff's *Patreque* and questionably still holds that while there is
an order of 'origin and derivation among the persons of the Trinity,
there is not an order of priority, precedence and sequence'.[84] I had
suggested that this statement cannot be defended. Hence, to see whether
the move to erase causal origins within the trinity is possible, I then
turned to Boff, who at least verbally did so, but did not further attend
to this issue except in positing *Patreque* as a necessary term within
trinitarian taxonomies. Mainly because of his erroneous step of divinizing Mary, however, Boff's trinity runs into all sorts of trouble. Hence,
to further explore this issue now, I will turn to Jürgen Moltmann, upon
whom Boff is so dependent. Moltmann is a contemporary Protestant
German theologian. One finds in Moltmann a most interesting strategy
which he employs to overcome Paternal Monarchy and the notion of
'origins' within the Godhead.

Moltmann's *The Trinity and the Kingdom of God* is a daring attempt to think God's triune being in relational political and gender terms.[85] At a crucial juncture of the book, Moltmann posits a distinction within the trinity regarding its *constitutive* level and the level of *relations* or *life* that exist in trinitarian communion. On the first level of constitution, the Father is properly seen as the origin of Son and Spirit.[86] On the second level, persons and relations are kept in reciprocal balance, such that their full equality and distinctiveness is retained. Moltmann's entire political theology depends on this relational, not constitutive, level of trinitarian life. Moltmann is only able to argue against hierarchic stagings, which involve subordinationism or modalism, on the level of relations. Boff follows him in this respect. Regarding the level of constitution, however, Moltmann seems to be fully aware of the difficulties, but unable to extricate himself from them, in his retention of a constitutive level:

> This thinking in terms of origin derives from cosmology and can therefore only be haltingly applied to the mystery of the Trinity, that is to say, in realization of its inappropriateness. It can only be used appropriately if the logical compulsion to monarchial reduction and the non-trinitarian notion of the single origin (both of which are inherent in it) are overcome.[87]

It is extremely odd, although not incoherent, to suggest that what is 'inherent' in a concept can be overcome through use of that concept. Surely, what is required is the further problematization of the concept, and the deconstruction of the questionable purposes it inappropriately serves. Moltmann seems unable to jettison the language of 'origins' and 'cause', even though he has been able to establish real trinitarian relations without origin and cause. Moltmann's retention of these two levels within the trinity leads to all sorts of problems, as Roger Olson has rightly pointed out.[88] Olson make the point that Moltmann violates his own principle that there is no God who is given apart from and above the events of salvation history and the cross, even though this is what his constitutive trinity amounts to. Furthermore, Olson argues that Moltmann's 'two-level conception of the Trinity also threatens to dissolve the unity between God and his acts which is a favourite theme of Moltmann's'.[89] Perhaps most importantly, for our purpose, is Olson's claim that Moltmann's entire political project is undermined due to his implicit 'ontological monarchism' in keeping the trinity of constitution.[90] This entirely undermines his divine authorization of non-hierarchical forms of social practice.

Moltmann is vigorously defended from this criticism by one of his pupils, Miroslav Volf, who suggests that Olson's criticism only works 'if one ascribes ontological status exclusively to the relations of origin, and not to the perichoretic relations'.[91] However, if one were to ascribe ontological status to both the constitutive and perichoretic levels, we would simply have two trinities: one hierarchic and cosmological and the other biblical and 'politically egalitarian' (in Moltmann's terms). The real question is: why retain the first level, especially if it is unbiblical? It seems that there is very little worth maintaining in the retention of this notion of originative causality within the Godhead, for it 'inherently' leads to a patriarchal cosmological 'father' that bedevils even Moltmann's progressive and radical re-presentations of the triune reality.

Furthermore, this contradiction in Moltmann's project resurfaces at the most crucial moment in Moltmann's re-presentation of a non-sexist trinity, in which the 'father' allegedly escapes patriarchal encoding. It is worth paying attention to this as it is a basic consequence of Moltmann's retention of originative causality within the Godhead. Moltmann (followed by Boff) develops the theme of the 'fatherly mother' and the 'motherly father' and both draw spurious authority from the Council of Toledo in 675 which stated:

> we must believe that the Son was not made out of nothing, nor out of some substance or other, but from the womb of the Father (*de utero Patris*), that is that he was begotten or born (*genitus vel natus*) from the Father's own being.[92]

From terms such as the womb of the father and many other references to the maternal nature of God, Moltmann develops the idea of the 'motherly father' and the 'fatherly mother'. Is this like the complex cross-gendered representations witnessed in the medieval period regarding Jesus, and that of the early Syrian church regarding the Spirit and Father? The answer must be both yes and no, for Moltmann's theological figurations fall foul of the problems that beset such earlier cross-gendered re-presentations. Moltmann's re-presentation fails precisely because his introduction of both gendered images *within God* threaten to become phallic appropriations of the feminine, rather than any real symbolization of difference.[93] Moltmann stages his fatherly mother and motherly father between patriarchy (pure monotheism) and matriarchy (pantheism). In a telling paragraph, he develops the central idea of the fatherly mother and the motherly father:

> If the Son comes forth from the Father alone, then this coming forth must be thought of as both 'procreation' and 'birth'. But that means that there must be a fundamental change in the father-concept. A father who both *begets* and *gives* birth to his son is not a mere male father. He is a motherly father. He can no longer be defined as single-sexed and male, but becomes bisexual or transsexual. He is the *motherly Father* of his *only-born Son*, and at the same time the *fatherly Father* of his *only-begotten Son* . . . [Here he cites Toledo (see above)] . . . The Christian doctrine of the Trinity, with its affirmations about the motherly Father, represents a first step towards limiting the use of masculine terminology to express the idea of God, without, however, changing over to matriarchal conceptions.[94]

While Moltmann is right to criticize both patriarchy and matriarchy, this paragraph is fraught with difficulties, not least because Moltmann has explicitly disavowed the generative/origins taxonomy as being operative at the level of relations about which he is now speaking.[95] This reflects the unresolved tension between his two trinitarian levels. Furthermore, Moltmann also unwittingly rewrites the Nicene Creed which has it that Jesus was 'born of' Mary, not of a heavenly bisexual, and was 'eternally begotten' of the Father. While Toledo was metaphorically daring in speaking of the womb of the Father, it also ran the danger of anthropomorphizing the Father, for it is far more startling to speak of an eternal begetting, which linguistically is like the sound of one hand clapping. To introduce a womb into the Father dangerously literalizes the metaphor beyond warrant, even if Toledo's employment of the metaphor can be historically contextualized. Nevertheless, without any explicit intention, Moltmann's positioning of the divine birthing ends up denigrating Mary's human birthing of the divine without whom salvation could not be shared with the world. Moltmann's inclusivism is enacted within a fundamentally male God ('He is the *motherly Father*'

– why not 'She is the Motherly father'?) who always includes woman
within *his own* taxonomy.[96] Hence, the 'he' has a womb while remaining
'he'. Irigaray, as already quoted, notices how the womb is often construed as the passive receptacle whereby the woman has no claims on
its workings, but only acts as container to the product made in the
father's name such that it is 'possessed as a means of (re)production'.[97]
Moltmann's wrenching of Mary's bodily womb into the body of a
non-sensible transcendental bears the marks of the phallic encoding of
the womb. This confirms Irigaray's early cited remarks:

> The problem is that, by denying the mother her generative power
> and by wanting to be the sole creator, the Father, according to our
> culture, superimposes upon the archaic world of the flesh a universe
> of language and symbols which cannot take root in it except as in
> the form of that which makes a hole in the bellies of women and in
> the site of their identity.[98]

Moltmann's dissolving of the female Mary in place of a heavenly
bisexual or transsexual therefore further replicates the very omission
that his trinitarian taxonomy supposedly promotes: realizing our 'co-
dependence' and 'interrelatedness'. That such terms as co-dependence
and interrelatedness are given only *theoretical* fleshing within
Moltmann's project is explained both in the missing (murdered)
mother's body – Mary – and the omission of the infant's vulnerable
love of the mother, a real relationship. In Irigaray's terms, is Moltmann
wishing 'To forget dependency?'[99] That the enfleshed relationship
between Mary and Jesus is transcribed into a heavenly gynaecology
overriding these particular male and female bodies signifies Moltmann's
failure to realize that trinitarian categories actually illuminate
enfleshment, rather than project a heavenly 'Karma Sutra'. The latter
is kept in place by Moltmann's retaining constitutive originating
relations, even though he then represses this formulation for the rest
of his book. However, as I have shown, this repression returns within
the significations of the conscious. Hence, the repressed manifests itself
in fathers who have wombs and historical mothers who disappear from
narratives. Such are the effects of retaining the metaphysical notion of
'origins' within the Godhead.

Amongst modern systematic theologians, Wolfhart Pannenberg is one who unequivocally advocates the jettisoning of the constitutive notion of the trinity, but for reasons almost entirely unconnected with gender issues. Pannenberg, a German Protestant, traces pagan infiltration into Christian theology when 'father' is envisaged as sole origin and fount of deity. Pannenberg advocates such a position in the first volume of his *Systematic Theology*. Pannenberg is also critical of Moltmann, regarding Moltmann's untenable distinction between the level of constitution and that of relation.[100] I am not concerned *per se* with Pannenberg's project, but want to look at his argument against constitutive relations of 'origin' to gain support for my own position regarding 'father'. There are a number of elements within Pannenberg's position that are inimical to my own intentions, not least his refusal to countenance the use of 'mother' for God on the basis of it's entailing Feuerbachian projectionism.[101] I shall return to this shortly.

Pannenberg gives a number of reasons for arguing against relations of 'origin'. First, they inevitably lead to either subordinationism or Sabellianism, for, in so much as the Father is seen as the fount and origin of deity, he will then be seen as prior and ontologically primary (subordinationism), or alternatively the Son and Spirit are simply modes of his will and activity, such as to detract from their equality in personhood (Sabellianism). If the relations between the persons are regarded as those of origins, 'one cannot do justice to the reciprocity in the relations'.[102] Perichoresis or circumincession, which were designed to check against this, failed to do so 'because of the one-sided viewing of the intratrinitarian relations as relations of origin'.[103] With these arguments, I am in complete agreement.

Secondly, Pannenberg suggests that the biblical evidence never renders any of the persons outside the context of their *relations*, and these relations are seen to be co-constitutive, such that the persons cannot be envisaged apart from their relations. He also argues that the biblical picture does not require or suggest relations of 'origins', and that 'father' is not a cosmological generative patriarch. Again, I am in complete agreement with this second argument and tried to develop it with the help of Ricoeur. However, while I am in agreement with the formal outcome of Pannenberg's biblical exegesis, there is still at the level of his particular exegesis a denigration of the Holy Spirit. To take just one important example, he says one must *start* with the relation of the Father and Son,[104] which clearly implies that this relationship is

envisagable apart from the Spirit, which it is not. It also implies that
there is a formal priority in this relationship (Father–Son), which is
not supported biblically.[105] The fact that the gospels narrate Jesus'
ministry in terms of his baptism in the Spirit (Luke 3.22), and that his
miracles and healings are seen as the outpouring of the Spirit (Luke
4.14), and view the proper exegesis of the scriptures as a result of
the Spirit's activity (Luke 24.13–25), all seem to be subordinated to
Pannenberg's historical-critical method of reading the texts. However,
Pannenberg's historical-critical presuppositions are also in part due to
his failure to anchor the doctrine of the trinity in ecclesiology, but
instead making it an item of knowledge capable of being understood
apart from the ecclesia.

Whatever the status of my critical comments, Pannenberg's conclusion regarding the Father–Son relationship is important, for he
realizes that since exegesis does not point to a father who is the origin
of all, then:

> Does that not mean that in some way the deity of the Father has to
> be dependent on the relation to the Son, although not in the same
> way as that of the Son is on the relation to the Father? The Father
> is not begotten of the Son or sent by him. These relations are irrevers-
> ible. But in another way the relativity of fatherhood that finds
> expression in the designation 'Father' might well involve a depen-
> dence of the Father on the Son and thus be the basis of true reci-
> procity in the trinitarian relations.[106]

The reader might recall that Weinandy's reluctance to drop 'origins'
was because of the subsequent perceived inability to distinguish the
persons, but here Pannenberg shows that this does not necessarily
follow. The relations are 'irreversible', and they follow from the economic self-revelation of God in history, not from cosmological notions
of origin. Hence, the Son is 'sent' in a way that the Father is not.
Clearly, their distinctiveness, if related to a specific narrative story that
remains unfinished, will be a matter of a complex network of relations
giving definition to each person. And if, as I have suggested, the completion of the story involves our own participation, the completion of
any *fixed* definition of relations is not possible. Pannenberg, with his
strong doctrine of God's eschatological history, suggests something

similar in his comment that the 'persons cannot be identical simply with any one relation. Each is a catalyst of many relations.'[107] One reason for this examination of Pannenberg has been to show that the arguments regarding the removal of constitutive originary relations is very much alive, and not simply in terms of gender concerns. I have also shown Pannenberg to be operating with particular blind spots precisely regarding gender, such that his argument in various details is difficult to sustain. I will return to this point again in a moment. Pannenberg has a Jesuit critic on precisely this point of his argument (abandoning 'origins'), however, and it will be worth closing this section with a brief look at these criticisms.

John O'Donnell criticizes Pannenberg for abandoning relations of 'origins' on the grounds that it just happens that some relations are 'unilateral', not reciprocal. The example O'Donnell cites is that the 'Son receives his hypostasis from the Father and not vice versa'.[108] He also criticizes this move in Pannenberg, as neither scripture nor tradition warrant this departure. Further, he argues that this move in Pannenberg is due to his making the immanent trinity dependent on the economic trinity. As I said earlier, I am not interested in Pannenberg *per se* but in establishing my argument against relations of origins, so I will only address O'Donnell's criticisms in so much as they bear upon my basic contention. His first objection clearly begs the point as Pannenberg is showing that there simply are no unilateral relations, but always reciprocal relations, even if they are irreversible and distinct. The example that O'Donnell cites requires far more critical attention to 'receives' (the 'Son receives his hypostasis from the Father and not vice versa') if it is not to fall prey to causal projectionism within the Godhead. Is the Son not co-equally subsistent, such that there is no ontological derivation, no hypostasis received that once was not? Furthermore, in one particular sense, O'Donnell appears to make an objection simply by stating it. Pannenberg's argument actually contests the making of just such statements ('the Son receives his hypostasis . . .'), so it is not helpful to simply state it in countering Pannenberg's argument. One needs to explicate it in the light of Pannenberg's criticisms.

With reference to his second criticism, while O'Donnell is correct in saying that the tradition actually contains such expressions of causal origins within the Godhead, certainly Pannenberg's biblical exegesis, and that of Ricoeur, Hamerton-Kelly and others, suggests that this is not actually warranted by scripture. Hence, elements within the tradition may be problematized, and Pannenberg's study makes it abundantly clear that there is no consensus in Christian history on these issues. O'Donnell would not, I think, contest this point for clearly all elements within the 'tradition' cannot always be held at the same time and with equal weighting. But it should also be realized that when the tradition has spoken of the Father as the unoriginated origin (DZ 1331) and the source and origin of all divinity (DZ 1331) to read these dogmatic truths exclusively of the Father or in purely casual terms is to misread them. Strictly speaking, ontologically, both the Spirit and Christ are of 'unoriginated origin' in so much as there never was a 'time' when they were not. There was no logical or chronological moment when the father was 'alone' – despite Smith's contention. However, it seems historically explicable that a major non-causally intended metaphor was employed within the tradition to distinguish the relations between the three persons and to safeguard their distinctiveness within their unity. What I am suggesting is that working with different metaphors to express the reciprocal relations may helpfully counteract the employment of an exclusively patriarchal metaphor within which to configure trinitarian relations. One manner in resisting a cosmological masculine taxonomy to encode the trinitarian event is to recognize that the three co-constitute each other, such that 'subsistent relations' really constitute deity. In the next chapter I will further explore this claim, for if we are created in the image of God then subsistent relations are also an important conceptual description of human persons being redeemed.

O'Donnell's third criticism takes us into Pannenberg-specific discussion, which I do not wish to pursue except to say that Pannenberg makes it absolutely clear that he questions Rahner's 'vice versa' in the axiom 'the economic is the immanent trinity, and vice versa', but rightly insists that the immanent trinity cannot be other than what we know through the economy, even if the fullness of this economic revelation has not come into its completion.[109] Hence, while acknowledging that the suggestion I am making regarding the reconception of the birth of the 'fatherhood' of God is open to many objections, I propose that in so much as it cleanses Christian thought of pagan patriarchy it is necessary. However, given that cleansing Christianity of pagan patriarchy is my main intention in advancing the argument, I should briefly attend to Pannenberg's objection to the use of 'mother'.

Pannenberg, when inspecting the New Testament evidence regarding the use of 'father', rightly concedes, far more than Ricoeur, that while the Israelites distanced themselves from cosmological patriarchs, the use of father does bear a semantic sense from Israelite patriarchal structures in that God the 'father's' 'responsibilities . . . are similar to the duty of a family head to care for the members'.[110] Pannenberg then poses the question: if family structures have changed, can we not change the use of 'father'? He suggests that the alternative use of 'mother' would simply presuppose Feuerbachian projectionism, for finally God's fatherhood questions all human notions of fatherhood. 'On the lips of Jesus, "Father" becomes a proper name for God.'[111] This latter claim about proper names is quite unsustainable. Furthermore, Pannenberg's first argument is clearly weak in initially acknowledging the use of father as having some analogical similarities (along with Hamerton-Kelly) deriving from Israelite social structures, and then claiming later that it undermines all analogical similarities. While Pannenberg does succeed in showing that the father of Jesus is not a cosmological generative patriarch, he does not succeed in his arguments against outlawing 'mother'. Why should it be that 'father' is safeguarded from the criticism of Feuerbachian projectionism, and the case not be made out for similar analogical circumspection in the employment of 'mother'?

I have already shown grounds for reservations about Moltmann's creative use of 'mother', not for the reasons Pannenberg gives but because of the patriarchal encoding of such usage. Pannenberg's prohibition against 'mother' is as arbitrary as Elizabeth Achteimer's argument that whenever 'mother' is used it leads to pantheism for it suggests that the world is God's body.[112] While Achteimer's point is extremely incisive in relation to Sally MacFague against whom she argues, it unwarrantedly generalizes from a particular. If early Christians had the sense to question Arius' similar literalism when it came to the Father–Son, which meant that, for Arius, by virtue of being Son Jesus could not be equal to his father in ontological status, then it is not clear why pantheism would *necessarily* follow as Achteimer claims from speaking of God as 'mother'. In fact it would usefully help to make clear the materiality of God's involvement with creation.

In this second section of Chapter 2, I have argued that the biblical 'father' is utterly relational, transgressive of patriarchal cosmological monarchs and has nothing to do with 'origins'. 'Father' is eschatologically oriented towards the future, a figure who draws us into new life, into a new kingdom, but only through co-operation and as co-redeemers. I have also shown that there are good arguments for dropping constitutive relations of 'origin' from trinitarian representation, for when they remain, even in the most gender-sensitive theologians, they affect the entry of cosmological patriarchy through the back door. If they go, they do not necessarily compromise the distinctions between the persons which can be safeguarded on the economic level, both biblically and through subsequent conceptual metaphorical developments.

Hence, one effect of my argument about 'origins' is that the father is 'born' into re-presentation through subsistent relations that exist with the Son and Spirit, and vice versa, even though the relations are not formally identical. The Council of Florence put it like this: 'Everything is one except when this is impossible because of reciprocal relations' (DZ 330). Hence, it is permissible to speak of the birth of the Father's re-presentation as being both dependent and related to that of the Son's and Spirit's. If we have seen how the latter two's histories of re-presentation have indeed been so fluid, then trying to stabilize re-presentation of the 'father' is rightly called into question. Of course, we will never know all three 'face to face' until the beatific vision, and until then we must remain content to re-present the triune God 'through a glass darkly'.

I want to conclude this section with a brief exegesis of a Johannine verse to show that giving 'birth to the father' is not an inappropriate metaphor, given that we only come to know the Father through the Son and the Spirit, through our ecclesial participation in the drama of redemption. In the prologue John suggests that the Word was 'with God' and 'was God', and through whom 'all things were made' (1.1–3). Having alluded to identity and difference between the Word and God, and the Word's functioning in the manner attributed to God (being light, life, glory), John then identifies this Word as Jesus, in whom 'the Word became flesh' (1.14). The outrageousness of this is further compounded when John closes the prologue with the words: 'No one has ever seen God; the only Son, who is in the bosom of the Father, he has made him known' (v. 18). Not until we come to share the life of Jesus, through the power of the Spirit, do we begin to know the shared love that exists between Jesus, the Spirit and the Father: triune, relational ecstasy. The Greek word used for 'known' in John's phrase 'he has made him known' (v. 18) is *exēgeomai* which is nowhere else used in the New Testament in this manner. *Exēgeomai* forms the root of our English word exegesis: to read and interpret. The root of the Greek word for knowledge is usually rendered with a 'gnosis' cognate: *agnoeō, epignōskō, ginōskō* and so on; or *agnōsia* (having no knowledge: 1 Cor. 15.34). But in this context the 'knowing' that John predicates is like that of reading a text and explaining, that is exegesis, describing and performing it, which within that very act the reality of Jesus' revelation is given. This textual-exegetical performance of the scriptures leads us into the relationship that we can only describe in the 'process', as Ricoeur puts it, rather than as an object of description that transcends all processes. *Abba* after all, as Ricoeur points out, is invocation, not description, a living relationship. It is significant that *exēgeomai* is employed in Luke 24.35 where the disciples on the road to Emmaus recognize Jesus only in Jesus' exegesis of the scripture (24.27) *and* in the breaking of bread (24.30–1). Luke, in verse 35, then tells of the disciples relating the Emmaus story to the others: 'Then they told what had happened on the road, and how he was *known* to them in the breaking of the bread.' This eucharistic practice is definitive for Luke's context of recognition. Both John and Luke, even with very significant differences, recognize that Jesus Christ *and* the Holy Spirit reveal the Father, and this can only be interpreted ecclesiologically.[113] For John and Luke, the Father is only known via the Son, who is not yet known by us in his fullness, for this continual exegesis *is* the life of the Marian body of Christ, whereby both his daughters and sons are led, like Jesus and Mary, by the Spirit into the fullness of life. Elsewhere, I have elaborated upon John's emphasis on the Spirit as that which means there is no closure in Christ.[114]

My re-encoding is an attempt to re-present difference between the personal relations without static identity, without closure. In this respect, the trinitarian taxonomy proposed in these two chapters makes no claim to static figuration or essential quality. I tried to show the importance of recognizing the politics of our language of divine re-presentation, and the numerous unexpected and legitimate ways in which trinitarian re-presentation constantly poses questions to our questions about gender politics and social configurations. This was true of all three persons of the trinity, the Spiritess, the Christa and the Mother. To freeze any of these re-presentations, or to give them exclusive privileged status runs the risk of idolatry. In engaging with Irigaray, I hoped to have shown both the immense truthfulness that her work is able to bring to a church that is so deeply enmeshed in pagan patriarchy and the way in which a church that has not totally lost its bearings might make a critical and creative response to Irigaray from within its own symbolic traditions.

Our engagement with Irigaray has also allowed the Spirit to take shape *in relation* to the embodied church of women and men, the church of the maternal Virgin, the queen, mother, bride and friend, the communion of women saints. This archaeological recovery of an imaginary that is so often captured and used for patriarchy's ends is a resource that might help to dismantle and address Christianity's patriarchy. But there is no bypassing the scandal of particularity, and this scandal calls into question a number of Irigaray's presuppositions. It is also a scandal that is made into a false scandal when the maleness of Jesus is used to exclude women from the priesthood, or any other form of analogical re-presentation of that new life that is God's gift. This is not to suggest that men and women are equal, but rather that they are different, even if the specifying of this difference is still part of the process of learning redemption. In fact the very re-presentation of Jesus in Christian history calls into question whether his anatomy determines any clear gender understanding. But the fact that Jesus was male might also be interestingly employed to address the very problematic that Irigaray's analysis reveals – as was developed in the first part of this chapter. Finally, I have tried to show that the main issue at stake in imagining the 'father' lies in the seductive metaphysical perpetuation of a pagan generative cosmological figure. The *ex nihilo* doctrine within Christianity checked against such tendencies, but the main problem remains an intratrinitarian one which then surfaces within all forms of cultural re-presentations. The biblical witness within the church allows us to offer a critique of such gross anthropomorphism, but this task is in its infancy. There are no simple answers, such as now calling God mother, which can also fall into all sorts of dangers (Feuerbachian projectionism, pantheism, patriarchal encoding); but not to call the 'first' person mother would be an impoverishment in our theology, social practices and worship. Neither father nor mother are finally applicable, for analogy always operates within a greater dissimilarity.

I want to turn now to a fictitious female trinity and a single male deity, posited as the foundational battle in the construction of Islam. In this fiction, the analogous battle between multivocal language and univocal predication is staged, and with it the human struggle against idolatry. Salman Rushdie rewrites Freud on religion and Irigaray on language. Language, gender and trinity are explored from a very novel angle in Salman Rushdie's *The Satanic Verses*.

3

Gendered divinity and Satanic fiction

1. Rushdie, Irigaray and Freud and the question of divine re-presentation

Irigaray's question mark against the closure of the incarnation as occluding the process of divinizing women and her problematization of the trinity provides an unexpected bridge to Salman Rushdie's fiction and his profound problematization of the divine. Rushdie's fictionalized exploration has led to his non-fictional disappearance, the assassination of translators, anonymous publishing conglomerates, intergovernmental negotiations and a plot that makes Rushdie's 'magical realism' look naturalistic. However, this metanarrative tragi-comedy indicates the power of Rushdie's fiction, how the 'imaginary' novel can contain the repressed taboos and divine idolatries that drive men to kill. Rushdie, like Irigaray, represents a confluence of important cultural forces with which Christians engage: postmodernism, psychoanalysis, sexuate language and cultural criticism. They are fused into a novel about feminine representation within the divine and within human culture, a novel about how language's relationality means that signification can never be fixed, be it for the human or divine. In this sense, *The Satanic Verses* is a profoundly apophatically religious novel. It also allows me to thematically develop aspects of the trinitarian issues raised in the previous two chapters.

My exploration here must remain in tension with what I have written elsewhere about Rushdie's *The Satanic Verses*.[1] There I argued that there may be good grounds for banning the book *in England* because of its 'Orientalizing' of Islam and the subsequent offence caused to marginal and vulnerable groups of Muslims. (By Orientalism I mean the portrayal of Islam in negative images generated in the context of the west's colonization of Muslim territories, following Edward Said.)[2] I suggested that Rushdie's novel was part of the universalizing discourse of *secular fundamentalism* and that it was incapable of recognizing its own dangerous totalitarian tendencies in ideologically reducing and ridiculing any claim that God has revealed himself in history. By secular fundamentalism, I meant a closed ideology that refused the possibility of transcendence, and therefore reconstructed religions within its own master-code. I now think that there is more to Rushdie than the 'Orientalism' and secular fundamentalism that I attributed to him, even if traces of both still remain in his work. Whether Islam really conforms to the images presented in the novel remains an open question.

But what of the Irigarian, Freudian and trinitarian bridge? In this chapter I will only consider exploring two crossings. The first revolves around the relationship between language and 'character' or 'person'. If language constructs us and is constructed by us, and language is utterly relational, then it follows that we only find a sense of who we are through our relationships with each other, the divine and the world. Furthermore, if language in its endless possible relationships cannot be given a frozen and singular signification then neither can we. Our meaning and significance is not and cannot be 'closed' by our very constitution within language. But Rushdie's exploration does not remain at a purely formal semiotic level. He explores our interrelatedness within signs in terms of our most primal relationships: that of relationships to our parents and to the divine. In short, there is a sense (not necessarily shared by Rushdie, but to be found in my engagement with him) in which the psychoanalytic theory of object relations might help us to purge idolatry from our representation of the divine and learn, through the Christian narrative, how to purify our relationships with fathers and mothers, wives and children, friends and relations, and those who form the 'church'. This will be the implicit argument of sections 3 and 5 below. I say implicit because I do not want to labour my theological points such as to *use* Rushdie's novel purely as a vehicle to advance my own project. I want the reader to enjoy the almost 'revelatory' status of this novel and the process of how the narrative and our close engagement with it yields insights that cannot be simply given apart from the narration. Hence, much of my 'argument' constitutes close textual

exegesis. In the postscript I will develop some of these insights in a
more theological manner.

The second theme that I explore follows on from the first and is
explicitly the concern of Section 4 below. I want to explore further
Irigaray's thesis about feminine divine representation and its socio-
political-psychoanalytic genesis and consequences. I do this by arguing
that Rushdie's novel is a reworking of Freud's *Moses and Monotheism*,
such that Rushdie both attends to the matricidal foundations of religion
(which Freud had repressed and Irigaray uncovers) and the gender
issues of divine representation. We will find Rushdie in both strong
agreement and disagreement with Irigaray, and this engagement
between the two of them also furthers my own engagement with the
issues. There is an intimate link between Rushdie's restless refusal at
univocal signification and Irigaray's epistemological unveiling of the
phallocentric economy of singular representation. Rushdie is profoundly
aware that this crisis in signification affects both the question of human
and divine representation. There are no divisions between the personal,
political and religious – such as modernity has deployed. Islam often
seems more able than Christianity to deconstruct these enlightenment
taxonomies. However, if there are no separate zones of life, then equally
the religious representations by which we live will also signify the
repressed concerns within our religious cultures. Freud was somewhat
reductionist and unilateral in seeing the process between representation
and neurosis as one way, such that religion (Judaism and Christianity)
could be analysed away so as to facilitate our entry into adult and
scientific maturity. Irigaray thawed out Freud's 'scientific' paralysis,
even though she may be in danger of both essentialism and instrumental
reductionism regarding the divine – as was suggested in the previous
chapter. Rushdie shares a similar ambivalence towards the 'religious',
as does Irigaray, and it is not always clear how to interpret this ambivalence.

Rushdie is as daring and wide ranging as Freud and Irigaray for
within his fictional text there is a questioning and probing of the constructions of western (and eastern) cultures, and with it their 'religions'.
It is within this intersection of interests that my conversation with
Rushdie is generated. But the reader might still ask: why engage with
a novel, a fiction; why not take on Freud, Islam and the various issues
in a straightforward fashion? The answer is simple. I am concerned

with the linguistic mediation of the divine. Irigaray's concern with sexuate language, *parler-femme*, alerted us to the fact that all cultural artefacts (philosophical texts, pictures, music, films) are important in Christianity's engagement with culture. The novel is especially important, for, like the Christian story, it construes its reality in a manner which makes us look differently at the world. Rushdie's book is profoundly postmodern at this very point for it explores a major tenet of postmodernism by employing it fictionally: that all meaning is mediated through signs, and signs are forever shifting; they have no stable home, no pure meaning and they can be put to an infinite number of uses, which, nevertheless, fail to exhaust their meanings (Derrida). There is no single overarching grand narrative that explains and stabilizes all signs, no foundational point from which to view the world (Lyotard).[3] If these tenets are true, then religions which claim that revelation has taken place in history (Judaism, Christianity and Islam) – *they* say that God has spoken – have a lot more accounting to do for such claims, given that all signs, all speaking, are humanly mediated and subject to indeterminacy. In short, can one really distinguish the Word of God from the words of man – and sometimes, but all too rarely, the words of women? In so much as 'revelation' tends to be constructed within the words of male mediators (priests, imams, rabbis, popes, roshis, bodhisattvas) and transmitted within their circles, Rushdie stages a questioning of the liberating power of such divine-male constructions. Rushdie's stance echoes Irigaray's, when she claims: 'God is being used by men to oppress women and therefore, God must be questioned and not simply neutered in the current pseudo liberal way. Religion as a social phenomenon cannot be ignored.'[4] Rushdie is asking profoundly 'religious' questions with a keen nose for detecting possibly idolatrous answers. Of course, Rushdie cannot be privileged as a conduit of truth, but I hope to show that many of his insights purify our own reception of revelation and also lead to an appreciation of the distinct Otherness of his own project.

If we ignore the question of the transmission of tradition and revelation, then terror is unleashed: 'From the beginning men used God to justify the unjustifiable. He moves in mysterious ways: men say.'[5] The context of this quotation is the narrator's pained amusement at the great patriarch Abraham being celebrated by the waters of 'Zamzam', even though this marks the site of his abandoning both Ishmael and

Hagar, his child and his child's mother, to die in the wilderness. Abraham's (and Sarah's) cruelty is occluded and instead Abraham's patriarchy celebrated, as a different story is retold by the waters of 'Zamzam', the site of the great Muslim pilgrimage. Rushdie's use of Zamzam cleverly recalls the celebrated well of Zamzam dug by the prophet's grandfather, 'Abd al-Muttalib. He like Abraham is called to sacrifice his son, 'Abn Allāh. However, unlike Abraham, he turns to a woman soothsayer for advice. She suggests that he bargain, and then gamble with the deity, the price of a human life to save his son. The going price is ten camels. However, 'Abd al-Muttalib is not too good a gambler, and is only eventually able to recover his son at the cost of one hundred camels. Interestingly, 'Abd al-Muttalib is driven to save his son by the imploring action of his daughters. The role of women in this counter-story further deconstructs the untroubled representation of the Abraham story.[6] History is constantly rewritten, and, as Rushdie notes in *Shame*, 'every story one chooses to tell is a kind of censorship, it prevents the telling of other tales'.[7] The unjustifiable justified in God's name finds expression in coercive power over others: 'personal', 'political' and 'religious'. There are of course no clear lines between any of these sites as each translates itself into the other as is seen, for example, in Gibreel: a character in the novel, an actor who represents India's cinematic psyche, the angel in the Mahound/Muhammed sequence, and thereby implicitly a figure who sanctions all sorts of power structures. The lack of demarcation between these sites, individual character, national psyches, angelic personae and Muhammed's life, also means that isolating any such phenomena as 'religion' is methodologically flawed.[8] All we have is our semiotic configurations by which we are constructed and which we construct. The divine cannot bypass this mediation.

In 'real life' Rushdie seems to have forgotten that divisions between personal, political and religious are inadmissible, when before the *fatwā* he said of the book:

Actually one of my major themes is religion . . . I have talked about the Islamic religion because that is what I know the most about. But the ideas about religious faith and the nature of religious experience and also the political implication of religious extremism are applicable with a few variations to just about any religion.[9]

Later, after the *fatwā*, he claimed that the book was not about Islam at all, but about 'migration, metamorphosis, divided selves, love, death'.[10] The book, of course, refuses such distinctions and it would be foolish to imagine that Rushdie has any special authority over his text, for this would commit the very fallacy the book explodes: that meaning is stable. If I am right in this, then my interpretation is certainly not exhaustive – nor could it be. In the next section I will briefly introduce Rushdie's fictional work and literary style to readers unfamiliar with his corpus. For those familiar with his work, proceed to Section 3. Since I approach Rushdie from a number of different but related angles, the reader will inevitably find interconnections, both intended and otherwise.

2. Introducing Rushdie

Rushdie's concerns with language and culture have inescapably meant a profound engagement with 'religion'. Rushdie had already employed Sufi traditions in his first book *Grimus* (1975). *Midnight's Children* (1980) deconstructs both Hindu and Muslim myths to unravel the political mythology of Independent India. Rushdie shows both religious and secular myths that populate the subcontinent to be forms of 'false consciousness'.[11] Attention to genealogies characterize Rushdie's work so that character cannot be constituted without an almost novel-length 'digression' about the 'main' characters' parents, grandparents, great-grandparents and even great-great-grandparents. Genealogy is important to Rushdie. It is significant that these genealogies refuse to work in patriarchal linear sequence, and mothers and sisters are powerfully, even often overbearingly, constructed. This almost feminist psychoanalytical reading of character construction is especially developed in *Shame* (1984) where Rushdie shamelessly disarms the military government of General Zia al Haqq and his predecessor, Zulfikar Ali Bhutto, through the characters of Ali Hyder and Iskandar Harappa respectively – especially in depicting their exploitation of women. In this respect, there is an Irigarian theme that the exploitation of women by men is the most fundamental form of oppression which subsequently generates other forms of exploitation. But Rushdie does not remain content with such foundationalism. Women are not essentialized, and *Shame* has a good measure of phallic mothers, especially in the shape of Chhunni, Munnee and Bunny Shakil, the 'three mothers', and in the figures of Sufiya Zinobia Hyder and Arjumand Harappa the 'virgin Ironpants'. We have here a vestige of the trinity of women goddesses later found in *The Satanic Verses*. In *Shame* Rushdie explores the way in which Islam in Pakistan constructed an edifice of power and control that kept political dictators and patriarchy in position, but never securely in place, for finally even dictators cannot fully control signs – even when they claim divine stabilization for (their) ordering of signs.

If *Shame* concerned the 'use' of Islam, *The Satanic Verses* (1988) pushes the question further: can Islam (or any religion) be understood detached from its many embodiments in history, apart from its many 'uses'? To those who would respond, 'but these are often misuses of religion', Rushdie replies, 'but signs in history are all we have'. There is no pure, divine, unmediated message which is then misinterpreted, but a string of contested interpretations, and no unpolluted Word, but endless sets of words claiming the reflected authority of the Word. When signs are treated ahistorically (univocally), as if they were not mediated, such exegesis denies history and our complex interrelated, multilayered, omni-storied world.

Rushdie's next novel, *Haroun and the Sea of Stories* (1990), although a 'children's story', is about censorship and repression, about strangling alternative stories, which leads to two-dimensional life (hence the car-toon character-like quality of so many of Rushdie's figures – holding a mirror to nature!). *East, West* (1994), his first collection of short stories, returns to the themes of the three big novels: cultural identity, power and the search for love.[12] *The Moor's Last Sigh* (1996) is organized around the fluid metaphor of the palimpsest, a construction whereby one picture after another is painted on top of the previous one, upon the same canvas. Hence, boundaries between time, people, inner and outer, private and personal are all erased: 'One universe, one dimension, one country, one dream, bumpo'ing into another, or being under, or on top of. Call it Palimpstine. And above it all, in the palace, you.'[13] This god's-eye view, up in the 'palace', is of course never clear or resolved, nor can it be within history. The book takes its title from a painting by Moraes' (the Moor's) mother, Aurora Zogoiby, who faces up to the 'treatment of her only son' in her multilayered painting which, with good Freudian timing, is stolen immediately after (and by?) her death.[14] The relationship between the Moor and his mother and father is central to the book. 'Central' is metaphorically possible because the image of the palimpsest allows for three generations of parental relationships to come into view. Similarly, the relationship between Saladin and his father and mother dominates *The Satanic Verses* and has its counterpart in Gibreel's orphan status. I shall be suggesting later that Gibreel can stage Saladin's unconscious, making clear the imaginary that guides Saladin, which is predicated upon the murder of both father and mother – and the enthroning of a narcissistic god: the self. It is for this reason that Saladin loses his faith precisely at the time when he openly hates his father. His 'implacable rage' would 'boil away his childhood father-worship and make him a secular man, who would do his best, thereafter, to live without a god of any type'.[15]

Having briefly placed *The Satanic Verses* within the textual corpus of Rushdie's fiction, let me say a brief word about his literary style and then finally outline the novel itself for those readers unfamiliar with it. Rushdie's restless employment of a palimpsest of interpretative frameworks and narrative styles refuses closure of meaning, defying any final act of 'reading' the novel – or life itself. This restless postmodernism bears close analogy with Irigaray's concerns in *parler-femme*, most primarily in the refusal of closure and therefore language's relationship to the divine. Since language relates to the 'Other' (woman, the outsider immigrant, or the divine) both Rushdie and Irigaray are deeply suspicious about our use of language, while also recognizing that in this use lies the seeds of redemption. Rushdie's 'magical realism' challenges the 'European realistic' novel, marking the end of the colonial 'imperial view' and its genres, the view from the 'palace', the imperial sense of control over stable territory. 'Magical realism' thus performs a transmutation of these idioms, a changing of 'traditional' signs.[16] This is seen within the novel when Baal, the failed poet, is escaping from Mahound. Baal reflects on the impossibility of his writing capturing forms that are not stable. The desert, that most powerful of postmodern metaphors, and one so central to the Semitic faiths, generates the following simile:

> How did one map a country that blew into a new form every day? Such questions made his language too abstract, his imagery too fluid, his metre too inconstant. It led him to create chimeras of form, lionheaded goatbodied serpenttailed impossibilities whose shapes felt

obliged to change the moment they were set, so that the demotic forced its way into lines of classical purity and images of love were constantly degraded by the intrusion of elements of farce.[17]

This is a wonderful description of the novel's own poetic prose and one reason for the demanding reading it can require. Rushdie's *style* shows that there are no pure signs, no unmediated 'realities', and therefore no constant pure meanings, and this includes 'ourselves', our 'divinities' and our 'signs'. The novel opens with two figures falling out of the heavens: a metaphor which captures angelic, satanic and earthly births, as well as the birthing of this novel. Saladin falls in 'the recommended position for babies entering the birth canal'.[18] Our descent down the birth canal into the cold air of 'reality', our 'fall' into the life of signs, into a fallen world, forms the opening of *The Satanic Verses*. But before looking at the opening sentences in more detail and beginning my exploration of the perichoretic nature and language and persons within the novel, I shall attempt a quick 'plot' description even though it runs against the entire novel for the process of reading, wonder, puzzlement and questioning is what makes it work, not its story line *per se*. But . . .

The book is divided into nine chapters, each broken into parts, mirroring the structure of the Koran. It contains many 'digressions', interconnections, changes of style and subject matter, almost like a 'clumsy patchwork'.[19] The citations are in fact those of Arberry speaking about the Koran, although they might equally and telling apply to the novel itself. Arberry goes on to defend the Koran from the charge of being a 'clumsy patchwork' (as we might well do of the novel) on the grounds that it is a reinterpretation of history, 'confirming what was before it', excepting falsifications.[20] He also notes the manifold style

swinging from the steady march of straightforward narrative or enunciation (tales of the ancient prophets, formulations of ritual and law) to the impetuous haste of ecstatic ejaculation (the majesty of God, the immanence of the Last Day, the torments of Hell, and the delights of Paradise).[21]

The first chapter is called 'The Angel Gibreel' and stages the descent of the two main characters into the novel, into England, and out of thin air. The two characters are: Gibreel Farishta (who is a womanizing Indian film star insomniac, fearful of his dreams, which also make up the inner life of other characters, including Mahound, the prophet) and Saladin Chamchawala (the sophisticated self-made Indian Englishman who loathes his culture, father and mother, and himself, and marries an archetypal English woman, Pamela Lovelace). Their his-stories are related as is the context of their fall: from an exploding jumbo jet, a metaphoric container of mixed identities, shuffling modern cities into each other and confusing static cultural identities. Chapter 2, 'Mahound', interlaces the modern story of Gibreel and Saladin with that of the 'origins' of Islam, in a similar way to Freud's fantastical restaging of the Moses story in *Moses and Monotheism*. It is set in terms of Mahound's (Muhammed) orphan background and his treatment of women as either mothers, lovers or/and subordinates. This treatment of women immediately relates him to the Gibreel of Chapter I, but all the more so as this same Gibreel finds himself in the prophet's dream world, identified with the Angel Gabriel who dictates the words of the Koran. These words are then dictated to another mediator, the scribe Salman, who later will change the W/words to see if Mahound realizes his trickery. The scribe most interestingly is Rushdie's namesake.[22] This fluidity of characters and language is in contrast to Mahound's 'terrifying singularity', his insistence on the authority of the Word, the Book, and his refusal to allow different stories to coexist – even though they do so in his own biography.[23]

This chapter also contains the incident of 'the Satanic verses' which is attested to in three authoritative Muslim sources: Ibn Ishaq's *The Life of Muhammed*, which is the most relied on account of the prophet's life by Muslims; al-Wāqidi's commentary; and Tibari's history of the life of the Prophet. Ibn Ishaq, the most authoritative of the sources, says that the believers, in hearing the verses which were eventually to be pronounced 'Satanic', were not 'suspecting a mistake or a vain desire or a slip' when they heard Muhammed recite them.[24] Guillaume argues: 'you cannot get behind these sources' and this incident was certainly possible to report 'before the doctrine of the eternity of the Quran became a rigid dogma'.[25] Indeed, Guillaume is typical of western scholarship in arguing that when 'we come to look at the external evidence there is considerable justification for the belief that the Quran was subject to alteration in its initial stages'.[26] Mahound compromises with the polytheistic Meccans and reports that the angel Gibreel has accepted the three goddesses of Mecca, despite all of Mahound's previous teachings. His follower Khalid is close to tears: 'Messenger, what are you saying? Lat, Manat, Uzza – they're all *females*! For pity's sake! Are we to have goddesses now. Those old cranes, herons, hags?'[27] Allowing the feminine entry into divine representation undermines the univocal, 'terrifying singularity' of the prophet's message. However, once this change in Mahound's strategy fails to attain his ends – acceptance within Mecca/Jihila, Mahound descends from the mountain with a different message, which forms Sura 53.19–21 of the Qur'an. Mahound claims the original recitation had been the devil's, thereby implicitly 'conceding' equivocal signification. However, Mahound simply attributes the falsity to Satan, and now claims that the angel has refused the three goddesses. In Rushdie's reading it is a matter of genealogical eradication. The satanic verse is the response given to the question about goddesses: 'Have you thought upon Lat and Uzza, and Manat, the third, the other?' Originally, Mahound had claimed the answer to be: 'They are exalted birds, and their intercession is desired indeed.'[28] After the faulty line of transmitting divine messages is 'fixed', the verse then reads: ' "Shall He have daughters and you sons?" Mahound recites. "That would be a fine division." '[29] Mahound's God, Allah, fails to challenge the cultural practices that suit the Messenger Mahound – and underwrite patriarchy.[30] Speaking of the 'rules, rules, rules'[31] dictated to Mahound that constitute parts of the Koran, the author's voice tellingly notes that authoritarian patriarchy also requires that sexually 'forbidden postures included all those in which the female was on top'.[32] Chapter 2 was, not surprisingly, one of the most 'offensive' to many Muslim readers.

Chapter 3, 'Ellowen Deeowen', phonetically producing 'London', is about Thatcher's Britain and contains a scathing political critique of Britain's 'empire within'.[33] Here we follow the fate of Gibreel and Saladin. Gibreel becomes angel-like in an act of betrayal of Saladin, who begins to transform into a goat and ends as the goatish Satan – a kind of caricatured polarity to Gibreel. His transformation works on a number of levels: it expresses Saladin's growing self-hatred; it metaphorically depicts the manner in which he is treated by the English, or at least the police and authorities that deal with him as an illegal 'immigrant'; and it expresses the metamorphic quality of 'character'. One of his fellow animal prisoners remarks of the authorities: 'They have the power of description, and we succumb to the pictures they construct.'[34] Immigrants often have fragile cultural identity from which to draw upon, to give themselves self-definition that will gain respect within an alien world, or alternatively they must acquiesce in the descriptions given to them by the more pervasive.[35] The pressure to hide otherness and difference is powerful. In this chapter we meet many characters including Saladin's wife, Pamela, who thinks he is dead and begins an affair with the aspiring but failed Indian poet, Jumpy Joshi.

Chapter 4, 'Ayesha', seems to start an entirely new novel with the account of the remarkable prophetess Ayesha – who also bears the name of the Prophet's favourite wife. But, before that, it also tells the story of an exiled Imam in London, who through an American convert runs a radio station to send messages of Islamic revolution back to his home country Desh. It has been suggested that the Imam is based on Ayatollah Khomeini. Ayesha's story is the magical and sinister account of a young orphan girl who begins to have visions and messages from the Angel Gabriel and authoritatively leads a group of followers into the sea which should part to give them passage, like Moses. It doesn't, and they are all drowned. We have to wait until Chapter 8 for the final part of this story. The incident is based on a historical one, that of Naseen Fatima and her eighteen drowned followers in Karachi. Some Shi'ites regarded her as a glorious martyr, but Sunnis uniformly condemned her. Both these tales are commentaries on the book, just as the book is a commentary on them. One important feature of this account of Ayesha is that it stages phallic women as equally and terrifyingly singular as those 'men' under the univocal phallic economy.

Chapter 5, 'A City Visible but Unseen', returns to London and the descent into the hell by both Gibreel and Saladin. Gibreel has a breakdown and cannot find love in his relationship to Pamela, for he constantly despises women. Tellingly, his hatred of women is mirrored by his dreaming in Arabic and his recitation during dreams: 'These are exalted females whose intercession is to be desired',[36] an engagement with 'other' than he unconsciously desires but also which he constantly thwarts. Saladin transforms back to a human person after the depths of his hate have wrecked the Hot Wax disco.

Chapter 6, 'Return to Jahilia', stages the victorious return of Mahound to Mecca and his controlled mercy and forgiveness – which cannot

extend to poets and whores,[37] for they both exemplify and generate
equivocal significations. Mahound's singularity and obsessive control
over signs and social practices leads to an underground brothel where
the whores become extremely wealthy in emulating the prophet's wives
(thereby undermining univocal predication). All the whores eventually
and ironically marry one man: the poet Baal, who acts as the prophet's
counterpart. Chapter 7, 'The Angel Azraeel', stages a very temporary
partial reconciliation between Saladin and Gibreel. Chapter 8, 'The
Parting of the Arabia Sea', concludes the Ayesha story with the death
of the pilgrims and Ayesha. Chapter 9, 'A Wonderful Lamp', is a play
on Aladdin's magical lamp and the mocking of happy endings. It is an
important chapter for it displays a real, but only partial reconciliation
(what else?) between Saladin and his estranged and now dying father
and deceased mother, and Saladin's birth into the possibility of love,
now that he has forgiven, been forgiven, loved and been loved. This is
the redemptive focal point of the novel which requires him to face
the perichoretic presence of 'others' that constitute himself: first and
foremost, his mother and father. This reconciliation incident also
coincides with the suicide of Gibreel in Saladin's father's home, which
perhaps signifies a resolution of the Oedipal conflict within Saladin
such that a new faith is possible. What this new faith might look like
is the unwritten margin where the novel ends.

What this new faith might look like, I suggest, is a bridge (a *preparatio*)
towards the trinitarian self-revelation of love that reconciles a fallen
creation through forgiveness, such that our own relations will be transformed through participating in the 'source' of love (as *Lumen Gentium*
put it): our entering into relations within the trinitarian relations. That
such entry into new relations may require the death and transformation
of the old man (Gibreel, the ego) into one in which dependence, trust
and vulnerability are required is the difficult story staged in the Christian narrative. It is the story that Irigaray's work also helps recover from
its patriarchal encoding.

But now having provided a potted plot, let me turn again to the
beginning of the novel to see how Rushdie shows us the interrelations
of all persons, through the interrelation of words and signs. In this
picture, Rushdie depicts a fallen world, Babel, that longs for a new
Pentecost, the marriage of the Spirit and Bride, the possibility of living
and loving difference. It is within this framework that we might more

fully understand the possible conceptual resources to imagine the centrality of perichoresis for trinitarian representation. That is, to imagine why it is that redemption is always a communal indwelling with all creation, in which each person is affected by all others. Language and history have no clear boundaries. The relational and perichoretic nature of the Christ event is nicely summed up in Paul's first letter to the Corinthians 15.12: 'As in Adam all die, so also in Christ, shall all be made alive' (see also Col. 1.20, 3.11). Psychoanalysis reveals the multiple levels of indwelling mediated always through our semiotic life. Rushdie's fiction embodies the same process.

3. Indwelling language

'To be born again,' sang Gibreel Farishta tumbling from the heavens, 'first you have to die. Ho ji! Ho ji! To land upon the bosomy earth, first one needs to fly. Tat-taa! Taka-thun! How to ever smile again, if first you won't cry? How to win the darling's love, mister, without a sigh? Baba, if you want to get born again . . .' Just before dawn one winter's morning, New Year's Day or thereabouts, two real, full-grown, living men fell from a great height, twenty-nine thousand and two feet, towards the English Channel, without the benefit of parachutes or wings, out of a clear sky.[38]

I will comment on this passage in some detail to show that Rushdie's postmodern understanding of language should not be read as a threat to revelation, but instead as an iconoclastic examination of idolatry, or closure, the attempt to capture and endorse the sacred in language. Rather than this indeterminacy being corrosive of revelation, it actually leads to the possibility of facilitating Christian revelation, centred as it is on 'relations'. That is, it shows how language (like the divine) only works relationally, reconfiguring itself in the company of other, such that they are not eradicated or repressed, but drawn into new 'relations'. Hybrid languages construct the book, in contrast to any attempt to maintain linguistic (and therefore equally religious, political, social and personal) purity, the Christian revelation that language has this power because all creation bears the image of God, which is the image of relationality, perichoresis and irreducible mystery that refuses closure.

However, let me return to the text. 'To be born again', Gibreel's opening lines, echoes variously throughout the novel. This is the plight of the 'immigrant' who moves from one culture to another constantly searching for and constructing 'identity'. Some like Salahuddin Chamchawala resist the father/land – Changez (his father) and his Bombay home – meticulously trying to reconstruct themselves, in Salahuddin's case, as English. Hence, while his Muslim name Salahuddin transmutes into the Anglicized 'Saladin Chamcha', he still ironically bears the name of the great medieval Muslim 'Saladin' who also conquered a culture, defeating the Christian Crusaders and restoring Sunni Islam to Egypt. Saladin enters enemy territory and tries to conquer England, but this time by assimilation. He has to eat 'smoked fish full of spikes and bones' at his inauguration into the English public school system. This ordeal takes him ninety minutes and a stern refusal to cry at his own humiliation. 'The eaten kipper was his first victory, the first step in his conquest of England.'[39] His refusal also echoes his refusal to cry at the separation from his mother and father. Saladin's attempt to deny his parents parallels his construction of a new identity via the conquest of England. However, this is a conquest which can never be won for it must confront 'the new empire within Britain': racism and class. This also parallels Saladin's hidden empire within himself. Saladin's accent changes because his classmates laugh at his Indian tones (which must now 'die'): 'he began to act, to find masks that these fellows would recognize, paleface masks, clown-masks, until he fooled them into thinking he was *okay*, he was *people-like-us*'.[40] On his return to Bombay, Indian accents keep leaking out of his character, until finally he can speak in fluent Urdu once he has forgiven and become reconciled to his father. The return to his 'home', to his 'mother' tongue and to his father signifies the possibility of real relations of love. But this return should not be conceived in unambiguous terms for there can never be a return to an original innocence and univocal transparency. The fact that he begins to speak Urdu, for example, is telling. Urdu is a hybrid language, Arabic and Persian grafted on to Hindi grammar. In one sense it represents the equivocal reality with which Saladin comes to terms. It contains the 'pure' language of Arabic, the language of the Koran, mixed into the profane, infidel language of the polytheistic Indians. In the novel's terms, this is the inevitable way in which 'the demotic forced its way into lines of classical purity'.[41]

For Rushdie the personal is the political, is the religious, is the novel. He juggles the theme of being 'born again' into cultural critique: people constantly construct and re-construct themselves, religiously, politically, culturally, economically and in every way they can. Saladin is a sign of his times, and signs, like people, use and are used in all sorts of ways. Some try to construct impossible pure cultural selves such as the British National Front, a racist fascist party, who must then necessarily efface both history and real people. The National Front's black counterpart is symbolized in Dr Uhuru Simba, the rather sinister leader of the Asian and African immigrants in England's invisible city. Simba has changed his name from Sylvester Roberts, 'from down New Cross way', and turns violent when his 'Africanness' is called into question.[42] Pure culture, like pure identity or meaning, is a fictional construct, for signs constantly change according to the company they keep.

However, those who question cultural/ethnic identity are equally problematized. For example, Saladin attends a political meeting to free the arrested Dr Uhuru Simba and is told by 'a young black woman' wearing a lenticular badge showing two different messages, according to the viewing angle, 'Uhuru Simba'/'Freedom for the Lion':

> 'it's on account of the meaning of his chosen name,' she explained redundantly. 'In African.' Which language? Saladin wanted to know. She shrugged, and turned away to listen to the speakers. It was African: born, by the sound of her, in Lewisham or Deptford or New Cross, that was all she needed to know . . . Pamela hissed into his ear. 'I see that you finally found somebody to feel superior to.' She could read him like a book.[43]

Saladin's desire to feel superior in noticing such cultural counterfeits, when he himself is one, is undermined by Pamela, while at the same time questioning such badge-wearing cultural identity that is skin-deep. Saladin has the same annoyance at the meeting, when they sing together the South African freedom anthem: *Nkosi Sikelel' i'Afrika* (this time Afrikans, not the Swahili of 'Uhuru Simba'): 'As if all causes were the same, all histories interchangeable.'[44]

The same 'predictable stink'[45] at questioning cultural identities is caused by Saladin's Bombay lover Zeenat Vakil's book, *The Only Good*

Indian. The unspoken remainder of the title is of course: 'is a dead one'. In it she:

> questions the confining myth of authenticity, that folkloristic strait-
> jacket which she sought to replace by an ethic of historically validated
> eclectism, for was not the entire national culture based on the prin-
> ciple of borrowing what ever clothes seemed to fit, Aryan, Mughal,
> British, take-the-best-and-leave-the-rest?[46]

As Zeeny puts it, 'Why should there be a good, right way of being a wog? That's Hindu fundamentalism.'[47] The BJP party in India are strongly featured in *The Moor* as encoding history within a univocal narrative that (violently) contests deconstruction. Further ironies are generated in the Zeeny incident. Later Zeeny will tease Saladin that his Anglicized name, English accent and contempt for things Indian are part of his loss of identity, and here she uses 'wog' quite differently: 'Your types got no culture. Just wogs now. Ain't it the truth?'[48] Signifi-cantly Zeeny, like the novel, makes no distinction between culture and religion, for 'both' are sign systems, and Hindu fundamentalism to her is no different from the British National Front. Both groups try to control, monopolize and name reality univocally. This type of naming must always exclude.

'To be born again' also further connotes a range of religious refer-ences. For example, Hindu reincarnation theory is exemplified by Gib-reel's 'unique [acting] career incarnating, with absolute conviction, the countless deities of the subcontinent in the popular genre movies known as "theologicals".'[49] Gibreel is quite happy to play god on and off the screen. Straight after this sequence, Rushdie reminds us that there 'are secular reincarnations, too', typically beginning with Gibreel's birth name: Ismail Najmuddin. This Muslim name provides further humour in staging a Muslim playing out Hindu deities. The name is significant, for it implicates him even more deeply into the story. In explaining the name, the authorial voice notes: 'Ismail after the child involved in the sacrifice of Ibrahim, and Najmuddin, star of the faith; he'd given up quite a name when he took the angel's.'[50] It is with his angelic name Gibreel, that he loses his faith,[51] when for a moment he begins to disbelieve in his own self-construction. Christians, Jews and Muslims are also born into and out of faith within the novel, but those who retain their faith unquestioningly are also those who are committed to univocal signification, such as Eugene Dumsday the Christian Creationist, Mahound, Ayesha the prophetess, the exiled Imam in London, Dr Uhuru Simbha and other figures who expend endless energy trying to control signs to keep their faith, their beliefs, in position. Pure religious identity is, like pure cultural identity, undermined. Every sign by which we are constructed is mediated so that after the fall (into culture) meaning is never univocal. This applies to the 'pure' revelation of God ... or was it Satan, or an angel, or both, or neither, or the Prophet himself? Rushdie's iconoclasm is deeply religious, but also always on the verge of postmodern nihilism.

The Imam who resides in London, probably based on Khomeini's exile prior to the fall of the Shah, exemplifies the impossible forgery of religious purity and certainty. The Imam believes that truth resides exclusively in the Book, even if at the same time, questionably, it is he that interprets what that truth is. All things alien to the Book and its culture are to be resisted and overcome. The Imam lives in Kensington surrounded by bodyguards. 'The curtains, thick golden velvet, are kept shut all day, because otherwise the evil thing might creep into the apartment: foreignness, Abroad, the alien nation.'[52] The irony is that the Imam cannot exist without foreignness, without relations. This is represented in his dependence on 'pure water' which in turn means a further hidden dependence. He has a glass of water every five minutes 'to keep himself clean', but 'the water itself is cleansed of impurities, before he sips, in an American filtration machine'.[53] His dependence on 'purity' requires his hidden dependence on 'Satan' (the United States). The Imam's purity taboo is also constructed upon his defeat of 'Ayesha', ruler of Desh from where he is exiled. Ayesha is a woman who drinks wine and is sensual. In this binary opposition, Rushdie elaborates upon the equivocal signifier, for the very name Ayesha is semantically related to a myriad of characters within the novel: the prophet's favourite wife (Ayesha); the whore who plays her part in a later sequence and adopts her name; and the name of the prophetess who leads the fantastical journey to the Arabian Sea and who receives uninterrupted instructions from Gabriel sanctioning her authority. Other than her etymological relations, Ayesha of Desh is also pictorially and symbolically related via the signs of her depiction: her drinking wine relates to Hind, who also loves wine, the woman who opposes

Mahound; and, via the Kālī-like image of her drinking blood from
skulls,[54] she is related to the Sikh hijacker, Taverleen, who is portrayed
with weapons of destruction terrifyingly threatening death. By this
technique of palimpsest writing, which we might call perichoretic writing, which also recalls the incident of the Satanic verses itself, Rushdie
indicates that univocal signification is impossible however much humans
seek to control signs – and each other. They cannot. The elusiveness
of signs, their sheer indeterminacy, is also the source whereby the
redemption from oppressive signs might take place. Rushdie, like Irigaray, knows that 'redemption' is only possible in the semiotic context
of our existence. This too is Christianity's contention, narrated via a
different but interrelated story to this one, of how an incarnate God
transforms all signs so that they may become the possibility of the
celebration of difference, of joy and of interrelated love.

The Imam's attempt to destroy women (Ayesha of Desh) as the
founding act of his religious authority is related to Mahound's refusal of
the three goddesses worshipped by Hind. This is also related to Gibreel's
inability to mourn his mother's death. Instead he chooses to compete with
his father. The end of this competition is also the end of his religious
faith.[55] I shall return to this theme shortly. In a humorous touch, the
Imam's preaching of Islamic revelation, *his* mediation of the Word ('burn
the books and trust the Book')[56] is via his own words being transmitted
by another: 'the voice of the American convert Bilal is singing the Imam's
holy song' over pirate radio to Desh![57] Put plainly, revelation cannot be a
closure of knowledge and praxis. This makes an idol out of a particular
cultural representation. Mediation in history is the condition of the Imam,
which for his very self-image he must deny. In the account of Bilal's
broadcast of the Imam's message, after his imprecations against Ayesha,
this denial is unmasked by the authorial voice:

> 'We will make a revolution,' the Imam proclaims through him [Bilal],
> 'that is a revolt not only against a tyrant, but against history.' For
> there is an enemy beyond Ayesha, it is History herself. History is
> the blood-wine that must no longer be drunk. History the intoxicant,
> the creation of the lies – progress, science, rights – against which
> the Imam has set his face. History is a deviation from the Path,
> knowledge is a delusion, because the sum of knowledge was complete
> on the day Al-Lah finished his revelation to Mahound.[58]

The claim that 'The sum of knowledge was complete' is important. It mirrors Irigaray's protest at the closure of the incarnation, and both Rushdie's and Irigaray's critiques are against univocal signification: the refusal to admit that signs are always mediated, always open-ended, and capable of being re-read and re-encoded endlessly. This openness to transcendence may lead closer to the divine than to nihilism, although postmodern writers are often unable to steer clear of the latter. However, the denial of questions, doubts, plural interpretations, ambiguous significations – history – is not a prerogative of any one religion or people. The American Christian creationist, Eugene Dumsday (eugenics, doomsday – modelled on Duane Gush of the Institute of Creation Research, California) is another such character like the Imam.[59] Both are caricatures of features shared by many other characters in the novel. It is not religion *per se* which is Rushdie's target, but also economics (see his equivalent portrayal of Hal Valance, the Thatcherite businessman), ethnic identity (Saladin's attempt at Englishness), *any* cultural construct that tries to preserve a single identity, fixed meaning, a purity against history. One might add to this list, those who resist any other word than 'father' for God.

The next seven words of the opening paragraph after 'To be born again' are: 'sang Gibreel Farishta tumbling from the heavens'. 'Sang'. Singing is one cultural mode of production, and is a generic form that unites a number of formative semiotic configurations: the recitation of the Koran (we've already seen how the black American singer Bilal sings over the airwaves); popular Hindi musicals and theologicals whose songs are known through the entire subcontinent, and stars who, like Gibreel, can cause the Prime Minister of India to cancel foreign visits (as did Indira Gandhi when the film star Amitabh Bachan fell ill); jingles used in advertising (Saladin is the voice of garlic crisps and frozen peas, where reality and pastiche are indistinguishable); political black rap which mobilizes the angry crowd in the Club Hot Wax;[60] and high poetry (his mock allusion to Eliot in the 'Tat-taa! Taka-thun!' of the opening paragraph).[61]

Singing is also what angelic beings do in heaven; the same beings who are infernal, devilish after falling, which is why Saladin, also falling out of the sky, shouts 'to the devil with your tunes' at Gibreel.[62] The connection between angels and singing is made by the Urdu name 'Gibreel Farishta', which translates into 'Angel Gabriel' (who recites the Qu'ran to Muhammed initially on Mount Hira), who is 'tumbling from the heavens'. The tumble suggests that he may in fact be a fallen angel. Hence, this tumble is what relates us to the angels: we, like they, fall into a world of unstable signs, such that one cannot always distinguish good from bad, angel from devil, being born from dying, smiling from crying, the divine from the human, and the human from the demonic. No wonder, then, that Gibreel plays deities on screen and eventually off screen, and that Saladin turns into a huge goat with putrid breath, horns and a massive erection – both characters, like humans, are made up of many signs including voices, songs and recitations.

Just as we are being sucked up into this vortex of fantastical images and associations, the (mock) voice of a realistic narrator enters, although this voice is really no different from that of the previous fantastical one. Precision and exactness calm our imaginations, a reporting of the facts: 'Just before dawn one winter's morning, New Year's Day'. Later in the novel during the reporting of the 'facts' by TV cameras at a 'race' riot (based on Brixton, London) we are reminded about how facts are always constructed from points of view, and therefore obstruct from view other images and stories. A TV camera 'requires law, order, the thin blue line. Seeking to preserve itself, it remains behind the shielding wall, observing the shadow-lands from afar, and of course from above: that is, it chooses sides.'[63] But before we can grasp at any solidity, any realism, any 'truth' in the precision of 'Just before dawn one winter's morning, New Year's Day', authorial omniscience is deconstructed with the addition 'or thereabouts'. To confound matters we are then given the exact height from which 'two real, full-grown, living men' fall: 'twenty-nine thousand and two feet'. The Himalayas house the gods and boast Mount Everest (the pilgrimage site of many European expeditions, the symbol of European colonialization of the east?) which is precisely 29,002 feet high. With this allusion to holy mountains, Mount Hira is also conjured up as is Mount Sinai. Hira is already established within the semantic field through Gabriel and the title of the novel, and soon we are to meet Gabriel's English lover: the conqueror of Everest, Allie Cone. Her name is a palimpsest for her 'real' Jewish name – Alleluia Cohen. Alleluia phonetically recalls 'Allah', and Hallelujah is the Jewish/Hebrew term of praise to God. Cone is an Anglicized form of Cohen,[64] for she is Jewish: hence another mountain – Sinai, the site of yet another 'pure' revelation. Cone also puns upon the Arabic for soothsayer: 'kahin'. In a comment on her Polish Jewish father who has changed all the family's names when they arrive in England in an attempt to repress their ancestry, Rushdie writes: 'Echoes of the past distressed him; he read no Polish literature . . . because for him the language was irredeemably polluted by history.'[65] He is not unlike Dumsday, Ayesha, Taverleen, the Imam and Mahound. His attempt to escape history ends in the death he continually lives: when he 'jumped into an empty lift-shaft and died'.[66] Suicides litter the book. People have the power to deconstruct themselves nihilistically with the same violence with which they construct themselves and are constructed. Saladin's reconciliation with his father and mother (the latter by proxy) suggests that there are other ways of both de- and re-construction.

A final comment, which takes us to Paradise and Babel. One might read the entire novel through its beginning, which indicates that it is not the 'beginning', but just one point within a complex interweaving narrative, signs mediating other signs, endlessly. We discover that Gibreel and Saladin are falling out of a blown-up hi-jacked jet: Bostan, Flight AI-420.[67] This hijack is based on an Air India jumbo jet blown up over Ireland in 1985, allegedly by Sikh terrorists – who also blow up the novel's jet. Two features are worth nothing. First, the fall from paradise into the babel of language is alluded to by the name of the jet: Bostan, one of the Islamic gardens of paradise. (Milton's *Paradise Lost* is also constantly alluded to in the novel.) It is significant too that Saladin is able to name the fruits and flowers of his own Bombay garden on return from England, something he could never do in childhood and something that establishes his distance and alienation from his parents: 'something had been lost which he would never be able to regain'.[68] Another significant garden in the novel lies within the house from which the Ayesha story develops, another of the gardens of paradise, 'Peristan'.[69] This is in contrast to 'Jihila' (the place of ignorance) from which Muhammed originates and eventually conquers, where there are no gardens at all.

Secondly, the jet is blown up because the terrifying Sikh terrorist, Tavleen, will not compromise. Her singularity, her unbending sense of her own righteous demand is metaphorically given a Durgā-Kāli image (the Hindu goddess of death and destruction) as she stands naked before the passengers 'so that they could all see the arsenal of her body, the grenades like extra breasts nestling in her cleavage, the gelignite taped around her thighs'.[70] And what does she demand which will cost the lives of all the passengers (but two)? 'religious freedom' and 'justice'.[71] ('From the beginning men used God to justify the unjustifiable'.)[72]

In this section I have tried to allow Rushdie's text to act as a commentary upon itself, partly to reinforce the relentless (postmodern) point that Rushdie is making: that language and signs work relationally and dynamically. They are not univocal signs which float above history with a purity of meaning. Rather 'meaning' and 'signification' constantly reconfigures itself in terms of further signs and mediations. And if characters are made up through signs, through language, then the notion of the 'person' is best understood in terms of 'relations' that are constantly 'open' to the future and to each other. In this sense, we might imagine the body of Christ coming into being, through the Marian church: the way in which the 'lack' in Christ's suffering (Col. 1.24) must be borne by those who are co-redeemers. This psycho-linguistic model may well offer resources for a modern attempt to rethink perichoresis and relations, for this openness within language betokens the indwelling that possesses linguistic being. And love is important, for it is the refusal to allow closure, despite our every attempt to stabilize signs, to transcribe them into what Irigaray called a hommosexuate language. Since divinity is also most often transcribed within such a hom(m)osexuate economy, it fails to liberate both men and women. Rather than language becoming a source of joyous celebration (prayer), it becomes an instrument to possess power over others. If a single language and culture are seen as the site of pure revelation, then this is almost indistinguishable from idolatry. This is the wrong scandal of particularity, and one from which Christianity needs to fully purge itself.

Interestingly, Pentecost, the moment (for Irigaray) of the marriage of the Spirit and Bride, is also the coming together of language, while also remaining distinct. Acts tell us how Parthians, Medes, Elamites and residents of Pontus, Asia, Prygia, Egypt, Libya and other places were all able to hear the word of God in their own 'tongues' (Acts 2.11). Babel cannot be replaced by another monolithic towering phallus that seeks to unite all under its power, but rather the Holy Spirit in Acts is able to facilitate a *relationship between* all these differences, so that a new community might be formed. In this community, all language is made into the possible site of God's mediation, such that language can also become the source of praise, healing and redemption; just as it could be the site of damnation. Pentecost is the refusal of a single divine language, but represents the co-creative power of the Spirit working through and with humans using their language(s).

Rushdie's use of language also relentlessly questions the notion of a fixed substance, as if a word could contain its meaning intrinsically, or have a fixed meaning. All language and signs are relationally constructed, as are persons. Postmodernism can take this infinite deferral of meaning into the philosophy of nihilism, while trinitarian language suggests that this constant opening up of signs is the risky invitation to co-create and co-redeem, such that Christian cultures might better facilitate representations that move women and men to worship the triune God, rather than an idol. This questioning of 'substance' prior to 'relations' is of course one tentative and not fully attained achievement within the Christian narrative as we saw in chapters 1 and 2. Rushdie mirrors this metaphysical argument in his construction of 'character', such that all characters in the novel are co-constituted by the telling and re-telling of the novel, and in each reading the sense of the inter-relationships and co-inherence between characters begins to grow. This is not unlike the liturgical retelling whereby stories of the saints, Mary and Jesus, and ourselves are constantly re-positioned within our lives in every performance of the eucharist. I have tried to depict this process in dense textual detail in relation to the opening lines of the novel, which requires for its interpretation the entire novel, which in turn is re-read via the opening lines. Rushdie's other novels and all fiction and culture are also drawn into the reading and rereading, so that it would not be incorrect to say that the process of reading is never complete. My own multiple readings are indicative of this. Hence, this is not only a formal structuralist point about language but also one about all that is borne within language: our lives, our loves and our gods. This also bears relation to the openness within the triune God, such that no single rendering of God could be final and definitive for all time.

In the next section I want to return to the construction of divine taxonomies with regard to the question of feminine representation by means of an argument that Rushdie's novel is a rewriting of Freud's

Moses and Monotheism. In this, Rushdie joins ranks with Irigaray's critique of Freud, but is also implicitly critical of various strategic poses of Irigaray.

5. Rushdie as the feminist neo-Freudian

I will now explore Rushdie's reworking of Freud's *Moses and Mono-theism* and show how Rushdie both employs Freud and goes unsettlingly beyond him, to reintroduce the maternal homicide at the 'origins' of religion (Irigaray), while at the same time refusing to allow the feminine to be unproblematized. In this limited sense, Rushdie's work may be an advance on Irigaray, and an advance which allows us to detect more clearly the possible idolatry in recasting the divine according to our human conceptions of gender. There is an equal danger in refusing the feminine within divine representation, however, for in so doing univocal predication is maintained with phallic rigidity. Maybe Rushdie's novel stands at the entrance to Irigaray's third age, and acts as an intimation towards a trinitarian metaphysics of elusive representation such as I have begun to develop within this book.

There are a number of arguments to support my thesis that Rushdie's novel is a rewriting of *Moses and Monotheism.* First, there are some remarkable similarities in the authorial context of both Freud and Rush-die that are worth noticing. We have two writers struggling with their own religious background which they recognize to be profoundly con-nected with parental relations: Judaism and Islam, respectively. Both are also 'exiles' from their 'native' religions in so much as they are not active practitioners. Take, for example, Freud's moving preface to the Hebrew translation of *Totem and Taboo*, written in Vienna and published in 1939, and his response to the anticipated criticism at *his* authorship: 'Since you have abandoned all these common characteristics of your countrymen, what is there left to you that is Jewish?' Freud replies: '"A very great deal, and probably its very essence." I could not now express that essence clearly in words; but some day, no doubt, it will become accessible to the scientific mind.'[73] This modernist essentializing of religion, and its detachment from practices that are perspicuous to the gaze of the 'scientific mind', is one of many blind spots that goes unquestioned in Freud, as is his claim to be more Jewish than the rest

– 'the very essence'. That same year in the opening lines of 'Moses an Egyptian' in *Moses and Monotheism*, Freud is subliminally aware of the uncanny resemblance between himself and Moses: great sons of the Jewish people who are found not to be Jewish! Patricide is in the air: 'To deprive a people of the man who they take pride in as the greatest of their sons is not a thing to be gladly or carelessly undertaken, least of all by someone who is himself one of them.'[74] The fact that Freud is writing about his own religion may also account for the lack of clear and ordered form in *Moses and Monotheism*, rather than the account given by Albert Dickson attributing this to external events.[75]

Rushdie's namesake in the novel, Salman the poet, also curiously mirrors Rushdie's own relationship to Islam, which is not unlike Freud's. First, it reflects the fact that Salman al-Farisi was a close companion of the Prophet and therefore that non-Arabs were there at the beginning of Islam. This is especially important for Iranian, Indian and African Muslims. Bilal, for example, is a Black Abyssinian Muslim. Freud's lack of 'purity' as a Jew and Rushdie's lack of 'purity' as a Muslim are thrown back upon the questioners. Secondly, Salman Rushdie in the novel begins to tamper with the words of the tradition, even the Koran, exploring the question of their origins. Salman has a dream one night and not surprisingly imagines himself to be Gibreel. But he recalls the 'incident of the Satanic verses' and exclaims: '"Maybe I was Shaitan." The realization of this possibility gave him his diabolic idea. After that, when he sat at the Prophet's feet, writing down rules rules rules, he began surreptitiously, to change things.'[76] Satirizing Freud's preface to *Moses and Monotheism* Salman acknowledges: 'So there I was, actually writing the Book, or rewriting, anyway, polluting the word of God with my own profane language.'[77] When Salman's increasingly grave 'mistakes' in writing down Mahound's dictated Word are not noticed by Mahound, Salman is shattered:

> There is no bitterness like that of a man who finds out he has been believing in a ghost . . . I had to choose, on that awful night, whether I preferred death with revenge to life without anything. As you see, I chose: life.[78]

Rushdie may have unwittingly and tragically 'chosen' both by writing his novel. Rushdie admits to being a Muslim only by cultural association. His one 'lapse' into 'submission' (Islam) was when he publicly wrote, after the *fatwā* had been declared, that he had become a Muslim. This was recanted a few days later, and was quite explicable given the appalling pressures Rushdie suffered at the time.

There are two further important biographically related points worth exploring. First, Salman's tampering with the Word means that the Word is now interspersed with words; singularity of predication, phallic representation, is forever undermined. The phallic order will of course not tolerate such disorder, in the same way that Al Lah (or Mahound) had reversed the acceptance of the three goddesses, so that He would reign supreme, alone, and unalterably masculine. As R. W. J. Austen puts it when discussing the feminine in Islamic divine representation, Allah is seen as 'an absolute identity-consciousness with an immutable, eternal and inalienable identity, who is always, significantly, called He'.[79] This is despite the fact that Muslims would refuse to attribute 'gender' to God. Part of my argument in the last chapter, which does not necessarily hold true of Islam, is that while the same is said in Christianity ('there is no gender in God'), the logic of sexuate language often leads to such gender attribution at the imaginary level. The importance of language is the reason why Mahound sentences Salman to death: 'Your blasphemy, Salman, can't be forgiven. Did you think I wouldn't work it out? To set your words against the Words of God.'[80] Rushdie, like Freud, is aware that he is touching on a taboo. This is always a dangerous move. Both Freud and Rushdie feared reprisals from religious groups, knowing that what they wrote was inflammatory: Freud from the Roman Catholic authorities of Vienna; and Rushdie from certain groups of Muslims.[81]

Secondly, another argument to support my thesis is that Freud applies psychoanalytic techniques used on individual patients to cultural and historical complexes to locate neuroses and disorders in culture. Rushdie, likewise, treats history as the patient. Interestingly, Freud's technique is not unlike that of the literary and cultural critic who must pay extremely close attention to texts, not just to their surface meanings, but also to the stories they repress. For instance, in speaking of the compilation of the Hexateuch, the partial textual basis for Freud's reconstruction of the murder of Moses 'the Egyptian', Freud focusses on 'noticeable gaps, disturbing repetitions and obvious contradictions . . . indications which reveal things to us which it was not intended to communicate'.[82] Freud predicates his reconstruction of the Moses story on the murderous desires towards the father. Rushdie likewise focusses on the single incident of *The Satanic Verses* in the history of the origins of the Quran, and begins to unravel its untold implications and 'noticeable gaps' for it gives access to a hidden story, a repressed trauma, which constantly resurfaces in Islam – a *different* story of its origins. A story of the semiotic murder of women. It is a story about the repression of the feminine, the control of women and their exclusively permitted role as mothers and sisters (a refrain regarding Mahound's relations to women),[83] who are always there for men, but can never be 'equal'.[84] It is also simultaneously the story of univocal signification, a refusal of plurality (the three goddesses) and the possibility of polysemic signification. This is why Mahound's religion is characterized by 'rules, rules, rules', the phallic desire to control and keep in place, rules that are enforced by divine writ and human punishments. This religion is predicated on the murder of women. Rushdie's rewriting of *Moses and Monotheism* also reveals Freud's repressed maternal murder, which Irigaray seeks to recover, a recovery that is vital to Catholic trinitarian theology.

Unlike Freud, however, Rushdie tries (but perhaps does not always succeed) to avoid reductionism in refusing psychoanalysis any foundational status.[85] Rushdie is able to explore the founding events of Islam by the telling strategy of making it part of a larger picture – Gibreel's imaginary dream world – thereby questioning Islam's own reading. Gibreel says of Mahound that it was 'not possible to say which of us is dreaming the other. We flow in both directions along the umbilical cord.'[86] This is significant in two ways. Gibreel can signify Saladin's unconscious so that Rushdie locates the 'founding' event of Islam in the unconscious, as does Freud of Judaism. Of course, for Freud, one main way in accessing the unconscious was via the analysis of dreams.[87] I must add a few words to justify this interpretation of Gibreel, which is not developed in any of the secondary literature consulted. Gibreel and Saladin are born together and their stories are closely interrelated throughout the novel. Gibreel is a man of dreams, quite literally, who in his own sleep enters the lives of others and who is a feature of the dreamlife of other characters in the novel. In this sense he is the unconscious. The narrator tells us of his extraordinary power: 'he could fulfil people's most secret desires without having any idea of how he did it'.[88] This is a classic description of the unconscious. His own character is made up of Oedipal configurations and secret desires: his mother had only eyes for him,[89] not for his father. His mother dies. His father's life was subsequently geared 'to defeat the son and regain, thereby, his usurped primacy in the affections of his dead wife'.[90] His father wins by dying first, and being reunited with his wife, excluding his son. Subsequently, Gibreel sleeps with every woman he can, exemplifying the unbridled sexual phantasies of return to the mother. Seen like this, we can understand why he features so centrally in Mahound, Ayesha and the Imam, who all deny the unconscious and are bulwarks of a black and white, dualist Islam. No questions or ambiguities are allowed. This eventually leads to socio-political psychosis and in Gibreel's case a psychotic breakdown, which ends eventually in his suicide.

This very account is far too clean, however, for Gibreel's 'suicide' is actually part of Saladin attaining some resolution of his emotional ambivalence towards his father and mother.[91] Freud defines the 'modern civilized man' as one in whom this ambivalence is diminished and taboos come to an end.[92] Freud's lack of analysis of scientific modernity is startling, and it is only perhaps with National Socialism that he begins to sense that there are problems with his 'scientific faith'. In 1938, the year before his death, he writes: 'We find to our astonishment that progress has allied itself with barbarism.'[93] Freud's astonishment reflects his complacent secular fundamentalism which Rushdie is at pains to resist, even if not altogether consistently. If Gibreel plays the unconscious, then Saladin certainly suggests the superego. He is characterized by his own self-construction, predicated upon his denial of his father and mother, and tries to make himself up according to the rules of Englishness, sprouting a new voice, new mannerisms, clothes, culture, identity and so on. He is impeccably respectable and begins to lose his sanity in the process of this construction breaking down. Hence, the mid-point of the book is Saladin and Gibreel's meeting again, which results in a terrible struggle between the two, with a brief and momentary partial reconciliation, when Gibreel saves Saladin from destruction by fire.[94]

To return to my argument about interpretative strategies employed by Freud and Rushdie; another manner of accessing the unconscious for Freud was via the analysis of language, its slips, omissions, puns and jokes.[95] Gibreel, and the author, cannot repress constant jokes, puns and playing with language. They both relentlessly refuse the univocal representation of the phallic economy of signs. This refusal begins to uncover the possibilities of different forms of representation, enacted in Saladin's reconciliation with his father, helped by Zeeny, and thereby generating the possibility of love *between* a man and woman: Saladin and Zeeny, and Saladin and his mother; and *between* men, Saladin and Chamcha (his father), and Saladin and himself. There is, interestingly, no important reconciling women–women relations within this novel (or any of Rushdie's others). It might be noted that since Saladin's mother is dead there is no reconciliation here, even if it is staged through the proxy second wife-mother. In Irigaray's sense, Rushdie fails to establish imaginary female genealogies, with most relations in the fiction revolving around male characters.

Thirdly, Rushdie rightly questions Freud's evolutionary distinctions between Judaism and Islam, and the distinctions drawn by Freud between animism and monotheism. For Freud, Islam is a pale reflection of Judaism. In *Totem and Taboo* Freud writes that animism, the stage allegedly prior to that of religious (monotheism) is characterized by men ascribing omnipotence to themselves:

> At the religious stage they transfer it to the gods but do not seriously abandon it themselves, for they reserve the power of influencing the gods in a variety of ways according to their wishes.[96]

Rushdie's portrayal of Mahound shows how this could be true of this very high form of monotheism (Islam). But he keeps with Freud in recognizing, although not reductively as did Freud, that the construction of religious images corresponds to the 'object-choice of which the characteristic is a child's attachment to his parents'.[97] Mahound, who has no father, but a very overbearing uncle, has a very overbearing God whose omnipotence (maleness and resistance to the feminine) is only matched by Mahound's.

Fourthly, Freud's basic thesis regarding monotheism, or totemic religion, is that it is founded on the two primal drives that constitute the Oedipal complex. After showing the relation between totemic animals and the father, Freud writes:

> If the totem animal is the father, then the two principal ordinances of totemism, the two taboo prohibitions which constitute its core –

not to kill the totem and not to have sexual relations with a woman of the same totem – coincide in their context with the two crimes of Oedipus, who killed his father and married his mother.[98]

Upon this edifice Freud constructs his thesis that monotheism is based on the primal murder of the father by the rival sons, who then overcome their guilt by exalting the father (God) and unconsciously construct taboos to ensure that the memory of this act is erased, but which is re-enacted in totemic meals. Thus religion bears the same marks of an obsessional and neurotic disorder, and can lead to psychosis in some cases. Most important, Freud uses this Oedipal foundational point to explain 'the beginning of so many things – of social organization, of moral restrictions and of religion'.[99] In short, culture is predicated upon the Oedipal complex. Rushdie is no less ambitious than Freud, even though, as we have seen above, he dramatically rewrites Freud so that *both* matricide and patricide are positioned in the generation of culture. Unlike Freud, however, Rushdie refuses any one archimedian point of explanation, which is where he is perhaps able to remain open to the 'divine'. More of this later.

Fifthly, Rushdie redraws the European imaginary so that the hidden other, Islam, and not only Judaism and Christianity, is brought into the cultural cauldron. In a curious sense Rushdie is both an Orientalist (in his critical stereotypical depiction of Islam) and strongly resistant to Orientalism. In Freud's single reference to Islam, Freud suggests that Islam is no different to Judaism except in its foundation: 'I may perhaps add that the case of the founding of the Mohammedan religion seems to me like an abbreviated repetition of the Jewish one, of which it emerged as an imitation.'[100] Freud shared the view of most Europeans at the time that Islam was a spent force. He puts this down to the fact that it 'lacked the depth which had been caused in the Jewish case by the murder of the founder of their religion'.[101] Rushdie's portrayal is that within Islam there is a murder of the founder, in the eradication of Muhammed's narrative complexity focussed in the story of the Satanic verses. This forgery of his memory is also enacted, as we shall see below, in the retelling of his death. Furthermore, the founding of the various branches of Islam do rely on 'murders' and 'deaths'. However, this contrast by Freud obscures the widely acknowledged historical implausibility of Freud's thesis regarding the murder of Moses and his lineage.[102] This particular point helps to plot Rushdie's extremely ambivalent attitude towards Islam. His 'fantastical' reconstruction (and assassination) of Mohammed/Mahound mirrors Freud's reconstruction (and murder) of Moses. Both are not trustworthy narrators, even though Rushdie is far more self-aware on this count.

If my argument that Rushdie is rewriting *Moses and Monotheism* begins to seem more plausible, I now want to illustrate some key parts of it in a little more detail, paying particular attention to the divine and the feminine. The incident of the 'Satanic verses' illustrates two key events. First, it could be seen as an Irigarian critique of Islam for it shows that Mahound's divine vision is based on repression and fear of women. The orphan Mahound has lost his mother (just like Gibreel, who refuses to grieve over her and thereby denies his loss).[103] He is raised in strong patriarchal traditions. In a telling linguistic omission, the narrator says of Mahound's first wife, Khadija: 'She is almost seventy and feels these days more like a mother than a.'[104] There is an inability to speak of women outside their role of servicing the patriarchal line. Mahound is incapable of dealing with women as equals, which is why Hind, who oversees the temple of Al Lat, is such a formidable enemy and will not accept Mahound's rules of patriarchy. She reminds him, 'I am your equal'.[105] The battle between the sexes, for this is in part what it is, is also staged in terms of the divine imaginary: the battle between Mahound's univocal controlling Al Lah (who is under Mahound's control?) and the multivocal female trinity of the city Lat, Uzza and Manat (who are under Hind's control?, but see also pp. 373, 8, 394). Lat, Uzza and Manat are the preeminent deities of polytheistic Jahilia, and reflect the three most popular goddesses in pagan polytheistic Mecca at the time. However, Rushdie is well aware that feminine divinity does not itself mean a change in the social order *per se*. When speaking of Mahound's powerful and wealthy first wife he says: 'It isn't easy to be a brilliant, successful woman in a city where the gods are female but the females are merely goods.'[106] Women are still commodities when female divinity is encoded within male sexuate culture, a point relentlessly made by Irigaray.

The Satanic verses incident is secreted within the sole instance where Mahound, in his desire to *share* power rather than have none, his one and only compromise in the book, gives the recitation in which Al Lah allows for the 'exalted birds' Lat, Uzza and Manat, 'and their

intercession is desired indeed'.[107] These words would have formed verse
21 of Sura 53 – assuring Mahound the cooperation of the Grandee of
Jahilia. It is this Koranic verse's disappearance from the Qur'an, its
palimpsestic painting-over that generates the stories of *The Satanic
Verses* and the origins of Islam. Between the account of the old verse
and the new, retold verse, there is a 'night of masks'[108] and 'certain
murders for which the first lady of Jahilia will wait years to take her
terrible revenge'.[109] The accommodation that has been made by Mahound's Allah to the female goddesses is one of masculine encoding,
controlled and ordered by Al Lah. Hind will not stand for this. After
telling Mahound that neither Abu Simbel nor Baal are Mahound's
equals, only her, she scorns Mahound's comment that she will not lose
temple revenues because worship of Manat, Uzza and Allat will be
permitted:

> 'You miss the point,' she says softly, coming closer to him, bringing
> her face very close to his. 'If you are for Allah, I am for Al-Lat. And
> she doesn't believe your God when he recognizes her. Her opposition
> to him is implacable, irrevocable, engulfing. The war between us
> cannot end in truce. And what a truce! Yours is a patronizing, conde-
> scending lord. Al-Lat hasn't the slightest wish to be his daughter.
> She is his equal, as I am yours'.[110]

Allah, like Mahound, cannot accept women as other than sisters, sex
objects and mothers; they remain within the male genealogical system;
and consequently the original verse that Mahound recited is deemed
satanic. The new verse ensures the genealogical eradication of the feminine, both divine and human: '"Shall He have daughters and you
sons?" Mahound recites. "That would be a fine division."'[111] In this
single verse, the feminine is repressed and murdered. Could God possibly act differently from men? Not this one. The subsequent taboos
and policing that develop ensures patriarchy, and Mahound uniquely
embodies the primal father who has both the mother and many daughters (sanctioning polygamy) to satisfy his desires. This also explains
Mahound's favourite two wives, Ayesha and Hafsah, the 'two halves
of his dead first wife: the child, and the mother, too'.[112] Mahound, like
most of the male characters in the novel, can only tolerate women in
these two modes, and Zeeny is virtually the only exception. She is

Saladin's helpmate through his odyssey/exodus/hajj/pilgrimage of reconciliation with his father.

The rather evident clue of matricidal foundations is related *immediately after* the new recitation. When Mahound returns home, his
motherly wife is dead.[113] She, alone among women, was able to be
'mother sister lover sibyl friend'[114] to him, but now he will forfeit this
relation to the feminine. There is no reason given in the narrative for
Khadija's death.[115] She just sits there, dead, and this will be the last
time that Mahound relates to an-Other with any glimmer of love.
Immediately a new economy of time is enacted: 'on this first day of the
new year at the new beginning of Time' – as Mahound leaves for
Yathrib, Medina, and so begins the Muslim calender.[116]

Time and history are measured from founding events. No longer will
Allat, the linguistic feminine counterpart to Allāh, have any autonomy,
co-equality, or even intermediary status. She is banished from the
linguistic universe of the Koran and subsequently Islam. There are no
neuters in Arabic, so the binary choices are pre-plotted. Indeed, Allat
will purely be represented by Allāh, etymologically, *the* god, and now
irrevocably, 'called He'. There is dispute among some scholars and
Muslims as to whether Al-Lat is the feminine form of Al-Lah. Al-Uzza
is the superlative form from the root '-z-z. Al-'Aziz (from the same
root) is indeed a masculine form of the name of God, meaning 'the
mighty, powerful' and is found in the Koran (2.129, 209, 220; 3.6),
even though the superlative masculine counterpart to Al-Uzza does not
appear as an epithet of God. Manat may etymologically and genealogic-
ally relate to the 'manna' found in the Jewish desert exodus. In Arabic
the root means grace, kindliness, generosity, and is only found in its
masculine form in the divine names as 'Al Manan'. However, it is more
likely to derive from the root m-n-y, which means to 'afflict' or 'make
happen to' and is associated with fate and death. Manat was the goddess
of fate and death worshipped by the pre-Islamic Arabs and is not used
as a name of God in the Koran, but is etymologically related to the
action of Satan who 'afflicts' men with false desires.[117] The name of
God cannot bear the feminine and is univocally male, and univocally
represents reality. The denial of the feminine divine representation
reflects also the refusal to allow women to represent themselves. As
with the divine, so with women. Women are represented according to
the economy of male desire.

The underlying argument is not entirely different from the one we inspected in the last two chapters, but here it is given vivid representation in a novel where 'art' and 'reality' have no clear boundaries – because there are none. But even as the incident of the hijra is related, the beginnings of male time, the repression can never be complete and Gibreel is attacked at the close of the chapter by three winged creatures, 'Lat Uzza Manat',[118] just as he is constantly attacked by the ghost of Rekha Merchant, another 'feminine' who refuses to Submit. It is not by chance that Rekha's ghost curses Gibreel with 'the repeated name *Al-Lat*' in the opening pages of the novel, which at that moment in the novel is an unintelligible signification as it takes place before any of the story of Al-Lat is narrated.[119]

The main part of the novel is framed within this founding incident (Chapter 2) and the return of the Mahound narrative in Chapter 6. On its outer margins we find birth and death (chapters 1 and 9). However, the second point about the incident of the Satanic verses, which relates to the first, is that the repressed will not stay comfortably repressed. To see this, I will focus on two incidents in the 'return' sequence. Most of 'Return to Jahilia' (jahilia: another 'name' for another 'time', a time of 'ignorance') is about Mahound's consolidation of patriarchy in Mecca. Salman, Mahound's scribe, and Rushdie's namesake, is deeply disillusioned about the Satanic verses incident, which he then replays in his own changing of the holy text. The other thing that makes him lose faith is Mahound's encoding of women. The Koran, called the 'Rule book' in these sequences, ensures that women must stay in the place designated to them by patriarchy, so that male desire can narcissistically expand:

> The revelation – the *recitation* – told the faithful how much to eat, how deeply they should sleep, and which sexual positions had received divine sanction, so that they learned that sodomy and the missionary position were approved of by the archangel, whereas the forbidden postures included all those in which the female was on top.[120]

Within the divine male economy of desire, in so much as it replicates male phallic postures, the woman cannot be allowed to transgress the space allocated to her. Mary, the mother of Jesus, is expounded as an ideal of submissiveness in the Quran. She is the perfect example of 'abudiyya', as opposed to 'khilafa', 'the principle of vice-regency represented by men'.[121] The opposites to this ideal are 'musafahit' and 'muttakidhat akhdan', promiscuous women who take lovers (such as Hind, Zeeny, Rekha), 'in other words those women who defy patriarchal controls and feel free to choose how and with whom they have sexual relations'.[122] Of course, as an assessment of historical Islam, the matter is far more complicated, and there are many legal protections provided for women, and some Muslim women have rightly questioned western feminism's universalizing gaze.[123]

Salman reiterates the point about phallocratic encoding when he tells Baal about Mahound's sexual proclivity in Yathrib, where Mahound also meets 'his match'. I shall give this extended quotation as it brings out most forcefully the semiotic themes I have been dealing with:

> The point about our Prophet . . . is that he didn't like his women to answer back, he went for mothers and daughters, think of his first wife and then Ayesha: too old and too young, his two loves. He didn't like to pick on someone his own size. But in Yathrib the women are different, you don't know, here in Jahilia you're used to ordering your females about but up there they won't put up with it. When a man gets married he goes to live with his wife's people! Imagine! Shocking, isn't it? [And now a reverse parody of Islam] And throughout the marriage the wife keeps her own tent. If she wants to get rid of her husband she turns the tent round to face in the opposite direction, so that when he comes to her he finds fabric where the door should be, and that's that, he's out, divorced, not a thing he can do about it. Well, our girls were beginning to go for that type of thing, getting who knows what sort of ideas in their heads, so at once, bang, out comes the rule book, the angel starts pouring out rules about what women mustn't do, he starts forcing them back into the docile attitudes the Prophet prefers, docile or maternal, walking three steps behind or sitting at home being wise and waxing their chins.[124]

But the more women are kept in this fixed position, the more repression is required to keep this position fixed. Static significations, univocal representation, require relentless denial of equivocality, the feminine imaginary. Perhaps one of the most startling (and offensive to Muslim?) incidents in the novel, which is not mentioned by any of the Muslim critics I have read, is the fact that Mahound's death is characterized by his conceding to the feminine.[125] Is it because in death Mahound has no power over signs?

After his defeat of the city, Hind comes veiled and begins kissing his feet, although this is no ordinary 'foot-kissery' for she 'licks, kisses, sucks' his toes.[126] This sensuousness initiated by a woman is too much for Mahound to bear, and eventually Mahound kicks out and catches Hind in the throat. However, this is not enough to stop her coughing out: 'There is no God but Al-Lah, and Mahound is his Prophet.'[127] She then reveals herself as Hind. Mahound, 'after a long instant', replies: 'You have Submitted. And are welcome in my tent.'[128] Submission, of course, is the word that translates 'Islam', and Rushdie plays on the ambiguity generated, for how is one to distinguish divine authority from male phallic authority? The response might be 'only when phallic authority is actually questioned by the divine', as trinitarian theology might, if it could break free from phallic captivity. Rushdie does not actually give an answer, but my own reading of the novel is that its apophatic religiosity sits at the feet of this answer. The novel's language actually suggests this answer – as I have been trying to show. No doubt, some Muslim scholars would argue that a response that counters feminists critiques is forthcoming on Koranic lines, either by questioning feminist assumptions, or by showing that the Koran is misread when read as misogynist.

Rushdie realizes, however, that the polarities are locked into a pragmatic dualist battle, for the phallic univocal order cannot tolerate otherness. As Hind earlier predicted, it is a battle to the death. After Hind's life is spared due to her employing multivocal signification, she recites one thing (Submission) and knowingly enacts another (revenge against the Prophet and his God Allah). She locks herself away for two years and comes out gleefully to celebrate Mahound's impending death. His death provides the other example that the feminine Other will not stay repressed, and like Rekha Merchant will continuously return to haunt the phallic spectre. When Mahound is on his death bed with only Ayesha tending to him, Mahound sees another figure in the room. He asks, 'Is it Thou, Azraeel?' (the angel of death):

But Ayesha heard a terrible, sweet voice, that was a woman's, make reply: 'No, Messenger of Al-Lah, it is not Azraeel.'

And the lamp blew out; and in the darkness Mahound asked: 'Is this sickness then thy doing, O Al-Lat?'

And she said: 'It is my revenge upon you, and I am satisfied. Let them cut a camel's hamstrings and set it on your grave.'

Then she went, and the lamp that had been snuffed out burst once more into a great and gentle light, and the Messenger murmured, 'Still, I thank Thee, Al-Lat, for this gift.'[129]

Mahound, in the vulnerability of death, is able to acknowledge Al-Lat, even though Ayesha, a woman, who overhears all this, goes out to the assembled company and perpetuates the phallic control of power: 'If there be any here who worshipped the Messenger, let them grieve, for Mahound is dead; but if there be any here who worship God, then let them rejoice, for *He* is surely alive.'[130] She will not acknowledge what has happened, and likewise perpetuates a religion predicated upon the denial of women.[131] This incident undermines any neat gendering of the divine (for the 'feminine' here is associated with revenge and victory) and any neat correlation between phallic power and men. Creation, both women and men, labour under the fixedness of signs which is re-enforced by Allah's (or Mahound's) univocalization: His Word, without human words, can only bear Submission. Rushdie's landscape performs relentless twists and turns, mirroring its 'main' characters, who both search for love, which requires Other, not hom(m)osexuate narcissism. Their semiotic quandary is not unlike that of Islam's.

It is perhaps the genius of the novel relentlessly to depict the depths of this predicament rather than to reach out towards easy resolution. My own suggested trinitarian 'resolution' is not a resolution in so much as the divine refuses closure (Irigaray's insightful protest), but a resolution in so much as it is the creative ground of a community called to celebrate the worthwhile 'sacrifice' of a love that abandons coercive power to bring about the power that is forgiveness and the redemption of relationships. This theme of hom(m)osexuate narcissism is interestingly plotted in Gibreel's own life. After being unable to grieve for his mother,[132] he instead enters into desperate competition with his father. This is classic Oedipal behaviour. His father dies, thereby defeating him – for he is robbed of victory over his father. Thereafter, Gibreel

begins to reconstruct himself, even dreaming in his step-parent's home
that he is the Prophet; and tellingly, besides marrying Khadija, he
imagines 'his new husband'.[133] This homosexual imagining brings
'shame' and a sense of 'impurity'.[134] He cannot bear to face this narcissism, and ever after he must keep his mind off 'the subject of love and
desire', so he becomes an 'omnivorous autodidact'[135] and sleeps with
numerous women. Here is the telling clue to his search:

> He filled himself up with God knows what, but he could not deny,
> in the small hours of his insomniac nights, that he was full of some-
> thing that had never been used, that he did not know how to begin
> to use, that is, love. In his dreams he was tormented by women of
> unbearable sweetness and beauty, so he preferred to stay awake and
> force himself to rehearse some part of his general knowledge in order
> to blot out the tragic feeling of being endowed with a larger-than-
> usual capacity for love, without a single person on earth to offer it
> to.[136]

This is almost an Augustinian vision whereby original sin has marred
all creation so that the lack of love is always passed on from generation
to generation, even amidst the desire to love and be loved. And even
in the depths of lack of love, there is still a hunger for love, for relationships that do not enact the cycle of destruction and unlovingness. The
same is also true of Saladin, who is unable to cry over his parents[137]
and subsequently builds up his self-construction. The telling passage
which makes this explicit allows Rushdie to show the multivocality of
representation:

> A man who invents himself needs someone to believe in him to prove
> he's managed it. Playing God again, you could say. Or you could
> come down a few notches, and think of Tinkerbell; fairies don't exist
> if children don't clap their hands. Or you might simply say: it's just
> like being a man.
>   Not only the need to be believed in, but to believe in another.
> You've got it: Love.[138]

That such a possibility (and it is no more than this) only happens
through Zeeny (whose mother has also died on her),[139] a woman who

can tease, joke and be equal to men, while not trying to 'defeat them', is telling. She helps Saladin back to his home where he is able to make peace with his father and dead (but reborn) mother. And this peace, even through and after death, is the possibility of loving relations. To imply any conscious reflection on crucifixion, resurrection and trinitarian relations would be absurd, but Augustine had already realized that the hunger for love was already a hunger for God and a hunger that was generated by the secret presence of the sought-after lover: the triune God.[140]

I shall stop at this point, for I have no wish to make an exact fit between Rushdie and Freud, which would also detract from my overall argument. Rushdie assimilates Freud within both a 'postmodern' and 'feminist' perspective and that is an altogether different Freud. In this reworking even minor details of Freud are corrected. For example, Rushdie overcomes Freud's cumbersome and implausible explanation of 'ancestral heritage' or communal memory traces via biological evolution to explain how various character traits are passed on.[141] Rushdie instead takes language as the answer: storytelling is the way in which characters and characteristics inhabit and shape our 'character'. 'Reality' is semiotically constructed and passed on in the same manner. Rushdie also pushes the question, in Irigaray's terms, of Freud's repression of the maternal. He rewrites *Moses and Monotheism* to show that the murder of the maternal feminine is central to the founding events of patriarchal religions and that such repression of the feminine from divine representation may closely relate to the subjugation of women within those religions. In one sense Rushdie presents a magically realistic world where we can see the dynamics that have been posited in the two previous chapters in relationship to divine (and human) representation, gender exclusion and the denigration of the feminine. We have also seen that Rushdie, unlike Irigaray, is able to posit the 'phallic mother', both in terms of the divine female triunity and in the many women that people the novel. Rushdie's envisaging a divine that liberates men and women lies in the space *between* male monarchy and female polytheism, in the *relation* between men and women, the note on which the novel ends, but without any 'happy' finish, just a stage in the process.

By developing the thesis that Rushdie rewrites Freud's *Moses and Monotheism* I have been trying to further the reflections of chapters 1 and 2 in the following ways. First, I have tried to deepen the exploration of the relationship between psychoanalysis, language, the divine and gender. I have tried to show that Irigaray's 'thesis' is both developed by Rushdie and also problematized by him. It is developed by applying it to Islam, whereas Irigaray primarily reflects on Catholicism. It corroborates her insights regarding the matricidal foundations of religion and culture and creates an imaginary that emerges out of this primary denial: the novel. The feminine divine meets the same fate as the human women: they are domesticated within the phallic order. Divine and human female genealogies are eradicated. With Irigaray, Rushdie also shows that such a domestication is never attained, and the repressed comes back to haunt the phallic order, especially through women who refuse submission of their sexuality (the whores of Chapter 6, and Hind) and through poets who celebrate the multivocality of language. Rushdie problematizes Irigaray in portraying the phallic mother, however, such that morphology and the symbolic cannot be strictly equated. He recognizes that a feminine divine might be differently problematic from a male divine, but problematic nevertheless. Rushdie, like Irigaray, however, sees the possibility of the divine being represented in the *relation* of love, between a man and a woman. Furthermore, Rushdie pushes Irigaray's exploration of language in a slightly different direction, such that *parler-femme* and the poet's language bear a close affinity to each other in their celebration of difference and embodiedness. For Irigaray, this was developed in terms of developing women's subjectivity – which allowed me to begin to explore Mary and the female saints in terms of Christological language. For Rushdie, it is developed in terms of showing how language cannot bear any closure – which has allowed me to allude to the perichoretic nature of language, whereby it becomes the site of mutual indwelling and the site, therefore, of salvation or dam-, nation – of being open to the other, or being singular, strong and monarchial.

In the next section, I hope to further my exploration of Rushdie's work, indicating the deeply spiritual quest in the novel precisely in its refusal of closure, of an ultimate explanation, an option missed by Freud the 'scientist'. In this restless postmodernism, there is the possibility of the divine and a refusal of nihilism, for after all the latter is closure and a grand narrative of endless violence. Christianity more positively suggests an alternative narrative, and one which thereby frames Rushdie's exploration as a *preparatio evangelica*, but one in which Christianity itself finds the self-gift of the divine in a purified manner. This is to say that theologians have much to learn from Rushdie even if he does not find much to learn from Christianity.[142] The refusal of closure in Rushdie requires the need of forgiveness and of love, the ability to see things differently, the ability to refuse language a fixed status, a frozen representation of reality.

4. The 'Scandal' of transforming characters

In this final section, I want to develop my initial claim that Rushdie's book is insufficiently analysed in purely 'Orientalist' terms, for it also poses a deeper, more troubling question: if all signs are mediated, then the semiotic configurations called 'revelation' are inevitably ambiguous, as are all signs. The problem is, as I have argued elsewhere, that if doubt and ambiguity become creedal statements, then a new faith, a new metanarrative, is born: postmodern nihilism.[143] However, I want to suggest that at one level within the novel the 'religious sentiment' within postmodernism becomes apparent (as it has in the later work of Derrida) in the strategic resistance against the closure of meaning. This distinguishes nihilist postmodernism, which after all is yet another closed narrative, from religious postmodernisms which preserve transcendence in differing ways in their resistance to closure. Such is the emerging re-presentation of the trinitarian God suggested in this book: a triune transcendence that can never be given definitive expression, but constantly requires construction and representation. Rushdie's resistance has an analogical similarity to a theological critique of idolatry. To imagine that we can adequately re-present God, by that which is not God, is idolatry and allows men to 'justify the unjustifiable' in the name of God, who is the unnameable.[144] Thomas Aquinas is not the only one to point out that while all speech about God is analogous, and analogy works by similarity, it always operates within a *greater dissimilarity*, a greater unknowingness.[145]

Two avenues within the novel open up this kind of reading. The first regards the psychoanalytic, and the second postmodern irony. Let me start with the second. There are a number of passages that question the narrator's clarity, his godlike point of view. Most obvious is Rushdie's own descent into the narrative in Gibreel's apparition[146] where it is not clear whether he is Ooparvala, 'The Fellow Upstairs', or Neechay-vala, 'the Guy from Underneath'.[147] The description of the apparition matches Salman Rushdie's own face and is confirmed when in a later passage the authorial voice comments on this intervention:

> I'm saying nothing. Don't ask me to clear things up one way or the other; the time of revelations is long gone . . . Don't think I haven't wanted to butt in; I have, plenty of times. And once, it's true, I did. I sat on Alleluia Cone's bed and spoke to the superstar, Gibreel. *Ooparvala or Neechayvala*, he wanted to know, and I didn't enlighten him.[148]

It is this refusal to allow any final resolution that allows Rushdie to escape secular fundamentalism or nihilistic postmodernism, both of which are resolved positions.

Another important example, as it touches on the question of religion, comes from an exchange between two characters. Swatilekha, a Bengali woman, criticizes Bhupen Gandhi, the poet, for being ambiguous towards religion and not unmasking the ways in which it has been used by the elites in Asia to establish and consolidate power. In many respects her argument summarizes what others have said of Rushdie's own approach.[149] However, she is undermined by Bhupen's reply. It is worth quoting in full:

> Society was orchestrated by what she called *grand narratives*: history, economics, ethics. In India, the development of a corrupt and closed state apparatus had 'excluded the masses of the people from the ethical project'. As a result, they sought ethical satisfactions in the oldest of the grand narratives, that is, religious faith. 'But these narratives are being manipulated by the theocracy and various political elements in an entirely retrogressive way.' Bhupen said: 'We can't deny the ubiquity of faith. If we write in such a way as to pre-judge such beliefs as in some way deluded or false, then are we not guilty of elitism, of imposing our world-view on the masses?' Swatilekha was scornful. 'Battle lines are being drawn up in Indian today,' she cried. 'Secular versus religious, the light versus the dark. Better you choose which side you are on.'[150]

Secular fundamentalist Swatilekha (swastika, Tilak, tilaka?) mirrors the religious groups who try and draw equally clear battle lines between good and bad, secular and sacred, right and wrong, and if Rushdie is in danger of falling into such polarities himself then one must acknowledge equally that he is painfully aware of their spuriousness. Bhupen, without romanticizing, keeps the questions open, whereas secular fundamentalism, in the person of Swatilekha, does not.[151] There are no real goodies or baddies in the novel, no secular or religious heroes or heroines, rather a canvas of complex, intricate, funny, scheming and sometimes tragic stories.

The sense that Rushdie is questioning 'religion' (as he does with ethnic, economic and political identity) when it denies its historicity, and therefore its semiotic mediation, is made even more strongly in an earlier incident. Gibreel is losing his identity to the angel Gabriel, his namesake (an angel of death, or an angel of light?), and is floating above a London park trying frantically to block out the complex and unresolved stories of his frustrated love affair with Allie Cone: 'he saw now that the choice was simple: the infernal love of the daughters of men, or the celestial adoration of God. He had found it possible to choose the latter; in the nick of time.'[152] This is a choice between love of other or displaced narcissism and univocal signification. Note the syntax at Gibreel's choice, his 'resolution':

No more of these England-induced ambiguities, these Biblical-Satanic confusions! – Clarity, clarity, at all costs clarity! – This Shaitan was no fallen angel. – Forget those son-of-the-morning fictions; this was no good boy gone bad, but pure evil. Truth was, he wasn't an angel at all! – 'He was of the djinn, so he transgressed.' – Quran 18:50, there it was as plain as the day. – How much more straightforward this version was! How much more practical, down-to-earth, comprehensible! – Iblis/Shaitan standing for the darkness, Gibreel for the light. – Out, out with these sentimentalities: *joining, locking together, love*. Seek and destroy: that was all.[153]

Rushdie's reference to the Quran 18.50 refers to the fact that while evil and bad jinn are metaphysically understood to be of a separate order from humans and angels, 18.50 actually creates confusion in this dualistic picture, for the leader of the evil jinn is in fact an angel that refuses to submit, despite the fact that all the others do. 'And [remember that] when We told the angels, "Prostrate yourself before Adam", they all prostrated themselves, save Iblis: he [too] was one of those invisible beings' (Quran 18.50).[154] Gibreel's choice is to reinterpret the verse, quite literally in Rushdie's rendering of the novel, to perpetuate and highlight a clear dualism.

To label, to keep the world in place, to divide good and evil, to deny the complex and multiple stories and voices that construct our lives, is 'more practical', but not the more truthful strategy. Clarity is a victory (always short lived) attained by imagining that signs are univocal rather than multivocal, that our lives – likewise. Rekha Merchant, who floats in and out of the novel on her flying carpet, signifying the unexorcized guilt of Gibreel (?) at betraying her (so that she leaps off Everest, her high-rise apartment, to her death), refuses Gibreel's clear-cut categories and mocks him: 'You played too many winged types for your own good.'[155] In an important incident she suddenly finds the voice of a comparative religion specialist. Gibreel realizes the 'real' Rekha incapable of such a speech, but it is a speech nevertheless that points to history and mediation and construction:

> This notion of separation of functions, light versus dark, evil versus good, may be straightforward enough in Islam – *O, children of Adam, let not the Devil seduce you, as he expelled your parents from the garden, pulling off from them their clothing that he might show them their shame* – but go back a bit and you see that it's a pretty recent fabrication. Amos, eighth century BC, asks: 'Shall there be evil in a city and the Lord hath not done it?' Also Jahweh, quoted by Deutero-Isaiah two hundred years later, remarks: 'I form the light, and create darkness; I make peace and create evil; I the Lord do all these things.' It isn't until the Book of Chronicles, merely fourth century BC, that the word *shaitan* is used to mean a being, and not only an attribute of God.[156]

The relentless postmodern point is that a closure of meaning, a settlement of signs, will always mask and construct tyrannical powers. Rushdie's narrative shows how falsely conceived certainties, be they religious, ethnic, economic, or class – lead to denial, the loss of love and the impossibility of forgiveness: 'Out, out with these sentimentalities: *join-*

ing, locking together, love.' Gibreel's clarity is that of the Imam's: 'Seek and destroy'; a kind of monotheism that resists trinitarian difference and relations, a '*joining, locking together*, love'.[157]

My reading of the novel suggests a profoundly 'religious searching', a refusal to bow to idols and a resistance to closure in created meanings. This, in tandem with Rushdie's exploration of evil, loss and love, his relation to his father and its analogue with faith, intimates other than secular fundamentalism and postmodernist nihilism. It is the possibility, suggested in the narrative, that love is the only way in which the story can be kept open – even if it is the most elusive of all realities, or perhaps precisely because it is.

I will focus on Saladin to explore this point a little further. Saladin is constructed out of his desire 'to escape' his father, Changez Chamchawala, who constantly outwits and humiliates him.[158] Changez's name is appropriate, for it is a derivative of Ghengis, alluding perhaps to the great Mongol infidel, Ghengis Khan, who sacked the thirteenth-century Baghdad Caliphate. Saladin's loss of faith in his father and in his religion confirms Freud's totemic thesis, but equally drives Saladin into an alternative (binary opposite) construction. In a humiliating and hilarious incident where he carries a take-away roast chicken (which will signify his heart) under his mackintosh in a hotel lift to his father (who has tricked him into paying for the chicken), he comes to a moment of revelation:

Chicken-breasted beneath the gaze of dowagers and liftwallahs he [Saladin] felt the birth of the implacable rage which would burn within him, undiminished, for over a quarter of a century; which would boil away his childhood father-worship and make him a secular man, who would do his best, thereafter, to live without a god of any type; which would fuel, perhaps, his determination to become the thing his father was-not-could-never-be, that is, a goodandproper Englishman.[159]

The novel follows him over this quarter century of 'implacable rage', not unlike Gibreel, trying endlessly to reconstruct himself. What Saladin and Gibreel share in common is their inability successfully to find and give love, for it was not (perfectly) found or given in their being constructed by their parents. If god is displaced, they must now play god.

'A man who invents himself needs someone to believe in him, to prove he's managed it.'[160] Hence, Anglicized Saladin marries the perfect 'English woman', Pamela Lovelace. Her name is a cocktail of heroines from the fiction of Samuel Richardson, the English realist novelist. Saladin is fixated on Pamela's 'Englishness' such that he never sees past her masks, like her upper-class smile, that 'brilliant counterfeit of joy'.[161] Her smile masks her own despair at not being loved by her parents, who had committed suicide.[162] The fall from love, meaning and clarity at the beginning of our creation is seen in every character (not least in five suicidal jumps).

Saladin's self-constructions mirror the bizarre and multifarious signs by which we create ourselves and want others to affirm. Rushdie names Saladin's drive in his godlike self-production: 'Not only the need to be believed in, but to believe in another. You've got it: Love.'[163] Of course, while Saladin is unable to love his father, which he cannot without rage for what has happened, so too is he doomed to a restless denial of him – trying endlessly to construct himself as an opposite to Changez and being trapped in such binary logic, as is the Imam (denying foreignness), Ayesha the prophetess (denying ambivalence), Mahound (denying Al-Lat), Gibreel (denying women), Hal Valance (denying poverty) and more or less every character in the book whose existence is predicated upon the denial of their own vulnerability. However, Saladin's inability to forgive contrasts with the easy forgiveness that Gibreel receives from the many women he sexually betrays. Such easy forgiveness only serves to condemn him further 'because their forgiveness made possible the deepest and sweetest corruption of all, namely the idea that he was doing nothing wrong.'[164] Denial and repression, it would seem, lead to univocality: a single story about who we are – which leads to personal and political tyrannies of multifarious varieties.

Multiple forms of betrayal, 'the unforgiveable', run through the novel: political, sexual, personal, economic, religious. At one point, Rushdie seems to attain a rare singularity:

What is the unforgiveable?
    What if not the shivering nakedness of being *wholly known* to a person one does not trust? . . . in which the secrets of the self were utterly exposed?[165]

While this nakedness alludes to birth and the sexual act, the double reference locates a site of betrayal, the possibility of love and the failure in love – a chain of relations that is passed on from one generation to the next, what in theological terms is partly understood by 'original sin'. The gospel story shows the possibility of this chain being broken through a naked vulnerable body that is wounded and crucified. Rushdie's novel shows the labyrinthine construction of the chains and the relations, and the near impossibility of transforming them. Nevertheless, this briefly attained singularity regarding the unforgiveable, is immediately deconstructed by the narrator: 'an idea of the self as being (ideally) homogeneous, non-hybrid, "pure", – an utterly fantastic notion! – cannot, must not, suffice.'[166] What Rushdie is protesting at is fixed persons, who are portrayed as never changing. Such a notion of persons belongs to Greek philosophy and enlightenment thought, but in the Christian narrative forgiveness is never a once off act, but is required in such vast mathematical proportions (seventy times seven – Matt. 18.22) as to indicate that the process of living life is all important, not just one single defining act.

Nevertheless, such an idea of the unforgiveable indicates one way in which the novel can be read, and why it ends, as it does, at Saladin's father's home, at Scandal Point, a return to the garden of his childhood, recalling that the Saladin character is born from a paradisal garden Bostan. (Saladin's ability to name the fruits and flowers of the garden – p. 45 – is taken as a sign of his exclusion from the garden, his unbridged distance, his fall from love.) This garden metaphor is important in Islam, as we have seen, and is the site of Paradise, the new Eden in the book of Revelation in Christianity (Rev. 22.1–3).

To get back to Scandal Point Saladin must go through multiple mutations. His implacable rage turns him into an infernal goat, not unlike Shaitan, in his slow recognition that he can never be 'English', not only because such an essence does not exist but also because it denies his own past. He becomes dehumanized (a goat) because he wears rather than subverts the identities and constructions given him in Valayet (land of foreignness), England. Hence his ritual humiliation with the fish bones as entry requirements for 'Englishness', and symbolically seen in his transformation into a goat in the back of a police van where he is beaten up. His rage at such namings will later help save him. His marriage likewise fails, as it is based on his desire to affirm

his Englishness, not on any real love of Pamela. While Saladin's transmutation operates on many levels within the novel, he is only returned
to human form after he learns rage against the coercion of his many
constructions, so that the image of his reconciliation to himself – which
is a process, not a single image – requires numerous reconciliations,
many of which are unattainable in terms of external relations, but are
always possible internally. The image of this transformation is also an
allusion to the image of his birth. He is found amidst the appalling
devastation he has caused at the Club Hot Wax (where transmutations
are the order of the day): 'mother-naked but of entirely human aspect
and proportions, *humanized* – is there any option but to conclude? –
by the fearsome concentration of his hate.'[167]

Saladin's reconciliation with his dying father, his ability to come to
terms with him (and the word 'forgiveness' does not appear in this
sequence) is a momentary fusion of Rushdie's postmodernism and, for
lack of a better term, his apophatic religious sensibility. That is, the
reconciliation is the point whereby Saladin realizes that love allows for
the possibility of keeping stories, signs, our futures, open. Univocal
signification is the choice of death in the middle of life. The Imam,
Eugene Dumsday, Ayesha and Mahound have all lived by closed stories,
resisting equivocality. In a powerful passage, knowing that his father
is dying, Saladin forgives him, and when he does so the image of the
child is inverted and makes possible the return of his father's love:

> Salahuddin suddenly longed to pick the old man up, to cradle him
> in his arms and sing soft, comforting songs. Instead, he blurted out,
> at this least appropriate of moments, an appeal for reconciliation.
> 'Abba, I came because I didn't want there to be trouble between us
> any more . . .' *Fucking idiot. The Devil damn thee black, thou cream-
> fac'd loon. In the middle of the bloody night! And if he hasn't guessed
> he's dying, that little deathbed speech will certainly have let him know.*
> Changez continued to shuffle along; his grip on his son's arm tight-
> ened very slightly. 'That doesn't matter any more,' he said. 'It's
> forgotten, whatever it was.'[168]

As he stays with his dying father, he finds his mother tongue, 'his Urdu
returning to him after a long absence', so that he says to the dying
Changez, speaking for himself and for his second mother who are sitting

at the bedside: '*We all love you very much.*'[169] In his new regeneration
attained through this reconciliation, Saladin recognizes two things: 'love
had shown that it could exert a humanizing power as great as that of
hatred; that virtue could transform men as well as vice. But nothing
was forever; no cure, it appeared, was complete.'[170] In Rushdie's refusal
to resolve the novel into a clear message, a clear narrative, a univocal
reading of life, he preserves a more vital hope; that while no cure is
ever complete, there may well be a cure in love, for it keeps open the
story, allows 'another chance', the possibility of a 'humanizing power'
that is not defeated by hatred. It is this kind of love that is impossible
under the phallic economy of signs. In the previous chapters I have been
suggesting that precisely 'another chance' is enacted by the narrative of
Jesus Christ, even though Christianity eschatologically awaits its own
full and faithful transformation. Such a recognition of ambivalence is
often missing from theologians prone to treating the church as other
than a pilgrim people, and Rushdie's affirmation of the tentative nature
of such 'humanizing power' is most appropriate.

The close of the story is indicative of this theme. After five hundred
and forty-seven pages Saladin's story is not complete, but his 'Childhood was over', and in his reconciliation with his father he steps out
of one narrative into another: the search for love with Zeenat Vakil, a
moving out of 'hell':

> 'Come along,' Zeenat Vakil's voice said at his shoulder. It seemed
> that in spite of all his wrong-doing, weakness, guilt – in spite of his
> humanity – he was getting another chance. There was no accounting
> for one's good fortune, that was plain. There it simply was, taking
> his elbow in its hand. 'My place,' Zeeny offered. 'Let's get the hell
> out of here.'
> 'I'm coming,' he answered her, and turned away from the view.[171]

That the novel finishes at the threshold of the third age, whereby the
Spirit and bride, the community of lovers, might flourish is only possible
because of the uncovering of male phallic desire, the critical exposure
of the death of female genealogies, the realizing of our perichoretic
indwelling of each other, and our gods, and the challenge to the ontological maleness of the divine. All this must happen before Saladin is able
to walk out of 'hell' with Zeeny. His inner world has had to change

dramatically so that he can begin to learn to relate to both his inner and outer world anew. To put it more technically, only when there is a recognition of our perichoretic relations, such that our internal object relations are seen to be most closely related to our religious representation and vice versa, can there be a movement towards really sharing in a divine life that is not of our own idolatrous making. Then we might relate not only to God more fully but also to our parents, partners, children, relations, friends and those who form the church. If we are made in the image of a triune God marked by subsistent relations and perichoresis, this need not be a surprise.[172] One might say that this is the beginning of a description of the eucharist. If the eucharist is the site of trinitarian representation, in so much as it enacts and invites participation in the paschal mystery, then it is also telling that the mass is celebrated with the entire community, both living and dead, and with all creation, as the various eucharistic prayers indicate. The eucharist is the site where we dimly imagine our indwelling each other, both 'brothers' and 'sisters' in this world, as well as the community of saints and sinners, both publicly declared and privately known. This indwelling is only possible through recitation of the lives of saints, the constant retelling of the stories of lives touched and transformed by the triune God, such that we linguistically and liturgically indwell the saints, and they us. The retelling of these lives, and others not officially declared, may be quite troublesome and unfamiliar, and may contain much that deconstructs and challenges us – just as a reading of Rushdie's novel might. Both processes are a way of invoking history, language and lives. Forgiveness and repentance are key themes in the creation of Rushdie's anti-saints, for they tell the story from the underside of history, the location of the everyday, the common. Christian saints belong in the same location, but tell their story differently, through each other's lives and through the triune God's life, the source of all life. I shall return to the eucharistic liturgical site in the postscript, and will do so in the next chapter where I shall begin to inspect a little more fully the triune nature of the church that celebrates the eucharist.

The depths of the fall have been staged in this monumental postmodernist novel with daring audacity, showing its disfigurement of the possibilities of our loving and being loved. The religious imaginary that shores up this disfigurement is encoded within an economy of singular desire and univocal representation: the order of the phallus in Irigaray's terms. The divine metaphysics alluded to, which might bear the fruits of love in the garden of our desires, has vestiges of resemblance to the trinitarian re-presentations that I have been engaged with and been developing in the previous chapters. It is about learning to live together, with our differences, in loving community. Rushdie's thick narrative description has facilitated a glimpse of just how far we are from describing such a metaphysics of representation. His book constantly signified that univocal prose is always likely to fail us. Are words any different from images? They are both semiotic representations. Let us see.

4

Icons and idols

1. Avoiding idolatry

Having focussed on gender, relations and the notion of perichoresis within the triune re-presentation, I want to explore these themes further in relationship to the problems of representing the trinity in art. Art, like music and speech, profoundly shapes the cultural imagination of communities and, like all signs, has the power both to re-present and occlude. Both Irigaray and Rushdie alerted us to the occlusion of the feminine, and in this chapter I want to explore the pictorial exclusion or inclusion of the feminine in both human and divine terms. In human terms, I will focus on the exclusion of Sarah from the pictured narratives of Genesis 18; and in divine terms, the divine representation, or otherwise, of the feminine within the triune God. The first two pictures, from very different contexts, deal with Genesis 18. The third picture represents another biblical text: John 1.14. Of course, it is as impossible to paint God as to name God, which was why Orthodox icon painters took their task with utter seriousness: both in their avoidance of idolatry (for God cannot be represented) and in their reverence for appropriate representation (some images were more acceptable than others). The only function of the latter was to draw the believer into prayer and contemplation. While not wishing to assimilate gender to race, we will see an analogous question being raised in this chapter: if Jesus is always represented in European terms (style of painting and facial features) might one begin to imagine God as European?

The question of relations and perichoresis have led us to explore the psychoanalytic supposition that primary object relations between the child and its parents is most important in the representation of the divine. This has worked, counter Freud, to help highlight the importance of male and female genealogies being preserved within theological taxonomies and historical retellings. Irigaray highlighted this in terms of pointing to the murder of the mother as the basis of western culture. I tried to show how Christianity is founded on a man who remembers his mother most creatively, and that the 'body of Christ' is both imaged in terms of the figure of Mary and cultivated and developed in the stories of women and men, both saints and sinners. I also tried to show that the three persons are all capable of being represented through both genders, not without difficulties and problems attending both types of gender representations. In the pictures I look at now, this same theme surfaces in ways that are interesting and unpredictable. For instance, it will bring us face to face with Christianity's murderous relationship to Judaism, as well as its utter dependence on Judaism. The question of Christian relationships to Jews will always be present. We will also be challenged by Hindu symbolics, as well as challenging patriarchal metaphysical encodings within Hinduism. The relation of Christianity and Hinduism will be constantly present. 'Relations' and 'perichoresis' will therefore take on further sets of significance, which shows both the creative and destructive possibilities that emerge from engaging with the other; and shows that what is at stake in such interreligious engagements is the proper representation of the trinitarian God.

The first two parts of this chapter are focussed on two corresponding images of the trinity based on Genesis 18 which seem to me to raise some profound questions concerning Christian 'negotiation' with the Other. This theme of negotiating with the other is carried through in the third picture which is a reflection upon John 1.14 within a Hindu context.

The word 'negotiation' is perhaps preferable to dialogue and very apt for the pictures I examine. In another context, Graham Ward has convincingly argued that 'dialogue' tends to be framed within philosophical idealism, ignoring the problematic socio-political contexts of 'exchange'. He employs Derrida's term 'negotiation' as it:

is more pragmatic and does not imply the *telos* of a truth to be understood. Negotiation suggests suspicion of intentionality (one's own and the other's); it suggests that each participant in any encounter comes heavily laden with presuppositions and previous contexts;

Figure 2: Andrej Rublev, *The Trinity* (c. 1411)

it suggests that the movement in the transfer being performed is slippery and not necessarily progressive. Negotiation is the economy of textuality itself.[1]

Both images deal with the question of the trinity in relation to other religious traditions, although otherness takes on fluid meanings as we shall see. The first image is the fifteenth-century icon, from the Russian Orthodox painter, Andrej Rublev, *The Trinity*. It raises the question of our making sense of God's presence in and to the Other and how we, as Christians, deal with this. Issues regarding negation, domestication, appropriation and transformation are raised, but not entirely resolved. The second (and third) images, which takes us into the modern period, are those by the Roman Catholic Indian artist, Jyoti Sahi. I will look at his wood cut *Abraham and Sarah Receiving the Three Angels* which forms an interesting contrast to Rublev – for both reflect Genesis 18.

I will also look at Sahi's painting *The Word Made Flesh*, reflecting on John 1.14 in the presence of Hinduism. These three pictures keep many of the same issues afloat and illuminate the complexity of our questions. With Sahi we shall of course change context from Israel and Russian Orthodoxy to Indian religions and Roman Catholicism.

2. Rublev's feasting triune God

Andrej Rublev's painting lives under three names: *The Hospitality of Abraham* or *The Old Testament Trinity* or *The Trinity* (see Figure 2). Rublev painted this icon for the monastery of the Trinity and St Sergius, probably between 1408 and 1425. It now hangs in the secular state-owned Tretiakoc Gallery, Moscow. Technically, it should be called *The Old Testament Trinity* in comparison to the two other standard forms of Orthodox trinitarian depiction: 'the Paternity' and the 'New Testament Trinity'.[2]

There is some humour in this icon circulating under three names, all of which are not inaccurate. There is also a rather remarkable theological point concealed here. Rublev's *Trinity* is in fact the metaphoric re-presentation of the three persons of the trinity *via* the Genesis 18 account of Abraham's and Sarah's meeting of three men/angels by the oaks of Mamre. It will be worth citing this account in full, as I shall constantly refer to it:

And the Lord appeared to him by the oaks of Mamre, as he sat at the door of his tent in the heat of the day. He lifted up his eyes and looked, and behold, three men stood in front of him. When he saw them, he ran from the tent door to meet them, and bowed himself to the earth, and said, 'My lord, if I have found favour in your sight, do not pass by your servant. Let a little water be brought, and wash your feet, and rest yourself under the tree, while I fetch a morsel of bread, that you may pass on – since you have come to your servant.' So they said, 'Do as you have said.' And Abraham hastened into the tent to Sarah, and said, 'Make ready quickly three measure of fine meal, knead it, and make cakes.' And Abraham ran to the herd, and took a calf, tender and good, and gave it to the servant, who hastened to prepare it. Then he took curds, and milk, and the calf which he had prepared, and set it before them: and he stood by them under the tree while they ate. They said to him, 'Where is Sarah your wife?' And he said, 'She is in the tent.' The Lord said, 'I will surely return to you in the spring, and Sarah your wife will have a son.' And Sarah was listening at the tent door behind him. Now Abraham and Sarah were old, advanced in age; it had ceased to be with Sarah after the manner of women. So Sarah laughed to herself, saying, 'After I have grown old, and my husband is old, shall I have pleasure?' The Lord said to Abraham, 'Why did Sarah laugh, and say, "Shall I indeed bear a child, now that I am old?" Is anything too hard for the Lord? At the appointed time I will return to you, in the spring, and Sarah shall have a son.' But Sarah denied, saying, 'I did not laugh'; for she was afraid. He said, 'No, but you did laugh.' Then the men set out from there, and they looked toward Sodom; and Abraham went with them to set them on their way. The Lord said, 'Shall I hide from Abraham what I am about to do, seeing that Abraham shall become a great and mighty nation, and all the nations of the earth shall bless themselves by him?'[3]

The account continues with the Lord promising judgment upon Sodom, and Abraham bargaining with the Lord to spare the city if first fifty, and then finally ten, righteous might be found in Sodom. Abraham is good at market haggling. I leave aside the complex matter of whether it was two angels and God, or three angels, or three men, or whether the trees were oaks or terebinths, and whether verse 1a is original or not, and many other disputed questions.[4] The first title, *The Hospitality of Abraham*, apparently respects the integrity of the 'historical story', but remains closed to any further signification. It is a static reading of Hebrew scripture. This is precisely the outcome of the historical-critical method when it applies itself exclusively as arbiter of meaning. For example, Claus Westermann claims in his historical-critical commentary on Genesis 18: 'There is no way in which one can consider the present event an appearance of God, though the majority of exegetes speak of it in this way.'[5]

The second title, *The Old Testament Trinity*, already reveals a Christian theological rereading of this Christian/Hebrew text; in fact not unlike the rereading and renaming that takes place *within* the story itself. We have the two main characters of the narrative undergoing name changes in the light of their transformative meeting with God: *Abram* becomes *Abraham*; *Sarai* changes to *Sarah*.⁶ This reminds us of the point regarding univocal signification that is so central to my trinitarian thesis. With God, signs are never the same, and their equivocal quality allows them constantly to transmute and re-signify such that they may become appropriate representations of the triune God. However, this hermeneutical rereading strategy inscribed within the 'New Testament' in relation to the 'Old' always bears within it the terrifying possibility, not necessity, of the Marcionite extinction of the Jews. This happens when univocal meaning is secured at the cost of suppressing polysemic signification. Marcion refused to accept the complexity of God's self-revealing through a long history of signs. He, like Irigaray's idolater of Jesus and Rushdie's Imam, wanted to freeze history and revelation so as to attain purity. Marcion claimed the Old Testament was idolatry, and most of the New Testament, except Paul and part of Luke. He excluded all biblical texts that were not in conformity with *his* view of God. We should keep in mind that anti-Jewish hermeneutics can take place not only exegetically but also figurally. I shall be suggesting this possibility within Rublev's icon. We should also recall that Rublev's work takes place in the context of what Ouspensky calls the 'heresy of the Judaizers', the phrase employed in the fifteenth century to denote various Christian reforming movements that denied the divinity of Christ and consequently the reality of the trinity.⁷ This heresy was identified linguistically with Judaism and, as all heresy is usually purged, we can see the potential genocidal logic always tempting Christians, and only slowly and recently acknowledged by the institutional churches after the *Shoah* or Holocaust.

In contrast, in God's renaming within the Genesis narrative there is transformation and change, and even death of sorts, but not extinction. Abraham and Sarah are reoriented and surprised, made new, but not by a denial of their histories, but by a reconfiguration of their lives. God constantly overturns their perspective on matters. Their renaming is not without specific cost, difficult demand and 'sacrifice'. For example, Abraham and Sarah employ a standard practice provided for by Nuzi legislation, and not found within Mosaic Law, to replicate Sarah's 'fertility': that is, they find an incubator for Abraham's seed, Hagar. The incident in Genesis 18 overthrows this planning, however, but also ensures that Hagar's line will bring forth the Ishmaelites. Sarah, despite her age, does give birth to Isaac because God desires it and unites his desire with theirs. It should be noted that within the accounts there is not a passive following of God's ways, but a constant wrestling with him: Abraham's haggling; Sarah's laughter.

The third title of the icon, *The Trinity*, represents an even deeper transformative re-presentation whereby Rublev almost seems to remove all traces of the Genesis story. There is no depiction of Abraham and Sarah despite the first title, nor the various foods laid on the table for the visitors.[8] The picture is often interpreted without any reference to Genesis 18, which might replicate a type of Marcionite anti-Jewishness. Calling Genesis 18 *The Trinity* is not entirely implausible, however, except when one is committed exclusively to historical-critical methods of reading the text. For most of Christian history, Genesis 18 was seen to be a foreshadowing of the trinity.

Let me comment briefly on the composition of the icon. The figures are represented in the usual taxonomic order. We find the Father first (as in eastern taxonomies), clothed in royal blue, with the 'house' in which there are 'many rooms' (John 14.2) above his head, indicating our *telos* towards our heavenly end. In the centre sits the Son, the second person, and he too is clothed in royal blue, showing the sharing of the same nature by the persons of the trinity. However, he has distinguishing features: the royal and priestly sash over his shoulder is bright orange, and the tree of the cross bends with the shape of his figure. He 'looks' towards the Father with his eyes, and towards the Spirit with his body. His fingers bless the cup at the centre of the eucharistic table. He is king and priest. The third person is last. The Spirit shares the royal blue, but also a delicate green, symbolizing life, vegetation, fecundity. The Spirit, like the Son, bows towards the Father but has her head also pointing towards the chalice and eyes, likewise, looking towards the chalice and the other two persons. The movement between the eyes and the bodies make us look from one figure to the other, not being able to fully focus on any single one, for that one sends us visually to the other. This perichoretic relationality is also focussed on the object that centres this rotational movement: the eucharistic chalice. The little niche at the front of the altar table is one in which an icon, like the one we are looking at, is often placed. Hence, the metanarrative enacted here reminds us that the niche, the space which frames the three, is one in which we are placed in our looking at the picture and one in which we are situated in our participating in the eucharist: we enter into communion with the triune God.

However, this removal of the Genesis narrative symbolized in the third title might well be to allow the story to be luminously more than itself, more than a *vestige* of the trinity. Rublev's sublime depiction becomes a holy icon, inviting us to participate in the inner trinitarian life of God glimpsed through the Genesis narrative. One might even call it an eschatological rereading of the Genesis story whereby our fractured histories and ambiguous incomplete lives are glimpsed, as it were, from God's point of view. But Rublev, we can be sure, would not have fallen into such idolatry at exactly its most tempting moment. The icon is not an idol, 'it is not a representation of the trinity itself, that is, of the three Persons of the Godhead, since in its essence the Godhead cannot be represented'.[9]

But let me return to the narrative of Genesis 18 which allows us to glimpse, before the incarnation of the Son, but only through the incarnation of the Son, the *presence* and *absence* of the triune God. The negotiations in this process are extremely germane to the engagements between Christianity and religious cultures. Such allegorical or analogical readings as I shall employ are replete within the early church and could also allow contemporary Christians to consider another form of relationship and negotiation with other religions and their texts and traditions.[10] Abraham and Sarah already represent the beginnings of the covenant community (Gen. 17.2), people in relationship, and their relationship is by no means passive. In Genesis 18 Abraham initiates the communing together with his angelic victors, though even here this is conditioned on the angels accepting Abraham: 'if I have found favour in your sight, do not pass by your servant' (18.3). Abraham and Sarah are extremely hospitable to their guests who are strangers. Westermann reminds us that this typical Near Eastern tradition of hospitality also held that 'The stranger comes from another world and has a message from it.'[11] Hence, Hebrews 13.2 also offers a commentary on Genesis 18, recalling the necessity of genuine and open hospitality: 'Do not neglect to show hospitality to the strangers, for thereby some have entertained angels unawares'. Rublev's depiction of the mutual sharing and self-giving within the trinity actually reconfigures the story of Abraham and Sarah's 'giving', highlighting their immense generosity amidst their failure of imagination regarding God's generosity; that is their disbelief in the impossible 'giving' which is God's promise to them, the gift of a son to Sarah who is barren. This gift prefigures the Son, Jesus, who comes forth from a different context of barrenness: a virgin's womb. Jesus marks the deepening and transformation of the covenant with Abraham and Sarah. This transformative rereading works both diachronically and synchronically, for now we must reread Elizabeth and Mary's stories which will in turn require a rereading of Sarah's story.

This transformative relationship between the primary narrative (Genesis 18) and its trinitarian re-narration is also enacted upon the physical elements constituting Abraham and Sarah's generosity. Abraham and Sarah bring before their guests the goodness of the earth (bread cakes, milk, curd and a tender calf). In Rublev's icon these foods are transformed, as in the eucharistic offertory the elements are transformed, into the sacred chalice which is placed in the centre of the table between the three figures. The gift of hospitality to the angels is returned and transformed into eternal Gift; the eucharist represents the continual self-giving of God's life. So Rublev not only sees in Abraham and Sarah the foundations of the church, but in their bringing forth the fruits of the earth (as good stewards of the gifts given to them) they prefigure the eucharistic return: participation in the loving perichoretic relations that constitute the triune God. In these transactions, active and passive roles are overturned into simultaneous reciprocity, recalling the novel and free gift of 'shared loved' within God, offered now to us by God.

Isaac is the gift within the historically narrated level. We find that God's presence is creative promise, is fecundity, the bringing of hope beyond human resources but, importantly, not without the cooperation of and creative response by human characters. Abraham is a hundred years old, Sarah ninety, and it is little wonder that Sarah laughs (18.12), as did Abraham earlier (17.17), when the promise of new birth is made to them. Laughter, as Aristotle and Freud both realized, is created through linguistic dissonance, through language's polysemic irrepressible 'surplus'.[12] In Romans 4.19–21 Paul suppresses the dissonance of this laughter and Abraham's laughter earlier in Genesis 17.17. In 17.17 Abraham falls to the ground in the presence of God, but his falling also conceals his laughter and disbelief at God's linguistic dissonance – God's promise. In Romans 4.9–21 Paul says:

He did not weaken in faith when he considered his own body, which was as good as dead because he was about a hundred years old, or when he considers the barrenness of Sarah's womb. No distrust made him waver concerning the promise of God, but he grew strong in his faith as he gave glory to God, fully convinced that God was able to do what he had promised.[13]

The laughter is theologically significant. The word 'laughter' suggests a telling play on the name 'Isaac', which comes from the Hebrew root 'yishaq' which means 'laughter'. This implies that Abraham and Sarah's actions, without their fully knowing it, anticipate that which is to come; their laughter, linguistically, anticipates Isaac.[14] Their laughter turns into a son. If ever there was an undermining of univocal predication we find it in this text where names, not unlike in Rushdie's novel, are constantly pregnant and indeterminate. But the gift of Isaac, this promise, also generates further significations: the continuation of Israel and the even greater Gift of God's love, Jesus, to be established with his covenanted people. The gift is out of all proportions to the expectation and imaginations of the human figures in the narrative.[15] The text, and the later Christian readings of it, tend to celebrate male genealogy: Abraham, then Isaac – and often, Sarah is forgotten. I will return to this shortly.

I want to suggest that Rublev's depiction of the trinity is deeply sensitive to the deep patterns within the Genesis story, and by contemplating the icon one is invited into a profound rereading of Genesis 18, which, rather than erasing the economic narrative in Genesis, negotiates it within the light of another narrative: the church. Here, a community of women and men are called to live in loving and forgiving relations, sharing the love that is shared within God, a costly sharing enacted at the eucharistic sacrifice where the revelation of the triune God is constantly represented. In this event, material creation is transformed and reconfigured – everyday. The sheer gift and miracle of our existence is celebrated in this cultic feast. My contention is that neither narratives are quite the same after such negotiation, nor should or could they be. As creation comes under the mercy and judgment of God, it cannot look the same, but neither is it destroyed and erased. This is a two-way process in which we cannot always predict beforehand what we will discover about the living triune God in the light of our negotiations with culture. Let me briefly elaborate.

Rublev reconfigures the hospitality, the generosity and the faith of Sarah and Abraham which are deeply nourishing and prophetic, for in their patterns of action such as meal giving, incredulity at God's 'giving', pleading for 'righteousness and justice' even to the point of getting God to budge (Gen. 18.22–33), they display both an initiative, response and reciprocity to the living presence of the trinitarian God. They become co-redeemers. All these patterns of action are taken up and recast within the trinitarian life of God, re-negotiating otherwise familiar texts to us, and revealing anew the unfamiliar presence of God in creation.

For example, meal-giving prefigures the sharing of the eternal life of God in the eucharistic meal that the Christian community are given to share. Incredulity at God's gift of Isaac is reshaped and transformed in the form of God's gift, Jesus, who together with the Spirit takes us into the presence of the Father within the icon. And Abraham's concern for righteousness and justice is echoed in the wood of the Cross via the depiction of the wooden oak of Mamre at the top off-centre of the icon. It is gently curved, nature shaped by grace, to follow the movement of the body of Jesus towards the Father, Jesus who in the events of the Cross is brutally and painfully undertaking the cost of separation from God – our choice of death and self-destructive sin – but displaying an alternative practice by refusing to perpetuate the violence of the phallus. Abraham's bartering with God to spare Sodom, if even ten righteous persons are found, is now turned into an account where only one righteous person, Jesus, justifies not only the saving of a city but also the redemption of all creation. Jesus brings new life – his fingers in the gesture of consecration point towards the sacred chalice. It is this sacrifice which traverses the space of our distance and alienation from God, such that through the death on the Cross, Jesus with the Spirit, returns to the Father, but now with us. We who participate in the eucharist are called to be 'his body'. Notice the movement of exchange established by Jesus' eyes tenderly looking at the Father while his body faces the other way, towards the Spirit. His action is not possible outside the relationship that already exists: the mutual love and indwelling between the persons.

As we have already seen, this should also remind us that Jesus' life is also impossible without his *relations* to his mother, father and disciples. At the foot of the Cross he is not abandoned, as so much theology traditionally has it. The visual arts have a better record in this respect, for the Cross is often portrayed (unlike some theological writings) in terms of Jesus' death being staged (recalling John's account) in the three-some figuration of Jesus, his mother and the beloved disciple. This reading is implicit in the context of Rublev's icon. It was painted for a monastic community's church; and the space at the front of the icon means that the three never have their backs to each other – or to us, but instead invite us to occupy the space that is opened in the viewing, which is also at the front of the eucharistic table. In this negotiation with Genesis 18, Rublev's own trinitarian narrative is trans-formed as well as the Genesis 18 narrative. Neither remains the same. However, the icon also raises some difficult questions which are equally important to notice.

Does Rublev's trinity represent anything other than an old-style fulfilment theology? Put bluntly: Israel is nothing but a prefigurement of the church, and, worse still, the occlusion of the two key Jewish figures from the Genesis narrative (despite the first title: *The Hospitality of Abraham*) is indicative of the potential genocidal logic in fulfilment theology. Very significantly, this occlusion is also prefigured by the double effacement of the feminine/woman: Sarah. She is both excluded from the verbal title (*The Hospitality of Abraham*, forgetting Gen. 18.6) and from visual representation. By contrast, one might compare the inclusion of Sarah and Abraham in the Russian Novgrod sixteenth-century depiction of the trinity, or the eighteenth-century Russian *Hospitality of Abraham*. This latter popular icon is interesting in a number of ways. It keeps the lively action of the Genesis narrative where not only Abraham and Sarah are figured but also the servant killing the calf. The simple tent where Abraham receives his guest is now an ornate Russian Orthodox church. The table is cluttered with both the implements of a normal meal as well as a clear eucharistic meal. Interest-ingly Sarah is aligned with the Holy Spirit and Abraham with the Father, and both share the royal and divine blue of the robes worn by the angelic figures. This may well represent their holiness, as well as their reflecting God's giving within their own lives. While this eighteenth-century depiction works more with the bustle of Genesis 18's narrative, it is perhaps arguable that Rublev, in an altogether different manner, has included all the actions and transactions of Genesis 18, while also showing us the other story that is hidden in the narrative.

Recalling the problem of anti-Jewish hermeneutics, however, this showing is never unambiguous. The triune God, for some, seems to obliterate historical mediation within Israel. I have tried to question this reading. One cannot entirely ignore the extent of anti-Jewish theology in fifteenth-century Russia, but I must leave the question of anti-Jewishness within the icon unresolved, for I only wish to signal a complex and unresolved issue when we encounter trinitarian reconfiguration. This question will not and should not go away, and the church must be ever vigilant against idolatry. The difficulties will remain even if I suggest that the icon can be seen to reinterpret history from a trinitarian perspective without distorting or effacing that history, but indeed transforming it and itself in the process of rereading. This process of rereading is of course never complete in history.

Another related issue, which runs beyond the context of Jewish-Christian relations, concerns the process of rereadings which takes place within any negotiation. To remain for the moment with written 'scripture', is it not inevitable that, while Christians should listen to and learn from how others practise and interpret their scripture, Christian readings and negotiation with such texts and communities will sometimes seem like gross misreadings?[16] However, such Christian 'misreadings' can also suggest that the original community's traditional readings are not the only possible readings. This process of course works both ways. Put bluntly, who 'owns' texts and signs, who owns creation? Rublev's depiction alerts us to the fact that Genesis 18 constantly signifies more than itself, significations that may be resisted by some interpretative communities but not by others. Judaism, Christianity and Islam are already part of that difficult intra-inter-textual set of relations whereby each one's sacred scripture asymmetrically belongs in part to the other, and is often interpreted in incompatible ways.

When we turn to Sahi we see the deeply political nature of this question in regard to Hindu-Christian relations. Here, the disturbing question of the manner of Christianity's appropriating its 'own' Jewish heritage has already been raised, such that throughout history Jews have been viewed as heretics, stubborn and perfidious in their refusal of Christ, and murders of God – all because they refused to interpret the texts as the church eventually did. To put it in this manner clearly simplifies a complex issue, but it at least indicates that trinitarian reconfiguration, if it is not to enfigure idolatry, cannot erase and disfigure the Other with whom it engages. Making judgments as to 'erasure' and 'disfigurement' are, however, usually retrospective events.

The question of the ownership of signs stares us in the face as we look at Rublev. The icon, not just Rublev's, has recently become an item of popular capitalist consumerism in contrast to its sacred function within its generative community: the church. The icon has been turned into an art object. The fact that Rublev's icon is now in the hands of the secular state as an art treasure makes the point well. Andy Warhol's immortalization of the Campbell's soup can in his icon to modernity makes the same point.[17] Society now worships the objects that capital can secure: the soup can, the icon as art treasure. In turning now to Jyoti Sahi, we are confronted with similar questions, and quite dramatically. Sahi has been involved in legal cases regarding his use of Hindu religious symbols in his Indian Christian art. The complexity of the problem is further illuminated by the fact that he has been prosecuted by both Christians and Hindus respectively for idolatry and profanity.

3. Sahi's ascetic and erotic trinity

Joyti Sahi's *Abraham and Sarah Receiving the Three Angels* (see Figure 3), as with Rublev's work, presupposes that the 'Old' Testament, the Hebrew scriptures, is part of Christianity's heritage. Put another way, the Word was made flesh within a very specific cultural-religious context, that of Judaism. Christianity in its inception was a process of rereadings, reinterpretations and negotiations with the Jewish culture out of which it arose in response to the triune God.[18] And, in these rereadings, there were plural readings of Judaism, some deeply negative to the heretical point of Marcion and some very positive to the problematic point of Ebionitism. This restless dialectic continued into Hellenistic culture which formed the crucible out of which Christians further negotiated their own identity. In conversation with the Greeks we then have the great creedal professions in a triune God as well as the unbaptized entry of pagan thought into Christianity – as we have seen in chapters 1 and 2. Christians responding to the triune God found themselves called into table fellowship that was *intended* to exclude none from sharing God's gifts of food and love together (even though the social reality was often quite different). These negotiations carried no

Figure 3: Jyoti Sahi, *Abraham and Sarah Receiving the Three Angels* (c. 1970s)

single assessment of the religious cultures within which Christianity lived and formed a part, although Christian responses were generally negative.[19] The point I want to make is that negotiation with other cultures and religions was part of the logic of learning to confess God as Father, Son and Spirit within these differing cultures, just as this book continues to try and do within a postmodern culture.

Not surprisingly, some modern Indian Christians living within the profoundly spiritual cultures of Asia have had to struggle to learn anew their practice, understanding and construal of their faith *in relation* to the religious cultures that surround them. If the Word was made flesh within a Jewish culture, thus generating an embodied church, the body of Christ is also becoming enfleshed within Asian culture, calling forth its own struggles and birth pangs. Of course, according to some traditions, Christianity has been present in Asia from the time of the disciple Thomas, but, until recently, most forms of Christianity in India have retained their European or Syrian liturgies, practices and beliefs such that, despite the surface changes enacted by DiNobli in the sixteenth century, it is only in the twentieth century that Indian Christians are seriously calling into question the way in which Christianity has meant Europeanization for Indian Christians.[20] There are very different reactions within the Indian church to the reality of India's religious pluralism, in part mirroring the early church, for example: the development of Nestorian Syrian Christianity for most of its history in splendid isolation from the Hindu culture within which it lived in South India; certain evangelical wholesale rejections of everything Hindu which bear some analogy to Marcionism; various indigenous experimentations which have had the charge 'Hindu Christianity' levelled at them, which may bear analogy with Ebionitism.[21]

Rublev should in part be interpreted by various rules followed by Russian iconographers, although to limit the power of his art according to such strictures would indeed be reductive, even if to ignore such strictures would always run the risk of anachronistic hermeneutics. Sahi provides a slightly different case, but not without analogy, for his art deeply engages with a complex, fluid mixture of Indian religious folk symbols, Jungian psychology and gospel stories and does not follow in any established tradition of Indian Christian art.[22] To begin to interpret his work requires a deep engagement with Indian folk cultures made up of Hindu, Buddhist, Sikh, Jain and Muslim elements – although, to make this exploration less diffuse, I shall only concentrate on the Hindu elements. In this respect, as with Rublev, we find that trinitarian confession forces the artist to engage and negotiate with other religious cultures. For the Indian Sahi, this 'other' in the form of Hindu symbols is already part of his 'own' make-up, as well as part of the deep psychic life shared with thousands of non-Christian Indians. In what follows I will offer a commentary on some of the forces at play in his Indian trinitarian depictions, drawing heavily on Sahi's own work concerning Indian folk symbols.[23] However, to be constrained by Sahi's prose would commit the crime of assuming that the meaning of signs resides in the mind of the artist. Rushdie rightly mocks this convention as we saw, and Irigaray's attention to the lacuna, blindspots and omissions within a text indicate that texts are never limited to authorial intention. Rather, signs, like words, take their meaning from the company they keep and such company always changes. Genesis 18 is now engaged in the company of Indian symbolic 'texts' in Sahi's portrayal. This changes both Genesis 18 and the Hindu symbolic world employed for its representations.

A few introductory words about Sahi are in order, as he is possibly less well known than Rublev. Jyoti (as he signs his name) Sahi was born in India to an English Christian mother and a Hindu father. He was baptized into the Scottish Presbyterian Church, but in his teens became a Roman Catholic when his mother converted to Roman Catholicism after reading Thomas Merton. He trained in England at the Camberwell School of Arts and Crafts in London where he became captivated by traditional Russian and Byzantine icons and contemplative monasticism. (He was much impressed by Rublev's trinity.)[24] Sahi met Dom Bede Griffiths, the now-deceased Benedictine monk, who was leaving England for India, and Griffiths invited Sahi to his South Indian Ashram where Sahi became responsible for various architectural and artistic designs.[25] Back in India, Sahi became closely linked to the Indian Christian ashram movement, immersing himself first in Indian classical, and, later, folk and tribal artistic traditions and mythologies.[26] Sahi had increasing reservations about his use of classical Brahminical Hindu symbols as they often excluded and alienated those converts who came from tribal and low-caste backgrounds, precisely to escape the oppressiveness of caste Hinduism. Sahi married an English woman in 1970 and moved to a village near Bangalore, where together they began an experimental school for local children on Tagore-Steiner lines. He also became closely associated with the National Biblical Catechetical and Liturgical Centre in Bangalore, which is a major centre for inculturation. One such issue in inculturation regards the depiction of the trinitarian God.

Sahi's artist-cultural dilemma has an interesting analogy with Irigaray's question regarding the representation of the divine as male, and whether such renderings of the divine empower men and demean women. Sahi presents an analogous version of this conundrum:

> If we only see Christ as a fair-skinned foreigner, it means that anybody with a different coloured skin, for example a Dravidian, or a person with Mongoloid features, feels alienated from the *body* of Christ, and therefore in some ways alienated from the Church . . . in the great

churches of Old Goa, in particular Bom Jesu . . . is a Christ who is very Portuguese. Christ and his disciples are clearly represented as fair skinned, wide eyed and with Mediterranean features. Indirectly this might have helped the Portuguese colonialists to dominate the local Church. Christ belonged to *them*, because he was represented as having their features. To represent Christ as having Indian features is to appropriate Christ to India; it is to say 'He is our Brother. He is one of us.'[27]

Sahi is well aware of the many problems in carrying out re-presentations of the gospel, for inter-culturally there are no easy one-to-one univocal semiotic interchangeable equivalents, nor can signs be removed from their broader context of associations to offer straight forward 'translation'. However, the alternative is to refuse translation and keep the purity of univocal signification (the kind of quandary presented in *The Satanic Verses*). This is both an impossible task and always in danger of idolizing western cultural forms. Alternatively, one can take risks with language and representation, but informed, poetic and inspired risks. Sahi speaks of inculturation in these terms, reminiscent of Rushdie's valuing of artists:

The task [of re-presenting the Gospel] would certainly be impossible, if it were not for the poet. The poet recreates language, as the artist recreates images. Every poet plays with the already existing words of a language, giving to them a new meaning. It is a dangerous task, one which is often resented. A true translation would have to be done by a poet, and not an ordinary poet either, but one who is himself inspired and imbued by the Spirit of Christ.[28]

The final sentences of this quotation could equally be applied to the visual artist, as indeed Sahi does at the beginning of the passage, and one which controversially applies to Sahi's own work. What is theologically invoked is the doctrine of the Holy Spirit leading the church into ever-new configurations of the body of Christ, such that, through women and men, the light of the triune God might shine anew. The obverse of this, as Sahi well recognizes, is idolatry and the destruction of the 'newness' of God's coming into history. If the gospel is simply assimilated into differing cultures within that culture's own terms, 'true

translation' cannot occur but rather a repetition of the original culture
with Christian dressing. Such has often been the case in various mission
fields.[29]

With this context in mind, let us now turn to the image of Genesis
18 to pursue Sahi's Jewish, Christian, Hindu process of 'negotiation'
in his work *Abraham and Sarah Receiving the Three Angels*. Forgetting,
for the moment, the 'strange' heads of the trinity, the narrated story
of Genesis 18 is very clear in the foreground of the depiction, a point
highlighted by Sahi's title. The old and frail figures of Abraham and
Sarah are bowing, almost genuflecting, towards the three angels. The
'tent' of the meeting is there as is the oak of Mamre. Despite all these
familiar references, there is something unsettling about the depiction
for it certainly does not resemble the traditional western portrayal of
this scene. One myth exploded immediately in this picture is the myth
of 'brute facts' or 'straight story'. As Rushdie noted in a not-so-different
context: 'every story one chooses to tell is a kind of censorship, it
prevents the telling of other tales'.[30] We saw good reason to question
the existence of a historical-critical level of primary meaning (*pace*
Westermann) and instead saw the possibility of non-identical repetition
whereby the story, like the revelation it discloses, is not an event of
the past, but always the possibility of revelation in the present through
its mode of inspired retelling and its graced reception. Sahi speaks in
a similar manner when discussing translation:

> If the word of God is to be revealed to the nations, it has to be
> revealed not just once to the prophets and evangelists of old but
> again and again in every translation, so that every poet translator
> [artist] has, in some measure, to become himself a prophet and an
> evangelist.[31]

I will initially comment on the arrangement of the picture and some
novel details which will lead us to the trinitarian depiction and to the
radical re-presentation offered by Sahi. First, Sarah has finally come
of age. Not only does she appear in the 'title' but she also stands in
the foreground with her whole body depicted in comparison to that of
Abraham who stands behind her. She is spatially nearer to God than
Abraham. This already offers a clue to a deeper reading and a different
set of symbolics. Sahi is allowing us to see the often-marginalized story

in this story, such that Genesis 18 is not about Abraham's paternity and the maintenance of patriarchy but the fecundity of God's life-giving gift to his creation, and the reception of that gift within a gendered community. Women's fecundity, by the grace of God, mirrors the divine fecundity and this careful attention to the theme of creativity out of 'sacrifice' is a mirror of the divine life. Sahi is treading a dangerous tightrope here. Just as Jesus' path entails the sacrifice of his life to bring forth new life so with Sarah, who must sacrifice her conception of the possibilities open to her and trust in the grace that gives her freedom and new life. Of course, this pictorial staging of Sarah/woman in 'submissive' terms, purely as passive receiver, is always in danger of simply replicating patriarchy, but here Abraham too adopts this pose of reception, thereby checking against patriarchal encoding.

Sarah and Abraham's bowed heads represent both awe and reverence, but also recall Abraham's bowing his head and laughing in disbelief at God's promise (Gen. 17.17), followed by Sarah's hidden disbelief (Gen. 18.12). This negotiation with the divine is configured at the geometrical centrepoint of the picture: the near touching of hands between the human and divine, the postures of gift and reception. In making these hand gestures (*mudrās*) between angels/deity and women the centre of visual attention, Sahi also evokes the story of the annunciation, the angelic visitation to Mary and her faithful reception of the Word, God's gift made flesh. The human and divine actually meet in the flesh of Jesus Christ. Here the meeting is prefigured and refigured.[32] Sahi, adopting Indian iconographical traditions, represents the divine with many hands each signifying a quality and characteristic of God's presence: the *varada-mudrā*, of the hand nearest Sarah, signifies charity and boon-giving; the *abhaya-mudrā* on the viewer's right signifies removal of fear and reassurance. (I shall use the viewer's right and left in what follows.) The other hand of Christ, like that of Rublev's Christ, recalls the priestly consecration of the host in the eucharistic meal.

Secondly, the tent which is traditionally depicted as a 'church' of varying styles in Russian icons is usually placed above God the Father's representation, usually to the left. Instead, Sahi presents some sort of building to the right of the picture. It might resemble the *gopura* structure, the entrance to a Hindu temple, or a two-storey house, but it is not very clear. The building is not located over the divine fraternity but above the human configuration. This could be read in a number of ways. It could imply a low and non-sacramental ecclesiology whereby the church is seen as a human construction and a community of people trying to follow God. Sahi's writings and his sacramental sensibility certainly counter such a reading, but we cannot be constrained by Sahi's prose. Alternatively, the structure could represent a learning and humble church, rather than a confident teaching church, a theme often expressed in Asian Christian writings, precisely because so many of the 'teachings' of the church require the process of translation and negotiation operating in this picture.[33] Rather than a church triumphant and eschatologically realized, as enfigured in Rublev's icon, this could be the church, living simply and in poverty so to embody – God. Contrast the garments of the eighteenth-century icon's depiction of Abraham and Sarah or the robes of divine splendour in Rublev (Figure 2) with that of Sahi's human and divine figures. However, I want to suggest that looking at this tent/building structure as church is to imagine that signs always follow the same economy (of western/Russian representation), thus failing to read the signs in Indian cultural terms. May be the church and the eucharistic sacrifice are actually represented via the tree (on the left-hand side) that occupies nearly a sixth of the total space of representation and under whose leaves and shade the divine presence resides. Let us look at the tree. I will return to the building below.

My commentary on the tree will take us, relationally, to the divine. Any Indian looking at this picture will have a number of associations triggered by the tree, many of which help recover the lost sense of sacred trees strongly present within the history of Christianity, and originally probably taken from Canaanite culture by the Hebrew people. By Rublev placing his tree over Jesus specifically, we have a clear reference to the cross. By Sahi placing the entire divine visitation under the huge shading tree, he invokes both the early Israelite's close relation to nature learnt through the Canaanites and Indian folk religion's relationship to trees from which modern Christians could learn much. (Clearly, the tree unmistakably evokes the cross of Christ.) Let us quickly recall the Hebrew negotiation: Abram had built an altar at Shechem, under the oak of Moreh (Gen. 12.16), and upon settling in Hebron also built an altar under the oaks of Mamre (Gen. 13.18), the site of the meeting with the angelic company portrayed in our picture. Later, in Genesis, Abraham will plant a tamarisk tree in Beersheba and there call upon the name of the Lord (Gen. 21.33). Most scholars are agreed that Canaanite altars were often built under shady groves or large trees, and this was not only for the shade provided to otherwise exposed nomadic communities in hot desert conditions, but Gray also suggests a close connection with agricultural fertility cycles upon which the people depended and relates this to the frequent theme in Cannanite art concerning the Tree of Life, which is sometimes configured in terms of the goddess Asherah.[34] That a female deity is represented in terms of fertility is significant, both regarding divine representation and also its human mirroring.

By placing the divine-human encounter between Sarah and Abraham and the three figures under a tree, Sahi recalls the early Hebrew reverence for the land and its fertility, also so important to rural India. At the same time he alludes to the long struggle the Hebrews had with the Canaanite traditions. This struggle is marked in Genesis by the incorporation of many religious Canaanite features amidst stringent criticisms of this tradition. Hence, the Hebrews adopted sacred pillars (Gen. 28.18; 33.20), sacred springs (Gen. 16.4), the teraphim (Gen. 31.19, 34), and the sacred tree/altar sites, as well as divine 'names' formed from the compound 'El', the name of the chief god in the Ugaratic pantheon, such as El Elyon and El Shaddai. By choosing to represent this particular narrative in Genesis 18 with Indian religious features, which are also consonant with the text, Sahi is thereby exploring the question of re-signification that takes place within the narration of Genesis 18 and its re-narrations within the Indian church, struggling with its own religious folk culture just as Abraham and Israel to be were struggling with theirs. This struggle characterizes the church throughout history. The struggle only ceases at the end of the journey, or when the church falls into cultural idolatry.

However, in the same way in which some of the prophets saw the presence of any Cannanite cultural elements as incorporating idolatry within Israel, so Sahi remarks that:

> the indigenous culture of the tribal or low-caste Indian, has not been looked upon favourably by the Church authorities, who have felt that many of the cultural practices of what we might call popular Hinduism or tribal religion, are pagan, or idolatrous in the extreme.[35]

This has often meant that a positive focus is placed on high-caste Brāhminical Hinduism, exemplified by some of the early Jesuits in the sixteenth century who were more keen to engage with sophisticated philosophical and priestly Hinduism than to address the popular folk culture within which the masses lived. In modern India, folk culture is mainly preserved in rural areas and relentlessly, but not successfully, eroded by the urban pressures of modernity.[36] Rushdie's novels reflect the cosmopolitan urbanity of Indian cities and their close resemblance with European cities, for both are products of modernity. Sahi deals with India's 'Other', the tribals and rural Hinduism.

This preference for folk culture and Sahi's pictorial critique of modernity might mean that the structure on the right hand side of the picture signifies urban sophisticated culture, the man-made stable dwellings, the 'Ur of the Chaldees' from which Abram and Sarai came. It may also recall their wandering in the 'hill countries', on the margins of urban centres. They leave the city, the static building, to come to the tree of life, to live close to the earth. This is powerfully signified by the lack of humanly constructed altars, thrones and buildings in Sahi's depiction – in contrast to the Russian icons of Genesis 18. Abraham and Sarah have their backs to modernity, and bow before a triune God who lives under the trees. However, such a reading is problematized for, even regarding caste Hinduism, Richard Lannoy argues that for traditional Brāhminical Hinduism the forest life is central in the first and third stages (*āśramas*) of *Brahmacārya* and *Vānaprastha*.[37] Furthermore, one cannot push this reading too far because of the irony that many of Sahi's works have been commissioned by urban religious centres which support just the kind of art he is producing.

One further point regarding Semitic trees. By prominently placing Sarah receiving the gift-blessing under the shelter of the tree, Sahi recalls the Genesis 'tree of life' in the bountiful pleasure garden of Eden ('Eden' in Hebrew = pleasure). We have seen in Rushdie the importance of the garden for the three Semitic faiths. In Sahi's evoking Eden, the picture also shows another woman, other than Sarah, reconfiguring Eve. In Sarah's cooperation with God, she brings redemption into the world; but not only Sarah but also the holy women of Israel such as Hannah, Deborah, Judith, Ruth and Esther, and eventually Mary, the mother of Jesus, and the many women that will follow her such as Edith Stein and Mother Maria Skobtsova. Many of these women are not biological mothers, but all of them 'give birth' to the church of Jesus Christ – in their various imitations of the divine. Through the creative power of the Spirit, they share this generative power with men in the church. The tree of Eden also evokes the 'tree of life' in the eschatological garden at the end of the book of Revelation (22.2). It suggests that while we may see now through a glass darkly, such that angels can refract the triune God, as can trees and wombs, then we will see 'face to face'.[38]

Having located some of the Semitic resonances of the tree, let me now turn to some of the Indian folk traditions that are evoked by the tree.[39] First, the tree recalls the magnificent palāśa tree which bears brilliant orange flowers, hence its common name: the flame of the forest. Its leaf consists of three leaflets, the central being the largest – and the *Śatapatha Brāhamaṇa* (II.6.2, 8) calls this central leaflet 'the priesthood', and upon it the sacrificial oblation takes place. The wood from this tree is also used for cultic and sacrificial purposes, such that the *Śatapatha Brāhamaṇa* (XIII.4.4, 5) requires that six of the twenty-one sacrificial stakes are made of parṇa wood (the palasa tree used to be called parṇa).[40] Secondly, the palāśa tree allusively refers to the wooden Cross and the three figures in the picture are not unlike the sacred leaf which is divided into three leaflets. (An eastern answer to Augustine's three-leaved clover!) The central leaflet usually used by the priest in sacrifice is emblematically the priest, Jesus Christ, who *is* the sacrifice. This reconfiguring of the palāśa recalls the Christological reconfiguring of the Jewish priestly sacrifice in Hebrews (especially Hebrews 6–9), whereby Jesus is no longer only the high priest who offers the sacrifice but is also the sacrifice. We shall return to this sacrificial theme shortly.

A further Indian tree reference relates to the divine presence, or of a holy person being often depicted under a tree. This probably has 'roots' in the Indus Valley Civilization where seals with a horned female figure in trees are thought by many scholars to be 'the earliest portrayals of the *yakshī*, the fertility-and-tree-spirit' that figure so strongly in later Indian art, both Hindu and Buddhist, and still persist in village Hinduism.[41] We will return to these Vedic origins in a moment, but let us stay with the figure of deity or holiness under the tree. The Buddha attains enlightenment under the Bodhi tree. Krishna consorts with Rādhā and the cowgirls under the kadamba tree, and also climbs into the tree with the latter's clothes when they are bathing so that they must come naked before him, as the devotee does to the deity. There is of course a significant sexual symbolics in the story. Kapila and Śiva often practise their yogic meditation under trees. By placing the three angels/trinity under the tree, Sahi is beginning to re-present the Genesis narrative in a way immediately intelligible to Asian semiotic patterns, and also reconfigures it to express the mystery of the triune God. He is also calling us to attend to the sacral folk traditions of India that are so often occluded from the Indian Christian tradition, perhaps at the cost of Christianity's own life and fertility in Indian soil. Western Christianity's frequent capitulation to modernity and its loss of embodiedness and relationship to the earth is called into question by Sahi's depiction, reminding the western church of its propensity to forget Christ's own tortured and earthly body. The cross-fertilization in this picture is not one way, however, for in placing the divine triunity under the tree Sahi invites the non-Christian Indian to ask: who is this deity? What are the *darshan* (blessings) being given to the couple in this pictured story? The presence of the tree already suggests an answer to the Indian mind.

One answer is profoundly connected with fertility and regeneration. I have already noted the possible origins of the sacred tree cult in the fertility goddess or female *yakshīn* tree spirits of the Indus Valley civilization who are able to bring fertility to barren women. That this meeting under the tree concerns the generation of life is therefore not without religious significance. I quote from Sahi's own exploration of tree symbolism and fertility:

> The trees grouped in sacred groves, under which snake stones (nāgak-als) have been erected, are centres of fertility. Childless women and men worship at such shrines, praying for offspring. The tree, growing from a seed placed in the earth, is itself a figure of birth and growth. The sap within the tree is like blood and the seminal liquid of man, or milk in the woman. It is the essence of life.[42]

By placing the tree in such a suggestive position, more authentically recalling the Genesis 18 story, Sahi succeeds in narrating much of the action via Indian folk symbols. A barren couple, Sarah and Abraham, are being given the gift of fertile life. The tree of life here is polysemic and cross-fertilizing. This negotiation with the religious folk tradition evokes a range of unresolved complexities. For example, here the life-giving deity is the Christian trinity in the form of the three angels of the Genesis 18 narrative. This raises the question: are the feminine *yakshī* obliterated and simply replaced by the divine trinity, as was Asherah by the male Ugaritic pantheon, as were the three female goddesses by Allāh in *The Satanic Verses*. The trinity here is 'male' in so much as there is a man's body in the foreground of the three figures. The central figure of the divine three-some which faces us in the form of a single human male body suggests itself to be Jesus, the Son, as is the case in a number of Sahi's *other trimūrti*-trinitarian representations.[43] Let me stay with this single question a little longer. To address it, I will have to comment on the three-fold face of the angelic/deity.

In Indian art, the *trimūrti* (Sanskrit: 'having three forms') is often used iconographically to represent the divine. The development and differences in these representations are extremely complex, with no possible single interpretation of the three faces (and one unrepresented face?) being considered definitive.[44] For the sake of some clarity, I will cite two brief definitions and note one famous representation to help us further address this issue. First, from a reliable Hindu dictionary, the *trimūrti* is seen as

The Hindu triad, the three manifestations of the Supreme Being, represented by Brahmā, Visnu and Śiva, each being associated with a specific cosmic function. Brahmā is the equilibrium between two opposing principles . . . Visnu primarily symbolizing preservation and renewal, Śiva disintegration or destruction.[45]

Brahmā is also often seen as 'creator', not just equilibriator. Sahi, following the art historian E. B. Havell, provides his own definition of the *trimūrti* which it is important to note:

In its basic form it can be seen as three masses, or spheres, which are given the structure of three heads emerging from one total mass. According to one theory, as the Trimurthy is generally represented as emerging from the body of the rock, as a sort of high relief, there is in fact a fourth unmanifest face (Brahman) facing into the body of the rock itself. Thus the Trimurthy can never be understood separate from the fourth, which is the Ground – or wholeness of the three which are meant to represent emergence (in the form of a feminine profile), fullness (the full face of Ishwara), and dissolution (in the form of a male profile).[46]

Sahi's interpretation draws heavily on the *trimūrti* tradition that facilitates feminine representation. This element might have been predictable given his representation of Sarah, and the feminine evocation of the *yakshīs* and Śakti. This feminine element is also found in one of the most famous depictions of the *trimūrti* in the Elephanta caves, near Bombay, where the eighteen-foot high Shiva Mahésamūrti is carved into dark brown sandstone. One side-facing head represents Shiva's wrathful and destructive aspect (Bhairavā), which is complemented on the other side by the feminine creative aspect (Vāmadeva). The central image is of Shiva Mahādeva, the 'great god' whose eyes are closed in contemplation and serenity. Sahi's *trimūrti* is not unlike the Elephanta configuration and Sahi's angel's hairstyles somewhat resemble the beautiful crowns worn by the Shiva *trimūrti* – but this detail is unclear.

For convenience I will simply work with Sahi's fluid definition which rightly reflects aspects of the Indian tradition to address the question that I have raised: are the feminine *yakshīs* simply replaced and effaced by the divine trinity, or is there an organic but critical symbiosis between the cultural symbols? To complicate matters, the trinity is already being re-presented by angels or men in the Genesis narrative and is now being re-presented via Hindu folk symbols, thereby evoking even further questions and deferred meanings. To follow just one avenue of exploration, however, if Jesus the Son and Lord, Īshwara, forms the body out of which the triunity is disclosed (as in the picture), then either the head facing the tree or the head facing the couple is the feminine face of emergence, creativity and growth and also possibly destruction. I suggest that it is the head facing the tree for three reasons. First, and most tenuously, it is the tree-facing figure who has the most feminine features. I would not want to push this too far. Secondly, if it is this figure, then might she represent the Spirit or, alternatively, God the mother? The former would make better theological sense for the Spirit generates the mirroring of the divine action in the human forms represented; what is called becoming 'Christ like' by the power of the Spirit, as we have seen in the last two chapters. For example, the posture and direction of this divine head is mirrored, though not exactly, in the postures of Sarah's and Abraham's heads. The fecundity and growth in Sarah's body, and the body of the church, are gifts given through the life-giving power of the Spirit who leads the church more faithfully into becoming the body of Christ. If I am correct, we find in this representation a profound attempt to relate the inner trinitarian life of God with the economic revelation of God within the community called church. Just as Jesus' own ministry was in the power of the Spirit, from his birth in the annunciation narratives through to the temptation, ministry, death and resurrection, the Spirit is what helps give shape to the Marian body – in Sarah's body and life, in Mary's practices, in Jesus himself, and in the many women and men who form and reform the body of Christ.

Thirdly, by facing this feminine emergence figure to the tree, further important significations take place. There is an acknowledgment of the *yakshī* tradition, and the preservation of various insights and practices within that tradition, while also developing them christologically: life is a fertile gift; we are utterly dependent on this gift, just as we are dependent upon the fertile earth, however self-made we might like to think ourselves; and this gift is always to be passed on, circulated, reciprocally shared. Furthermore, the feminine *yakshīs* are also associated with the divine śakti, the feminine creative energy of God, which contains within itself both life and death, and is often terrifyingly depicted in the figures of Kālī and Durgā.[47] Sahi brings together this loose set of associations which reconfigure elements in the Genesis narrative. For example, the divine creativity in regard to Sarah is matched with the destruction that is to take place at Sodom. The divine creativity involves both fecundity and destruction, both terror and awe.[48] Hence, I suggest that the Indian traditions of the *yakshīs* and the divine Śakti are reconfigured and also questioned, but not erased, by representing the Spirit in feminine terms and placing 'her' alongside the Son. Both originate from the tree of life, which is also the tree of the Cross. That the images originate from a woodcut itself nicely makes the theological point being explored.

This reconfiguration of the Christian trinity, the Genesis narrative and Hindu symbols has the result of posing unresolved questions to the Indian tradition while at the same time requiring the western church to rethink trinitarian representations and relations. The gift given to

Sarah of new life is related to offerings to the three angelic strangers. This has a resonance with Hindu symbolics and the offerings made to the gods in *pūjā*. But there is also dissonance, for the gift this picture prefigures and enfigures is the gift not of children, good fortune and protection from harm, but the very gift of the giver himself – in the flesh of a man who was impaled on a tree by the receivers of this gift. If Sodom is destroyed because even ten righteous persons cannot be found in the entire city then one righteous person, Jesus, gives the gift of the Holy Spirit to sanctify all life, by his own death on the Cross. This was the macabre 'offering' made to God, the human response to God's offering of love; but nevertheless Jesus' life is lived within a dark and unsettling love, and transfigured by his death (our 'no') into our redemption (God's 'yes'). By placing the feminine Spirit facing the tree, the tree of life in every sense, the tree represents earth's paradise-like beauty and fertility (recalling Eden) and the misuse of the earth (recalling the Fall) to construct a Cross made from the wood of life. Jesus is tortured and killed, and the utterly gratuitous gift of God's loving presence in the Holy Spirit is given, She who transforms the wood of the cross into the fertility of the resurrected body of the risen Christ that is there to serve the wretched and the powerful of the earth, but never on their own terms.

If the picture does indeed pose a troubling evangelical question to Indian folk religion in proclaiming the crucified Christ, amidst an enormous amount of learning and growth from its location within those sacred folk traditions, there are still more disturbing questions that remain. One of them could be formulated: 'Is the use of the *trimūrti* a kind of robbery from the stores of religious Hinduism, replicating the economic pillage of the Europeans from that same land?' This is to repeat the Rublev question: who owns signs? Rushdie's reconfiguration of Muslim signs and stories reminds us of the immense political and emotional power this question holds, as does Irigaray's problematization of sexuate signs. Our question could be recast to ask a slightly different one: 'Precisely because these folk symbols belong to religious cultures other than Christianity, are they not likely to simply proclaim their own gospel, despite the good intention of the artist?' The talented French nun and artist who lived in India, Sister Genevieve SMMI, also experimented, like Sahi, with Indian symbols in her Christian art up until the mid-1970s. She eventually came to reject and criticize her own earlier work in the growing conviction that Hindu culture could not be used for Christian purposes. Thus there is the question whether Sahi's employment of the *trimūrti* entails his prophetic 'risk' turning into offence (rather than evangelical scandal) in regard to some Hindus, or even being turned into uncritical syncretism. Both these charges have been dramatically enacted, for Sahi has been taken to the court over precisely the representation of the trinity as *trimūrti*. The *trimūrti/* trinity picture in question was placed within a Christian church that had commissioned it.

A group of Roman Catholics charged Sahi with bringing a Hindu idol into a Christian church and therefore creating religious offence through desecrating sacred ground. A Hindu judge had to preside over a case brought by some Hindus with the charge against Sahi that, by including an image of the Hindu *trimūrti* in a church, Sahi had stolen a Hindu sacred image and used it in an alien place, thereby desecrating it. The judge declared that the reverent use of the image in the church could not constitute disrespect, let alone desecration, but this was a legal, not theological decision. In some ways, one could argue that disrespect does take place because the *trimūrti* is emblematically 'used' to represent something other than itself. Of course, the angels in the original narrative suffer the same fate, and one has to ask whether anything represents itself with such semiotic purity. Sahi's interest in the fourth hidden face of the *tri*(sic)*mūrti* within the rock might not necessarily indicate modalism, but rather a good and proper apophatic sensitivity that reminds us that representations are inadequate to represent the divine, while knowing, nevertheless, that we have no alternative. Thematically, this follows the Orthodox distinctions between icons and idolatry. However, such alleged double desecration calls into question Sahi's entire project and with it many questions about the politics of trinitarian representation. Theologically, it calls into question whether God's trinity is indeed the universal Lord of signs, such that all creation, all signs will find their final meanings in the praise and glory of the triune God.

I cannot of course offer any historical resolutions to these complex questions, and they have faced the church in every moment of its long development within different religious and non-religious cultures. We have seen such a crisis in regard to an engagement with postmodern psychoanalytic feminism: are trinitarian representations of the divine

idolizing the 'male' rather than the living God? We have seen such a
crisis in Rushdie's writing: is his iconoclasm an undermining of the
possibility of revelation, or does it unveil the idolatry so often mistaken
for revelation? And now, we are faced with the question in regard to
Judaism and Hinduism, not that Christianity's relationship to each is
symmetrical: does the trinity either obliterate or recapitulate and transform the religious cultures with which Christians are engaged? I do not
think there is a generalized answer possible, for each encounter will
generate different moments of representation and signification. Historically, Christian hands are not clean, but neither are they utterly sullied.

One may of course wonder whether Sahi occludes the connections
whereby the *yakshī* and *Śakti* traditions are also related to elements
within Indian culture (not unparalleled in the west) whereby women
are counters which circulate within a male economy of desire: they are
receptacles for reproducing the patriarchal line; they are objects of erotic
desire; and, if they are faithful to their husbands, they have no reason
to live once their husbands have died. Sahi's untroubled interpretation
of *satī* (the widow's self-immolation) in rather lofty spiritual terms is
disturbing, given its contemporary practice precisely within folk culture.[49] He is perhaps on the verge of a Gandhian romanticization of
folk Hinduism and also pre-modern agrarian life, although this criticism
too easily dismisses many wise insights and practices that he seeks to
recover. Nevertheless, one may wonder whether Christianity's distinctiveness has much chance in the symbolic 'swamp' of Hinduism, to use
Shusaku Endo's metaphor of Japanese culture in relation to the possibility of Christianity's survival in Japan.[50] Hinduism's assimilating powers
helped eradicate Buddhism from India, and the religions that have
survived in India have been defined more by their lack of synthesis and
borrowing from Hinduism. Is there really a transformation of Indian
folk culture into genuinely Indian Christian culture in Sahi's paintings,
or do such representations actually allow and encourage the perpetuation
of non-Christian religious traditions in their own terms, but now in
cross-dress?[51]

Alongside these questions, there is the terrifying idolatry that the
church may perpetuate if it claims that the trinitarian God can only be
represented in western European forms, as if these *per se* were divinely
privileged. Why did the Christians who took Sahi to court not also
complain about the Portuguese Jesus in the cathedral of Bom Jesu, Old

Goa? Why do those same Christians still have Christmas trees in their houses? Why did the Hindus who took Sahi to court not also return the *trimūrti* to Buddhism, where many think it originated? To imagine univocal semiotic representation and the ownership of signs by a single community is to imagine the universe created by a God who does not offer creation as a gift, such that all signs and all creation belong to no single person, but only find their fullness in giving glory to God, by being able to re-present the triune God. To imagine univocal semiotic representation is also to imagine that we are God with the power of a final naming of signs. If all creation cannot reflect the glory of the triune God, then, to put it crassly, Jesus is indeed only the redeemer of Europeans and those who assimilate themselves to western culture. However, in the tentative reading I have offered of Sahi's picture, and in the light of the argument of my book, I hope to have suggested that this cross-fertilization of Catholic culture may facilitate possibilities of truthful re-presentation of trinitarian life and faithful Indian Christian discipleship; and a re-presentation which might also call into question various western trinitarian representations – as well as some configurations within Hindu life.

I now want to turn from Genesis 18 to John 1.14 (and thus again back to Genesis), in examining my final picture from Jyoti Sahi: *The Word Made Flesh* (see Figure 4).

4. The palimpsest church made flesh

This painting was made for a seminar on the 'Relevance of St John's Gospel in India Today' in 1974 and pre-dates the one we have been examining.[52] The title indicates that the painting is an exploration of John 1.14: 'And the Word became flesh and dwelt among us, full of grace and truth; we have beheld his glory, glory as of the only Son from the Father.' This text will also take us back to Genesis, for the beginning of John's Gospel ('In the beginning was the Word') recalls the beginning of Genesis ('In the beginning God created the heavens and the earth').[53] I shall argue that this trinitarian painting is about beginnings, 'being born' constantly, in the power of the Spirit, into 'Christ-like' forms, into communion with the divine life. I shall focus on one element in an extremely complex painting: the feminine

THE WORD MADE FLESH

Figure 4: Jyoti Sahi, *The Word Made Flesh* (c. 1973)

representation regarding this process. It will help us learn how Hinduism can help Christians relearn and re-envisage the divine feminine within trinitarian representation; and how Hinduism's and Christianity's own divine feminine is not unproblematic. Hence, this entire negotiation is not without troubling ambiguities.

At one level the painting depicts the Christ child being nourished by the Virgin, tenderly enfolding, in a graceful circular fashion, the suckling infant. Her oval form, constituted by circular movements, plays with and echoes the huge oval blueish-white egg, or womb, or moon, within which the mother-child image is framed. Mary's colour is the orange *kavi* of the holy man within the Indian tradition, not the royal blue of western depiction, and this colour also infuses the infant. Already, there is a similar striking note as with the portrayal of Sarah, for here a human woman constitutes the focus of the picture, wears the colours usually reserved exclusively for men in the Hindu tradition, and even though she has no recognizable face she is taken from a narrative that situates her historical enfleshment.

Intersecting from above there is a shape much like the dove of the Holy Spirit, made up of three crescent shapes fused together, that sweeps over, perhaps even gently kissing, the Virgin's neck, breathing life into the Word that she nourishes in her arms and by her breasts. The curves of the dove create a rhythmic dance of forms between Mary, the child, the womb-earth-egg-moon and the waters (?) upon which the Virgin is borne. The dance is nicely balanced by a crescent shape near the dove's neck and above Mary. Straight forms are rejected in this cosmic dance, possibly implying rejection of the linear logic and rationalizing of the mystery that besets modernity; a theme that we have already noted in Sahi's work.[54] At the bottom of the picture we have what could be the waters of creation above which the dove hovers, recalling creation in Genesis (Gen. 1.2), the dove from Noah's ark (Gen. 8.8), and which is now re-configured by John (John 1.14) and by Sahi in terms of Christ's new-creation and his role in the creation of the world. The shape is admittedly ambiguous, but the colour could resemble the dark, swirling waters from which form and new life are shaped.

If the reader were to ask why I consider this a trinitarian depiction when only Mary, Jesus and the Spirit are represented, two answers might be suggested. First, in the economy of revelation we only come to the Father (who is not explicitly represented) through the Son and the Holy Spirit (who are explicitly represented). I have spoken earlier of the birth of the Father, and Ricoeur also speaks of this sign signifying a process, not a static essentializing. John's prologue reiterates this: 'No one has even seen God; the only Son, who is in the bosom of the Father, he has made him known' (John 1.18). In the painting, the Son resides at the bosom of the mother, and it is by the light of the bright crescented moons of the Holy Spirit that we see Jesus in the tabernacled arms of Mary. This refusal at causal prioritizing of the Father allows the Father to be configured in the as yet unrepresentable space that the Son, Spirit and mother/church opened up to the viewer. Like Rublev's icon, the viewer is invited into a living relationship with that which is depicted. My second answer would be to quote an interesting comment by Sahi on the figure of the child in Indian art, which does draw on human causality, but only to run it up against the difference (pictorial analogical predication) that God constitutes: 'The child symbol is an image, making visible the invisible, or, as he is known in Hindu myth, "Guha", born of the "secret place".'[55] The Son is the visible image of the invisible Father, the source of all life. The Son together with the Spirit realigns all other signs to reflect the triune love within the divine life, to reflect the sign that is only known in relation to other signs, never in itself *per se*.

John 1.14 is represented to Asian and non-Asian alike in this painting, not unlike the primary action of Genesis 18 in the previous pictures. One need not be a specialist in Indian art to appreciate the painting. However, here, as before, Sahi's picture is entirely constructed out of Indian religious symbols and, in so doing, sets in motion a complex negotiation between different cultures and religions without any attempt at resolution. I will trace some of these unresolved issues set in motion in the painting by the light of the moon.

The moon is doubly or even trebly represented: in the oval shape constituting the background; in the three crescents of the dove; and in the single crescent near the dove's neck. The moon is a highly important Indian religious symbol – and is varyingly bisexual and transsexual in resonance. There are at least three evocations worth noting. First, the moon is related to the menstrual cycle and women's fertility. There are many popular depictions of Krishna and Rādhā (or Krishna and the *gopīs*) courting in the moonlight by the trees of the Vrindāvan forest.

This is not just sentimentalized romance, for in Indian folk art the moon is often depicted in terms of its three stages with associated colours and *guṇas* (spiritual qualities) for each stage: 'white being the moon in its ascendant phrase, red the full moon, connected with the menstrual blood and the fullness of life, and black being the moon in its receding phase'.[56]

The white moonlight of the ascendant phase in this painting clearly signifies the fertility of the birth that is depicted in the foreground. White signifies purity, and represents *sattva guṇa*, the highest of the three *guṇas* that constitute 'nature' (*prakriti*). The three *guṇas* (*sattva, rajas, tamas*) entrap the spirit, the *purusha*, and, in Sāmkhya metaphysics, the basis of most Vedantic thought, liberation is constituted by an escape from nature (the flesh). Hence, Zaehner says of *sattva* that it 'most nearly approaches to the nature of *purusha* and is the agency through which Nature promotes *purusha's* liberation from herself'.[57] In Sahi's painting, however, the *sattva guṇa* actually drives the Spirit and Logos/Sophia *into* human flesh, rather than being liberated *out of* human flesh, thus inverting Indian metaphysics, calling into question the metaphysical denigration of the created order in the main Vedāntic schools deriving from Sāmkhya, where liberation is envisaged as an escape from flesh. In Sāmkhya, *prakriti*/nature is understood as feminine, and, in so much as *purusha's* escape from nature is the source of liberation, there is also an inversion of this potential metaphysical denigration of the feminine in placing the female form of Mary, the church, at the centre of this redeeming process. It is through her flesh that the redeeming flesh of Christ is able to transform all flesh. Irigaray recalls this theme strikingly in her commentary on Roman Catholic occlusion of women from the priesthood, when the priest offers the food of life.[58] Here, the use of Indian signs creates major disruption to their usual significations by means of those same significations being employed to tell a very different story, the story of the 'Word made flesh'.

We must guard against reading the picture as a metaphysical anagram decoding social practices, however, for, as I have tried to argue, the process is far more complex. Nevertheless, such metaphysics do permeate daily cultic and social practices and the unspoken assumptions of many worshippers, such that the negative questioning of Hinduism must be heard at the same time as the positive affirmation of various features within Hinduism in the portrayal of John 1.14.

A second unresolved evocation lies in the shape of the three (or four) lunar crescents constituting the Holy Spirit, the hovering dove. Here we have a double reference. First, we are again taken back to fertility, for one of the most famous representations found on the seals at Mohenjo-daro is that of the meditating *yogi* figure who seems to have three masks or faces (and is thus seen as a prototype of Shiva), and who wears a large three-horned crown. A number of scholars have suggested that this triple crown may be a prototype of Shiva's three-pronged trident; the threeness recalling the three visages of Shiva as *trimūrti*.[59] The fertility connection is further evoked by the many animals that surround the meditating *yogin* with his erect and prominent phallus. By evoking this set of associations to configure the Holy Spirit, Sahi brings into focus that which Shiva so strongly balances in the Indian tradition: eroticism and asceticism.[60] This conjunction is interestingly employed in portraying the birth of Jesus from the Virgin, for the child always requires for her/his existence an erotic sexual meeting, but this child has been conceived in asceticism – through prayer and Mary's fertile human response to God's initiative, not through sexual inter-course with Joseph. However, this asceticism is balanced now by the erotic love (not necessarily genital love) that is released and enfleshed in the incarnation, such that all creation can be the source of the abandoned and ecstatic rapturous love by which Christians can com-mune with their lover: the triune God.

This depiction is of course taut with ambivalence in potentially making the female an incubator for God the 'Father', and also potenti-ally denigrating human sexuality. It is unclear whether Sahi has been able to steer clear of these difficulties, but his positioning of the feminine in a redeeming manner in contrast to the feminine *prakriti* makes it clear that the negotiation is a complex and challenging one. That Sahi is aware of the issues underlying such politics of representation is seen in a remark he makes when discussing the symbolism of the moon:

> The world-process, known in India as samsara, is thought of as feminine. Between this world-process and the all-transcendent Father there is an eternal dialectic. In the highly developed metaphysics of the later medieval schools, the term adhara, meaning support, con-tainer, is supplied to the feminine, as opposed to adheya, meaning that which is to be supported, meaning here the masculine principle.

Thus, although the feminine according to one viewpoint is understood as the relative, maya, seen in a different way it is the container of all that can be known, the very substance of all that is (sati).[61]

I presume that for Sahi this 'different way' of seeing is at least provided by Christianity, as is envisaged by the picture I am presently discussing. Throughout this book, we have seen that the question of the feminine divine within Christianity is unresolved. It is unclear whether and how Hinduism is able to readjust its hierarchical metaphysics of sexual difference. Such readjustments are to be found in certain recent Hindu 'liberation' movements which have tried to recover a positive feminine representation from the narrated portrayal of women in the popular epic, the *Rāmāyana*.[62] The least that can be said for Sahi is that in choosing not to represent the 'Father' as 'male' or 'person' he creates symbolic space for reconsidering *divine creativity* in alternative terms of female imagery which pulse through Indian religious folk symbolism. Sahi's bisexual and transsexual Holy Spirit, like Shiva's bisexual and transsexual *trimūrti*, suggests that sexual representation is crucially important in the representation of the divine, even though the different politics inherent in such representations are not always susceptible to static classification and univocal meaning.

Finally, the further configuration evoked by the Spirit, which takes into special consideration the fourth crescent, is that of the *aum* symbol. Admittedly, the fourth crescent could stand for the fourth face of the Shiva *trimūrti* that I discussed earlier, which would be quite in keeping with the reading being suggested and even provides an illustration of perichoresis; that is, even in one person of the trinity, all three coinhere. However, what the shapes of the dove certainly mimic is the holy Sanskrit word, *aum*: ॐ. *Aum* is said to be the eternal sound/syllable out of which all creation arises and dissolves. It therefore becomes apt in this Johannine picture. The *Chāndogya Upanishad* (2.23, 2–3) and the *Taittrīya Upanishad* (1, 8) assign the origins of language to Prajāpati, from whose meditation arose the threefold knowledge (the three *Vedas*). From Prajāpati's meditation on the *Vedas* arose the three syllables: *bhūr*, *bhavah* and *savār* (earth, atmosphere and sky), from which then originated the sacred syllable *aum*, which coordinates all speech and represents the totality of the world.[63] The creation of the world from the Word, God's uttered love (John's Gospel), and the Spirit (Genesis/

John) is powerfully fused and mediated in this picture, ironically not by language and sound (Word) but by its cognates, movement and form, without which language and sound would not be possible. It is by the Spirit's movement and giving form, the function of the Spirit in the Genesis account, that the Word is sounded in the world, giving testimony and praise to the formless chaos of our lives. Sahi's visual configuration underlines that of the persons of the trinity as utterly relational and co-constituting. The Son is not possible without the Spirit and the Spirit is not possible without the Son, and both are not possible without the 'Father', although all are distinct, yet in unity. He reverses phallocentric taxonomies, and in visual art makes the medium the message.

Interestingly, his own interpretation of *aum* draws upon *tantric* art, which also takes sexual difference extremely seriously, such that he describes *aum* in erotic metaphors and generative nuptial terms. Sahi here makes a link with the three lunar associations I have been exploring.

> According to tantric thought, the 'A' component in the cosmic sound Om (or Aum) is associated with the upward-pushing fire and light of the cosmic lingam. The sound U is thought to be the womb of nature, or the cosmic waters (jalahari) and the marriage between the two has been related to the sound 'M'. This 'M' is the bindu or drop from which creation arises . . . In the light of the moon, according to tantra, the word [*aum*] becomes visible, Pasyanti. It is this movement from cosmic sound to the visible that is characterised by the sign of Om which is perhaps the most sacred sign in India. It has been suggested that this sign is itself based on a moon symbol, namely the three mountains above which is the crescent moon, symbolic of the three phases of the moon. The cosmic resonance which emerges as light enters into the womb of space, and concretizes, crystallizing like the diamond into the geometry of matter. This last movement into the physical is characterised in Indian thought as the dance.[64]

Sahi, in this complex negotiation invites the Indian church to engage critically and conceptually with its own cultural and symbolic life, seeing in this the exciting possibilities of focussing on various neglected elements within its own European Christian heritage.

The sexual symbolics within this tradition that I have been focussing upon allow Sahi not only to play with the metaphor of generation, knowing that God is not generated like us, but also in so playing to represent both the feminine and the Spirit in a most powerful manner suggesting how we might rethink trinitarian taxonomy. Because Sahi is a visual artist the Word becomes image and form before it is concept – through the power of love (the Spirit). This biblical reorientation and Sahi's restaging the representation of the trinity via Hindu symbols, giving such focus on the Spirit and the feminine, confirms in a limited, but not unambiguous, manner the argument that I have been trying to advance in regard to the feminine and the trinity. Representing the divine without the feminine is always in danger of making the male equivalent to a narcissistic divine. The reverse is true with purely female trinities. Divine couples are in danger of idolizing heterosexual monogamy. But in a trinitarian representation that allows us to see that multi-gendered metaphors are appropriate, while all fall short of the divine *per se*, we have the chance to be open to the way in which the divine might reconfigure our understanding of gender relations and the perichoretic relations that we inhabit. That the negotiation I have been examining is ambiguous, unfinished and multi-directional is testimony to the power of Sahi's art and the difficult, unresolved questions it raises and with which we have been dealing.

Finally I want to comment on one further feature of this painting: the breastfeeding infant. In Bynum's discussion of breastfeeding, she notices how this configuration is extremely important in late medieval art for it portrays the nourishing of the church and even allows that Jesus has breasts and feeds the church, just as his mother fed him.[65] Sahi's depiction of this incident in the Indian context brings about further complexity to this transaction between mother and child. Mary's breasts are swelling and fecund, and here Sahi echoes the Indian feminine:

The Indian feminine figure is depicted with swelling breasts. This again is thought to show her overflowing fertility, rather than her specific relation to a child whom she is feeding. It is almost as if the Indian feminine figure has been abstracted beyond any personal relationship, which is the intention behind the highly personalized depictions of the mother and child images of Christian art. For here the woman is the all-embracing principle of nature, and even the milk that fills her breasts is described as 'the essence of water and of the plants'.[66]

In depicting the child suckling from the mother's breasts, in a stroke Sahi employs the richness and universalism of Indian symbolic language (the overflowing fertility of God's relationship – as feminine – to us), but characterizes it in the particularity of personal love between Mary, Jesus – and the Holy Spirit. Sahi manages to balance, in terms of artistic economy, two aspects. First, in the generalized picture of the fecund feminine who is not in 'specific relation' to a child and not an erotic object for male desire woman is portrayed in her own fertile creativity and enjoyment, not as encoded by men and not purely in relation to being incubator. Secondly, at the same time Sahi links fecund creativity to a particular person, Jesus, who is born from Mary's fertility and God's creative fertility.

The power of this fusion shows that being Christ-like is in one sense also deeply feminine; it is the nourishing of the body, the tender glory in God's creation seen *in Mary's relationship to Jesus*. The church, as we have seen earlier, is often represented as Marian in western art and theology and the church's mission is to nourish a Christ-likeness through the grace of the Spirit. Earlier I argued that this 'maternal' theme is always in danger of rendering women into incubators, but need not do so. However, such a maternal relationship, as Mary has to Jesus, may well help Christians, as both men and women, to reconfigure their lives and relationships into giving birth to God's love. The pain of the Cross is a reminder that this birthing cannot be 'easy', for it recalls the shadow cast over all creation through a constant rejection of God's love.

There is an important and dark, even ambiguous, echo in this breastfeeding depiction, one which touches upon the harrowing death (and resurrection) awaiting the infant, for it evokes the myth of Krishna who as a baby was at one time 'nurtured' by the demoness Pūtanā who gave the babe her breast which was filled with poison. Here is the phallic mother if there ever was one. However, Krishna drank all the poison, draining the demoness dry, and thereby defeated Pūtanā. While this story may reflect a powerful murderous desire towards the mother/ feminine shared by both male and female, it nevertheless is also capable of generating a further level of engagement with Hindu myths and symbols. This story evokes the important myth of creation, where Śiva drinks the dark poison generated from the churning of the cosmic ocean (the bottom of the painting?) to save the world from destruction.[67] Is there a creative tension between these stories and the one revealed here? Here the Son takes unto himself the evil and sin of the world, not by crushing the opposition (like Krishna), nor by wondrous deeds (like swallowing the ocean), but by the patient, painful and joyful living out of an ordinary life in which especially the poor, marginalized and social outcasts were made to feel that Jesus and those who follow him might be the location where love can really be found and reciprocated. But to do so also meant the slow ignominious death borne in history upon a wooden cross. It is this action which begets and nourishes a new creation. Sahi comments on the Krishna and Shiva accounts: 'Both myths probably relate to an ancient concept of recreation by swallowing, but here food is given a negative value – as poison it cannot be absorbed, but has to be transformed through a ritual death.'[68] I am not altogether convinced by Sahi's distinction between absorbing and transforming, but ritual death is certainly evoked in all three stories. However, in one story, ritual death is not symbolically 'acted' out, but historically undergone by a human figure. It is now 'acted' out in the eucharist; which requires the historical lives of persons in the church participating in this eucharistic food to 'take up their cross' and be Christ-like. This is not to devalue the important positive symbolic role of such myths in Hinduism, but to underscore the historicism within the Christian narrative and the participative sacrifice and suffering that the church is called to live out to make up for the 'lack' in Christ's afflictions.

In this painting, the Indian mind can see a rich set of associations being triggered regarding the relationship of this *iṣṭa devatā*, Jesus, to the many popular gods such as Krishna and Shiva. How is this one child related to the many other gods within Hinduism, many of whom have shared his childhood state? Sahi seems to suggest a deeper organic connection between the Word made Flesh in Jesus and the creative power of the divine found within differing aspects of Hinduism embodied within different gods.[69] This refusal to suppress difference but to take it up into a new relationship with the trinitarian God is refreshing. Sahi does not conceal an interesting series of differences, some of which we have noted. Iconographically, it is quite significant that this God, Jesus, is portrayed with his human mother in contrast to the main iconographic feminine representation in Hindu art: the male gods with their divine consorts. Not that this latter is uniform or entirely suspect, but it lends itself to an easier suppression of the mother, the root of the hom(m)osexuate trinity, that we have called into question. That Christianity has not escaped this difficulty despite its alternative representation should remind us that the complexity, ambiguity and surplus within signs refuses easy stabilization and redemption.

It is perhaps appropriate that we should finish this chapter where we started: the eucharistic meal (of Rublev's monastic community and now of Sahi's Indian church). Shiva's and Krishna's consuming of poison requires that Hindu worshippers still offer food to their gods, and then leave the temple with *prasāda*: sweet foods to recall the blessings of their Lord. Sahi's picture depicts eucharistic food as the mother's milk. It is not poisonous when given in love, although it can be poisonous in the real relationships between mothers and their children. In drinking of it, the earth is transformed, just as Shiva's drinking changed him and the oceans. The church, of women and men, is called to imitate a human mother called Mary, by the grace and gift that is bestowed by a bisexual and transsexual Spirit, to imitate and grow more like its cross-gendered Lord. This Lord, who 'became flesh' had the vulnerability and trust of a new-born child, showed that love is there to nurture our co-dependence on each other, and our utter dependence on God. He also showed us what such 'love' looks like when displayed in human history. By eating the eucharistic meal with this Lord, Christians are called to transform all signs into signs of redemption, forgiveness and love. That Rublev and Sahi have in part achieved this indicates that, through their eucharistic participation, their art is able to reflect something of the divine love, if even through a glass darkly.

Clearly, we will only learn about the riches of the trinitarian God in our openness to the multiplicity of representations of the infinite mystery, representation that will take up all creation in ways that our best artists and theologians have only sometimes imagined, and which will allow the church to continually reimagine. Taking the risk of imagination can lead to syncretism, heresy and idolatry. Not taking the risk can also lead to false cultural and religious purity, another form of heresy and idolatry. Taking the risk can lead to the redemption of the signs within which we live, and thereby also the lives that are lived within those signs. Taking the risk is like Sarah's unexpected conception of Isaac and, in her child, in another, finding anew the image of God and finding laughter; just as with Mary's unexpected conception of Jesus and, in her child, in another person, finding anew the image of God. I finish with a quote from the Hindu poet, Rabindranāth Tagore. In one of his poems about children, the child asks his mother, 'Where have I come from?' The mother's answer indicates something of the complexity of our negotiating with trinitarian signs and the design of love that can transform signs:

> She answered, half crying, half laughing, and clasping the baby to her breast, 'You were hidden in my heart as its desire, my darling. You were in the dolls of my childhood's games; and when with clay I made the image of my god every morning, I made and unmade you then. You were enshrined with our household deity, in his worship I worshipped you.'[70]

5

Postscript: A never-ending vigilance

> The Trinity itself, that crown jewel of theological sophistication, evokes, beyond its specific content and by virtue of the very logic of its articulation, the intricate intertwining of the three aspects of psychic life: the symbolic, the imaginary, and the real.[1]

Julia Kristeva poignantly highlights the pervasive power of the trinity to construct human lives at every possible level. Looking at the confluence and flotsam when theology, psychoanalysis, gender and culture come together, we have been able to see the complex whirlpools and currents present in the life of the church deriving from constructions of the trinity. There are many who feel wrecked and abandoned, half-drowned, and have left the church. There are some who feel beached and numb but have nowhere else to go, believing that, within these same waters, one might drink and taste eternal life. There are others, situated variously, including those who feel that the influence of psychoanalysis and gender are modernity's children that ought to be subject to serious questioning from Christian discourse. I have written this book treading water, occupying on occasion all these differing positions. However, to the latter and former groups, the approach developed in this book might evoke Stevie Smith's lines (replacing 'I' with 'He'): 'I was much further out than you thought/And not waving but drowning.'[2] The gestures, even contortions, contained within this book require such a sea change within the Catholic Church that some might say they are no more than the hallucinations of a drowning man. Nevertheless, I write in the company of others, men and women, who feel that the traditions of the church, both repressed and explicit, within the imaginary and the symbolic, might disclose a reality that genuinely brings embodied new life, forgiveness, hope and love in the midst of death, loss, alienation and longing.

In this postscript I want to bring together some of the tentative discoveries made in the previous pages and show how they are related to a historical community called the Roman Catholic Church (where I happen to find myself). Even while this book is addressed to all Christians, and those dipping their toes in Christian waters, and those having left these waters with relief, I lay much of the blame for misogyny and the responsibility for change at the doors of the Roman Catholic Church. I have no other location from which to write. But I also see the resources for regeneration within the symbolic history of this church. I refer the reader to the 'Preface' for a rendering of the argument of the book in linear terms, as it was presented in the previous pages. Here I want to present the argument in a different fashion: one that looks back at the journey and reconfigures, rearranges and assimilates, anticipating further steps and different questions.

There is a direct trajectory between Paul's startling comments in Colossians 1.24 ('and in my flesh I complete what is **lacking** in Christ's afflictions for the sake of his body, that is, the church') and sections of Pope Pius XII's encyclical *Mystici Corporis* (1943) on the *Mystical Body of Christ*. Pius directly cites this Pauline passage.[3] Pius's encyclical was a formative document behind Vatican II's *Dogmatic Constitution on the Church* (1964) – *Lumen Gentium*. Pius's encyclical, perhaps even more than *Lumen Gentium*, provides a pneumatological vista from which the doctrine of Mary and the saints that I have been advancing might be developed. In *Mystici Corporis*, one may even say that women saints and Mary are *necessary* for the full development of Christ's body, for the full description of any Christology. Paul's 'lack' in Christ that must be completed is here rooted in the lives and bodies that have formed, and continue to form, Christ's body, the church. The notion of the incarnation as complete and finished, in both human and divine terms, is called into question by Pius XII, such that Irigaray's critique can be met in a creative ecclesiological fashion. This in no way suggests that the rereading of the figures of Mary and female (and male) saints as advocated in this book would find support from Pius XII. Nevertheless, such readings have already begun and if the Christian community does not engage with them seriously it risks perpetuating an idolatrous hommosexuate symbolic.[4]

In *Mystici Corporis* Pius reflects on Paul's teaching of the Body of Christ (in Romans, Corinthians, Galatians and Ephesians) in which all the members of Christ's body are *organically related* to each other and *dependent* on the Head, Christ, and are *animated* by His Spirit, the Holy Spirit. Pius follows a typical western trinitarian taxonomy and its hierarchical ecclesiology. There is no Marian body and no decentring of a gendered trinity. In a very uni-directional fashion Pius writes that 'after Christ's glorification on the cross, His Spirit is communicated to the Church in an abundant outpouring, so that the Church and each of its members may become daily more and more like to our Saviour'.[5] However, Pius goes on to develop this idea in a startling fashion:

> This communication of the Spirit of Christ is the channel through which all the gifts, powers, and extraordinary graces found super-abundantly in the Head as in their source flow into all the members of the Church, and are perfected daily in them according to the place they hold in the Mystical Body of Jesus Christ. *Thus the Church becomes, as it were, the filling out and the complement of the Redeemer, while Christ in a sense attains through the Church a fullness in all things.*[6]

The unilateral dependence of the church on Christ is now turned around: the church is a filling out and complement to the redeemer. The 'as it were' simply checks against making a straightforward identity claim between the divine life and the church on earth. The process of our becoming more like Christ is made less straight forward. It is less an approximation to a fixed standard that is set solidly above time and history, a male celibate resolutely denying women, but a communal process negotiated with the help of the Holy Spirit through the vicissitudes of history, so that the church may fill out and complement the Redeemer. Then, not only male celibates, but sexually active women, caring fathers, founders of religious orders, women painters and architects, and male nurses might also fill out and co-create Christ. To fill out and complement Christ is to point to a lack, to a refuse a closure on the incarnation, such that both women and men might now be co-redeemers. Mary, a companion, mother, daughter, friend, lover and queen of heaven, is Co-Redeemer, pre-eminent amongst all creation.

That the church, in Mary, its saints, sacraments and holiness might be called Co-Redeemer is clearly the import of the second qualification, 'in a sense', which allows that Christ's fullness is actually dependent on the church: 'while Christ in a sense attains through the Church a fullness in all things'. If Christ's fullness is really so dependent on the church, as *Mystici Corporis* and Paul make clear, then the doctrines of the trinity and church that I have been developing are not perhaps entirely repressed within the tradition.

To counter any impression of eisegesis, I want to turn briefly to the Italian Jesuit Paulo Molinari's exegesis of Pius XII's *Mystici Corporis*. Molinari's commentary is especially important as he was Peritus (theological advisor) to the Theological Commission of Vatican II and served as Secretary (and drafter) to the special Subcommission which was responsible for Chapter 7 of *Lumen Gentium*, on the saints and the eschatological nature of the church. In his book, *Saints: Their Place in the Church*, Molinari takes the passage cited above from *Mystici Corporis* to argue two points: first, that the *humanity* of Christ is being filled out and complemented in the human lives of those called 'saints'; and, secondly, that in those lives *the divine work of redemption is continued, fulfilled and perfected*.

Working from a Thomistic anthropology, Molinari suggests that Pius's encyclical must imply that the humanity of Jesus Christ is incomplete, just as all men and women are incomplete in that they are limited and open to perfection:

> If, then, by reason of his metaphysical make-up every man, inasmuch as he is an individual being, can and must receive from other men and be completed by them; so, too, the man Jesus Christ, inasmuch as He is truly man and therefore an individual human being, can and must receive from other men and be completed by them. If, by reason of this same constitution, a man cannot, as an individual, live all the concrete modes in which the specific perfection of human nature can exist, and can realize the maximum of human perfection only in union with other men, mutually complementing one another, then not even the man Jesus Christ, inasmuch as He is an individual, can realize by Himself, in His humanity, all the concrete modes in which specific perfection can exist.[7]

Leaving aside Molinari's Thomism, his claim is clear: humans are constructed through relations; they are therefore dependent on each other;
and even Jesus Christ is constituted through dependent relations on
others in human terms (and in divine terms through subsistent relations
with the Spirit and Father).[8] (This anthropology is complemented and
filled out by the object relations so fundamental to Freudian psychoanalysis.) However, Molinari is also saying that the description of who
Christ is, in his human perfection, is always necessarily a description
of the women and men (called the saints) that are being brought into
holiness through the Holy Spirit. Hence, the description of the humanity of Christ is never complete, and the lives of Eve, Sarah, Anne,
Mary, Priscilla, Joan of Arc, Hildegard of Bingen, Bridget of Sweden,
Dorothy Day of New York, Mother Theresa of Calcutta and many
others are necessary in describing Christ's redeemed humanity. Without
these women, Christ's humanity is incomplete. This cross-gendered
humanity, without erasing the specificity of the biologically male Jesus
Christ, is important. It deconstructs the question 'can a male saviour
save women?' into further questions: can salvation be possible without
women's genealogies, and has the Christian church failed to save its
Redeemer from hommosexuate representation, such that it has obscured
the on-going process of redemption? Molinari's concerns are not with
gendered saints, but with a doctrine of Jesus Christ and the church
which allows the historically specific person, Jesus Christ, to be also
the corporate mystical body, the church.[9]

In my own argument, I sought to show that the story of Jesus cannot
be told without the stories of those women and men of Israel, and even
before them the story of Adam and Eve. Neither could Jesus' story be
told without the stories of Mary, the women by the cross, and the
stories of the many lives that mediate God's action in history. My
purpose, like that of Molinari's, is to question the incarnation as an act
of closure, a once-and-for-all event, but instead to see it is a way of
reconstruing all other events together, in a harmony, such that they are
genuinely interdependent and constantly illuminate each other in new
ways. All signs: theology, liturgy, art, music, storytelling the lives of
saints, ethics, and so on, are involved in this reconstitution. The boundaries of traditional disciplines are also likely to be called into question,
as will many of the methodologies employed. Closure on these questions
is impossible until the eschaton. If the story of Sarah is repressed or

occluded, then the story of Jesus Christ is likewise misrepresented and incomplete. If the liturgy does not celebrate both women and men, both in terms of the human and divine, then the liturgy cannot be the praise of God by the entire church. Neither is it simply a matter of politically correct liturgies, as I have already indicated. Inclusivism, or equalism, is not what is at stake, but the creation of a new ecclesiological economy of redeeming signs, so that the Marian body of Christ might provide a different story. The story will not sound the same.

Rushdie relentlessly shows that the telling of a story is always the repression of another, so that we should be clear that we are never in possession of the full story. He also shows that the telling of any one character's story is always then the telling of the stories of their maternal and paternal genealogies, the stories of their lovers, friends and secret desires, and the telling of their divine imaginary. The linguistic membranes that distinguish character are fluid, permeable, osmotic and open-ended. Rushdie also shows that differing constructions of the divine generate different social patterns, and that the gender of these constructions are vital to the resultant practices, even though there is never any predictability to either constructions or practices. Our study of artists (Rublev and Sahi) illustrated this in relation to visual culture, such that the visualizing of the incarnation requires the creative and critical interaction with all types of human picturing, be it the written text (Genesis 18 or John 1) or the artistic typologies of the Jewish, Russian and Hindu traditions. Through Rushdie we saw the danger of essentializing gender either in human or divine terms, a problem which Irigaray is not always able to avoid, and with it we saw the difficulty of offering any stable portrayal of the divine or human in gender terms, while also recognizing the inevitability and even necessity of such portrayal. Christians require a never-ending vigilance regarding their construal of the divine and women and men.

Telling the story of Jesus Christ, as I argued in the opening chapters, is a story that explicitly refuses matricide, for this son does not repress or deny his dependence upon this mother, but brings into the semiotic world a different configuration of how the real, the imaginary and symbolic might look. There is no male hero who stands alone, but one whose mother is hailed as Co-Redeemer, along with his mixed rag-bag of 'friends', those proclaimed as saints – and those whose memories have no clear herstory. There is no mono-theism, no single patriarchal heavenly Father, who is sole origin and controller of everything, but instead perichoretic subsistent relations of indwelling love and forgiveness that are displayed in this trinitarian story of God's incarnation. The trinitarian life of God need not be one in which a Father–Son team occlude the maternal or feminine. Rather, this trinitarian 'jewel' requires a participation in charity and hope such that the light of created women and men together illuminates the divine darkness and allows the splendour of divine light to shine through specific gendered bodies in their particularity, interrelations and indwelling love.

This takes us back to Molinari's second point: that the divine salvific work of Christ is continued through the saints. Recalling Pius's point that 'Christ in a sense attains through the Church a fullness in all things', Molinari explains this sentence through Pius's recognition of the activity of the Holy Spirit that continues the work of redemption. Molinari is far from guarded when he explicitly claims that it is through human lives of holiness that salvation is developed, consolidated and amplified. This is what belonging to the mystical body of Christ implies. God

> wants us to be associated with his salvific work, contributing to it by applying His redemptive merits to individual human persons. By living and working in His members, through His Spirit, He extends and prolongs His life and activity among men through time and space. His aim is to live in His members those concrete forms of existence, activity, and love which His individual nature could not realize, and in this way *complete His salvific work, develop it, consolidate and amplify it extensively and intensively*.[10]

Here Molinari indicates that the lives of the saints actually develop, consolidate and amplify the redemptive process initiated in Jesus such that 'co-redeemers' would be an entirely apt term, even though Molinari does not use it himself. However, Molinari employs Colossians 1.24 to develop his own argument that the lives of holiness lived by women and men who suffer for Christ's sake allow 'Christ Himself the possibility of *living His Passion in a new form*, namely, according to the peculiar modalities in which only this person can live it'.[11] Leaving aside the unquestioned valorization of suffering and its gender-related problems,[12] Molinari nevertheless indicates that not only the human nature of Christ is completed within the saints but also the divine mission of redemption. In this sense, our reception of certain graces is to be attributed to the fact that this or that pre-eminent member has or is co-operating effectively with Christ for our benefit. Without his co-operation, without his personal contribution of work, prayer and suffering, we would not have been accorded what we have in fact received.[13]

What is so important about the two points established by Molinari is that together they bring into question a closure of the incarnation, both in human and divine terms. Molinari shows how the *human* person of Jesus is never complete until the eschaton, and only comes to completion in the process of human becoming – both male and female. Molinari also shows that *divine* redemption, while always gift, is also a process that is utterly dependent on human cooperation, so that ordinary women and men become co-redeemers. Such a process is publicly recognized and signified in the making of saints, even if the process of making saints and the types of saints produced is open to many critical questions.[14]

For all this, Molinari's study, like Pius's encyclical upon which it expands, displays a hommosexuate configuration. The church is only ever the 'Body of Christ', never the Marian church, nor construed by the many alternative metaphors generated within the tradition. The church is always the spotless nuptial virgin with Christ as its groom, allowing his or the Father's will to take control over the feminine body so that it may serve 'him', especially through suffering for him.[15] *Lumen Gentium* at least began to offer resources to correct some of these imbalances: by inserting its reflections on Mary as the last chapter on the church, thus showing how Mary defined the church and was its primary archetype; and in its multiple employment of various biblical and patristic images of the church, and therefore its decentring of any one single metaphor for the church and the process of redemption.[16] Furthermore, Molinari's distinctions between Jesus' human nature and his carrying out the work of divine redemption are problematic, for the incarnation is about the inseparability of the two, without confusion and mixture. If the human person isn't complete then neither is divine embodiment which only works through the human persons. This distinction in Molinari's work might reflect a deeper metaphysical anxiety, that is overcome in Molinari's concern to rehabilitate the saints as mediators of the divine. Molinari is also gender blind to the politics of sainthood, both in terms of the process of canonization (exalting uncritically the 'heroic virtues') and the types of figures that are typically exalted. One could extend this list of criticisms (especially in regard to Pius XII), but what I have tried to show by focussing on their work is that, regardless of such criticism, their writings mediate the recovery of powerful traditions that might serve to dismantle the hommosexuate economy by which Christianity is so often portrayed. There is no easy clarity, no politically correct redeemed, or unambiguous way forward, only the patient, slow working together as a community that is both fallen and redeemed. Dismantling a hommosexuate economy facilities very different language, metaphors and constructions, such that the creed 'from the trinitarian nexus to its "political apparatus"' the church (as Kristeva puts it) might be a very different social, psychic and divine reality.[17]

It may be that Irigaray's *'wedding between the spirit and the bride'* is beginning to take place.[18] It certainly might take place in a church that celebrated both women and men, not encoded within a hommosexuate economy of signs. It might take place in a church which celebrated and encouraged the flourishing of female genealogies within its symbolic world: women as mothers to daughters, as lovers to other women, and as friends to each other; women as artists, authors and architects; women who are priests, queens and prophets. Mary and the saints provide just these symbolic possibilities. The Catholic Church has at least nurtured the possibility of the reclamation of such symbolic traditions, even if they have been preserved overwhelmingly within patriarchal patterns. When Irigaray laments, 'there is no *woman* God, no female trinity: mother, daughter, spirit', she is surely right to mourn the lack of female genealogy – and to realize that without the divine, human subjectivities, both male and female, cannot flourish.[19] However, I have argued that in Christianity there should not be a 'man God' nor a 'woman God', for both constitute idolatry. At the same time, the representation of the trinity cannot escape sexuate symbolization, such that the church must remain ever vigilant against a double closure: either making God male or female or denying that both male and female might equally, but *differently*, represent God's redeeming activity in history. If the church turns its signs into fixed essences, an ahistorical idolatry follows.

Signs, as we have seen throughout this book, have no essence or fixed stability. Sahi's liberating Mary might also be a patriarchal mother; or his inculturated *trimūrti*-trinity might also be the cause of (false) scandal, even litigation, to some Hindus and Christians. His redemption of Sarah from the Genesis 18 narrative is able to transform the shape of the narrative bringing to the fore all sorts of unforeseen and unpredictable motifs. Margaret Argyle's female *Christa* refuses a single gendered body to represent the divine, calling the church's political practices into question, while at the same time she is criticized by some feminists as perpetuating male fantasy by placing a woman on the Cross within bleeding vaginal lips. Signs interpret other signs, in never-ending configurations, for history is open and full of surprises. Rublev's divine threesome, gracefully transmuting creation in the eucharistic elements, while also transforming Genesis 18, can mask a genocidal logic regarding the Jewish figures of the original narrative, especially Jewish women. Rublev, Sahi, Argyle, all wrestle with signs which will not stay still, signs which can become the source of our redemption or the place of entrapment, matricide and genocide. Rushdie, perhaps most of all, showed us the fate of those who essentialized signs: an idolatrous worship of false gods – human egotism, in both male and female forms, various and chimerical, both personal and political. If all signs are polyvalent, then little wonder that the great 'crown jewel of theological sophistication', the symbol of the living God, the sign of redemption, the trinity, can also turn into a hommosexuate rod of slavery and domination regarding gender and its cultural patterning. Without a never-ending vigilance, the church might fall into the greatest error it has stubbornly resisted: worshipping a false god of man's creation.

And yet, God subjected the divine life to us, in birth, blood, wood, death and food, such that men and women creating love together might allow flesh to reflect the darkness of divine light. If Rublev turned text into icon, let me finish with Rublev sculpted into poetry by Rowan Williams:

Rublev

One day, God walked in, pale from the grey steppe,
slit-eyed against the wind, and stopped,
said, Colour me, breathe your blood into my mouth.

I said, Here is the blood of all our people,
these are their bruises, blue and purple,
gold, brown, and pale green wash of death.

These (god) are the chromatic pains of flesh,
I said, I trust I make you blush,
O I shall stain you with the scars of birth

For ever. I shall root you in the wood,
under the sun shall bake you bread
of beechmast, never let you forth

To the white desert, to the starving sand.
But we shall sit and speak around
one table, share one food, one earth.[20]

Bibliography

Abbott, Walter M. (ed.), *The Documents of Vatican II*, New York: Guild Press 1966.

Achebe, Chinua, *Things Fall Apart*, African Trilogy, London: Picador 1988.

Achtiemer, Elizabeth, 'Exchanging God for "No Gods": A Discussion of Female Language for God', *Speaking the Christian God*, ed. Alvin Kimel Jnr, pp. 1–16.

Akhtar, Shabbir, *Be Careful with Muhammed! The Salman Rushdie Affair*, London: Bellew Publishing 1989.

Allen, Sister Prudence, RSM, *The Concept of Woman: The Aristotelian Revolution 750 BC–AD 1250*, Quebec: Eden Press 1985.

Amaladoss, M., T. T. John and G. Gispert-Sauch (eds), *Theologizing in India*, Bangalore: Theological Publications of India 1981.

Appignanesi, Lisa and Sarah Maitland (eds), *The Rushdie File*, London: Fourth Estate 1989.

Aquinas, Thomas, *Summa Contra Gentiles*, tr. English Dominicans, London: Burns, Oates & Washbourne 1927.

— *Summa Theologiae*, London: Blackfriars/Eyre & Spottiswoode; New York: McGraw-Hill Book Co. 1976.

Arberry, Arthur J. (tr.), *The Koral Interpreted*, New York: Oxford University Press 1964.

Argyle, Margaret, 'Interview with Margaret Argyle' (with Julie Clague), *Theology and Sexuality*, 1995, pp. 57–68.

Asad, Muhammad, *The Message of the Qur'an*, tr. and explained by Muhammad Asad, Gibraltar: Dar Al-Andalus 1980.

Asad, Talal, *Genealogies of Religion: Discipline and Reasons of Power in Christianity and Islam*, Baltimore: Johns Hopkins University Press 1989.

Attwater, Donald, *Dictionary of Saints*, 2nd edn, London: Penguin 1983.

Auerbach, Erich, *Mimesis: The Representation of Reality in Western Literature*, Princeton: Princeton University Press 1953.

Augustine, St, *Confessions*, tr. R. S. Pine-Coffin, Harmondsworth: Penguin 1961.

— *The Trinity*, The Fathers of the Church, Vol. 45, Washington DC: Catholic University Press of America 1963.

Austen, R. W. J., 'Islam and the Feminine', *Islam in the Modern World*, ed. Denis MacEoin and Ahmed Al-Shahi, New York: Croom Helm 1983, pp. 30–43.

Babb, Lawrence A., *The Divine Hierarchy: Popular Hinduism in Central India*, New York: Columbia University Press 1975.

Baker, Derek (ed.), *Medieval Women*, Oxford: Blackwell 1978.

Balasuriya, Tissa, *Mary and Human Liberation: The Story and the Text*, ed. Helen Stanton, London: Mowbray 1977.

Beane, Wendell Charles, *Myth, Cult, Symbols in Śākta Hinduism: A Study of the Indian Mother Goddess*, Leiden: Brill 1977.

Beattie, Tina, *Rediscovering Mary: Insights from the Gospels*, Kent: Burns & Oates 1995.

— 'Sexuality and the Resurrection of the Body: Reflections in the Hall of Mirrors', *Resurrection Reconsidered*, ed. D'Costa, 1996, pp. 135–49.

— 'Carnal Love and Spiritual Imagination: Can Luce Irigaray and John Paul II Come Together?' *Sex These Days: Essays on Theology, Sexuality and Society*, eds Jon Davies and Gerard Loughlin, Sheffield: Sheffield Academic Press 1997, pp. 160–83.

— 'A Man and Three Women – Hans, Adrienne, Mary and Luce', *New Blackfriars* 79, 924, 1998, pp. 97–105.

— *God's Mother, Eve's Advocate: A Gynocentric Refiguration of Marian Symbolism in Engagement with Luce Irigaray*, CCSRG Monograph Series, No. 3, Bristol: University of Bristol 1999.

Beckett, Samuel, *Waiting for Godot*, London: Faber & Faber 1956.

Bell, Rudolph, *Holy Anorexia*, Chicago: Chicago University Press 1985.

Berry, Phillipa, 'The Burning Glass: Paradoxes of Feminist Revelation in Speculum', *Engaging with Irigaray: Feminist Philosophy and Modern European Thought*, eds Carolyn Burke, Naomi Schor and Margaret Whitford, New York: Columbia University Press 1994, pp. 229–46.

— 'Kristeva's Feminist Refiguring of the Gift', *Post-Secular Philosophy*, ed. Phillip Blond, 1998, pp. 318–33.

— and Andrew Wernick (eds), *Shadow of Spirit: Postmodernism and Religion*, London: Routledge 1992.

Bingemer, Maria Clara, 'Reflections on the Trinity', *Through her Eyes: Women's Theology from Latin America*, ed. E. Tamez, New York: Orbis 1989, pp. 56–80.

Blond, Phillip (ed.), *Post-Secular Philosophy: Between Philosophy and Theology*, London: Routledge 1998.

Boff, Leonardo, *Trinity and Society*, tr. Paul Burns, London: Burns & Oates 1988 [1986].

Børresen, Kari Elisabeth, *Subordination and Equivalence: The Nature and Role of Women in Augustine and Thomas Aquinas*, Lanham, Maryland: University Press of America 1981.

Bosch, David, *Transforming Mission: Paradigm Shifts in Theology of Mission*, New York: Orbis 1991.

Bourbon-Parma-van Oranje Nassau, Irene de, 'What Do I Think of When I Say the "Our Father"?', *Concilium*, 1981, pp. 117–19.

Brennan, Timothy, *Salman Rushdie and the Third World*, London: Macmillan 1989.

Brock, Sebastian P., 'The Holy Spirit as Feminine in Early Syriac Literature', *After Eve*, ed. Janet Martin Soskice, London: Marshal Pickering 1990, pp. 73–88.

Brown, Raymond E., *The Gospel according to John. I–XII*, London: Geoffrey Chapman 1971.

— *The Gospel according to John. XIII–XXI*, London: Geoffrey Chapman 1971.

— *The Community of the Beloved Disciple*, London: Geoffrey Chapman 1979.

Buby, Bertrand, *Mary of Galillee*, Vol. 3, *The Marian Heritage of the Early Church*, New York: Alban House 1996.

Buckley, J. J., *Female Fault and Fulfilment in Gnosticism*, Chapel Hill: University of North Carolina Press 1986.

Bultmann, Rudolf, *The Gospel of John: A Commentary*, tr. G. R. Beasley-Murray et al, Oxford: Blackwell 1971.

Burke, Carolyn, Naomi Schor and Margaret Whitford (eds), *Engaging with Irigaray: Feminist Philosophy and Modern European Thought*, New York: Columbia University Press 1994.

Burnham, Fredrick (ed.), *Postmodern Theology: Christian Faith in a Pluralistic World*, San Francisco: Harper & Row 1980.

Burrell, David, *Aquinas: God and Action*, London: Routledge & Kegan Paul 1979.

— *Knowing the Unknowable God: Ibn-Sina, Maimonides, Aquinas*, Notre Dame: Notre Dame University Press 1986.

Butler, John F., *Christian Art in India*, Madras: Christian Literature Society 1986.

Butler, Judith, *Gender Trouble*, London: Routledge 1990.

Bynum, Caroline Walker, *Jesus as Mother: Studies in the Spirituality of the High Middle Ages*, Berkley: University of California Press 1982.

— *Fragmentation and Redemption: Essays on Gender and the Human Body in Medieval Religion*, New York: Zone Books 1991.

— *The Resurrection of the Body in Western Christianity, 200–1336*, New York: Columbia University Press 1995.

— Stevan Harrell and Paula Richman (eds), *Gender and Religion: On the Complexity of Symbols*, Boston: Beacon Press 1986.

Caputo, John, *The Prayers and Tears of Jacques Derrida: Religion without Religion*, Bloomington, Indiana: Indiana University Press 1997.

Carr, Anne and Elizabeth Schüssler Fiorenza, *The Special Nature of Women?*, *Concilium*, 1991.

Catechism of the Catholic Church, London: Geoffrey Chapman 1994.

Certeau, Michel de, *The Mystic Fable*, Vol. 1, tr. Michael B. Smith, *The Sixteenth and Seventeenth Centuries*, Chicago: Chicago University Press 1992 [1982].

Chanter, Tina, *Ethics of Eros: Irigaray's Rewriting of the Philosophers*, London: Routledge 1994.

Charlesworth, James Hamilton (ed. and tr.), *The Odes of Solomon*, Oxford: Clarendon Press 1973.

Chopp, Rebecca, 'From Patriarchy into Freedom: A Conversation between American Feminist Theology and French Feminism', *Transfigurations: Theology and the French Feminists*, ed. Maggie Kim et al., 1993, pp. 31–48.

Clément, Catherine, *Opera, or the Undoing of Women*, tr. Betsy Wing, London: Virago Press 1989 [1988].

Coakley, Sarah, 'Gender and Knowledge in Western Philosophy: The "Man of Reason" and the "Feminine Other" in Enlightenment Thought', ed. Anne Carr and Elizabeth Schüssler Fiorenza, *The Special Nature of Women?*, *Concilium*, 1991, pp. 75–84.

Cohn-Sherbok, Dan, *The Salman Rushdie Controversy in Interreligious Dialogue*, Lampeter, Lewiston: Edwin Mellen Press 1990.

Congar, Yves, *I Believe in the Holy Spirit*, tr. David Smith, 3 vols, London: Geoffrey Chapman 1983 [1979, 1980].

Contemplating Icons: An Introduction to Icons and Prayer, a video from St Paul Multimedia Productions, UK, 1989.

Cornille, Catherine, *The Guru in Indian Catholicism*, Louvain: Peeters Press 1991.

Craven, Roy C., *A Concise History of Indian Art*, London: Thames & Hudson 1976.

Cunningham, David, *These Three Are One: The Practice of Trinitarian Theology*, Oxford: Blackwell 1998.

Daly, Mary, *Beyond God the Father*, Boston: Beacon 1973.

Davies, Jon and Gerard Loughlin (eds), *Sex These Days: Essays on Theology, Sexuality and Society*, Sheffield: Sheffield Academic Press 1997.

D'Costa, Gavin, 'A Hindu Christianity', *The Tablet*, 10 December 1983, pp. 1203–4.

— (ed.), *Christian Uniqueness Reconsidered*, New York: Orbis 1990.
— 'Satanic Discourse and the Clash of Faiths: "The Satanic Verses" in British Society', *New Blackfriars*, 1990, pp. 418–32.
— 'How Far Can an Artist Go?', *The Tablet*, 23/30 December 1995, pp. 1648–9.
— 'One Covenant or Many Covenants? Towards a Theology of Christian-Jewish Relations', *Readings in Modern Theology*, ed. Robin Gill, London: SPCK 1995, pp. 173–85.
— (ed.), *Resurrection Reconsidered*, Oxford: Oneworld 1996.
— *The Meeting of Religions and the Trinity*, New York: Orbis; Edinburgh: T&T Clark 2000.
— 'Church and Sacraments', *Blackwell Companion to Theology*, ed. Gareth Jones, Oxford: Blackwell forthcoming.
de Lubac, Henri, *The Church: Paradox and Mystery*, tr. James R. Dunne, Shannon: Ecclesia Press 1969.
Denzinger, Heinrich, *Enchiridion symbolorum: Definitionum et declarationum de rebus fidei et morum*, 32nd edn, Barcinone: Herder 1963.
Derrida, Jacques, *Of Grammatology*, tr. Gayatri Chakrovorty Spivak, Baltimore: Johns Hopkins University Press 1976 [1967].
DiCenso, James J., *The Other Freud: Religion, Culture and Psychoanalysis*, London: Routledge 1999.
DiNoia, Joe, Review of LaCugna, *God for us*, *Modern Theology* 9, 2, 1993, pp. 214–16.
Dissanayake, Wimal, 'Towards a Decolonized English: South Asian Creativity in Fiction', *World Englishes* 2, 1985, pp. 233–42.
Dogra, Bharat, *Towards a Liberation Theology of Hinduism*, publication details not given with circulated manuscript.
Dunn, J. D. G., *Jesus and the Spirit*, London: SCM Press 1975.

Eck, Diana and Devalai Jain (eds), *Speaking of Faith: Global Perspectives on Women, Religions and Social Change*, Philadelphia: New Society Publications 1987.
Eliade, M. (editor-in-chief), *The Encyclopedia of Religion*, London: Macmillan 1987.
Eliot, T. S., *Collected Poems 1909–62*, London: Faber & Faber 1963.
Endo, Shusaku, *Silence*, tr. William Johnston, London: Penguin 1976.

Fergusson, James, *Tree and Serpent Worship or Illustrations of Mythology and Art in India in the First to Fourth Centuries after Christ*, Delhi: Indological Book House 1971.
Fleck, Andrew, 'Crusoe's Shadow: Christianity, Colonization and the Other', *Historicizing Christian Encounters with the Other*, ed. John C. Hawley, 1998, pp. 74–89.

Ford, David F. (ed.), *The Modern Theologians*, 2nd edn, Oxford: Blackwell 1997.

Frei, Hans W., *The Eclipse of Biblical Narrative: A Study in Eighteenth and Nineteenth Century Hermeneutics*, New Haven: Yale University Press 1974.

Freud, S., All references, except when otherwise stated, to *The Standard Edition of the Complete Psychological Works of Sigmund Freud*, 24 vols, ed. and tr. James Strachey, in collaboration with Anna Freud, assisted by Alix Strachey and Alan Tyson, London: Hogarth and the Institute of Psychoanalysis 1953–74:

— *Jokes and the Relationship to the Unconscious*, 1905, Vol. 8.

— *Obsessive Actions and Religious Practices*, 1907, Vol. 9, pp. 115–27.

— *Totem and Taboo*, 1913, Vol. 13, pp. 1–161.

— *Introductory Lectures on Psychoanalysis*, 1916–17, Vols 15 and 16.

— *The Ego and the Id*, 1923, Vol. 19, pp. 1–69.

— *Moses and Monotheism*, 1939, Vol. 23, pp. 1–138.

Friedman, Sandra and Alexander Irwin, 'Christian Feminism, Eros and Power in Right Relation', *Christian Perspectives on Sexuality and Gender*, ed. Adrian Thatcher and Elizabeth Stuart, Leominster: Gracewing 1996, pp. 152–67.

Frye, Roland M., 'Language for God and Feminist Language: Problems and Principles', *Speaking the Christian God*, ed. Kimel, 1992, pp. 17–43.

Fuller, Reginald C., Leonard Johnstone and Conleath Kearns (eds), *A New Catholic Commentary on Holy Scripture*, London: Nelson 1969.

Gallop, Jane, *Feminism and Psychoanalysis: The Daughter's Seduction*, London: Macmillan 1982.

Gebara, Ivone and Maria Clara Bingemer, *Mary: Mother of God, Mother of the Poor*, tr. Philip Berryman, London: Burns & Oates 1989 [1987].

Gill, Robin (ed.), *Readings in Modern Theology*, London: SPCK 1995.

Gispert-Sauch, George, 'Asian Theology', *The Modern Theologians*, ed. Ford, 1997, pp. 455–76.

Gray, J., 'Legacy of Canaan', *Vetus Testamentum*, Supplement, 1965, pp. 156–8.

Gray, Janette, 'Celibacy These Days', *Sex These Days*, ed. Davies and Loughlin, 1997, pp. 141–59.

— *Sexual Subversions: Three French Feminists*, Boston/Sydney: Allen & Unwin 1990.

Grosz, Elizabeth, *Jacques Lacan: A Feminist Introduction*, London: Routledge 1990.

Guillaume, A., *Islam*, London: Penguin 1954.

Gunton, Colin, 'Proetus and Procrustes: A Study in the Dialectic of Language in Disagreement with Sallie McFague', *Speaking the Christian God*, ed. Kimel, 1992, pp. 65–80.

— *The One, the Three and the Many: God, Creation and the Culture of Modernity*, Cambridge: Cambridge University Press 1993.

Hacker, Paul, *Kleine Schriften*, ed. Lambert von Schmithausen, Weisbaden: Steiner 1978.
— *Theological Foundations of Evangelization*, St Augustin: Steyler 1980.
Halbfass, Wilhelm, *India and Europe: An Essay in Understanding*, Albany, New York: State University of New York 1988.
Hamerton-Kelly, R., *God the Father: Theology and Patriarchy in the Teaching of Jesus*, Philadelphia: Fortress Press 1979.
Hampson, Daphne, *Theology and Feminism*, Oxford: Blackwell 1990.
Hamson, Verna, 'Perichoresis in the Greek Fathers', *St Vladimir's Theological Quarterly* 35, 1991, pp. 53–67.
Hanson, A. T., *Jesus Christ in the Old Testament*, London: SPCK 1965.
Hargreaves, Cecil and Christopher Duraising (eds), *India's Search for Reality and the Relevance of the Gospel of John*, Delhi: ISPCK 1975.
Harris, J. R. and A. Mingana (eds and tr.), *The Odes and Psalms of Solomon*, 2 vols, Manchester: Manchester University Press 1916, 1920.
Harrison, Beverly Wildung and Carter Heyward, 'Pain and Pleasure: Avoiding the Confusions of Christian Tradition', *Sexuality and the Sacred: Sources for Theological Reflection*, eds James B. Nelson and Sandra P. Longfellow, Louisville, Kentucky: Westminster/John Knox Press 1994, pp. 120–31.
Harrison, Peter, *'Religion' and the Religions in the English Enlightenment*, Cambridge: Cambridge University Press 1990.
Harvey, Sarah Ashbrook, *Asceticism and Society in Crisis: John of Ephesus and the 'Lives of the Eastern Saints'*, Berkley: University of California 1990.
— 'Feminine Imagery for the Divine: The Holy Spirit, the Odes of Solomon and Early Syriac Tradition', *St Vladimir's Theological Quarterly* 37, 2/3, 1993, pp. 111–39.
— and Sebastian P. Brock, *Holy Women of the Syrian Orient*, tr. & intro., Berkley: University of California 1987.
Hassan, Hassan Ibrahim, *Islam: A Religious, Political, Social and Economic Study*, Beirut: Khuyats 1967.
Havell, E. B., *Indian Sculpture and Painting*, London: John Murray 1928.
Hawley, John C. (ed.), *Historicizing Christian Encounters with the Other*, London: Macmillan 1998.
Hijab, Nadia, 'Nadia Hijab Speaks on Women in the Arab World', *Connections: An International Women's Quarterly* 28, 1988–9, pp. 79–85.
Hoskyns, Edward, 'Genesis 1–3 and St John's Gospel', *Journal of Theological Studies*, 1920, pp. 210–18.
Hughes, Robert, *The Shock of the New: Art and the Century of Change*, London: BBC 1980.

Huzinga, John, *The Waning of the Middle Ages: A Study of the Forms of Life, Thought and Art in France and the Netherlands in the XIVth and XVth Centuries*, New York: Doubleday 1956.

ibn Ally, Muhammad Mashuq, 'Stranger Exiled from Home', *Rushdie Controversy*, ed. Dan Cohn-Sherbok, 1990, pp. 131–49.
Irigaray, Luce, *Speculum of the Other Woman*, tr. Gillian C. Gill, Ithaca: Cornell University Press, 1985 [1974].
— *This Sex Which Is Not One*, tr. Catherine Porter and Carolyn Burke, Ithaca: Cornell University Press 1985 [1977].
— *The Irigaray Reader*, ed. Margaret Whitford, Oxford: Blackwell 1991.
— *Marine Lover of Friedrich Nietzche*, tr. Gillian C. Gill, New York: Columbia University Press 1991.
— *An Ethics of Sexual Difference*, tr. Gillian C. Gill and Carolyn Burke, London: Athlone Press 1993 [1984].
— *Je, Tu, Nous – Towards a Culture of Difference*, tr. Alison Martin, New York: Routledge 1993 [1990].
— *Sexes and Genealogies*, tr. Gillian C. Gill, New York: Columbia University Press, 1993 [1987].
— *Thinking the Difference*, tr. Karen Montin, London: Athlone Press 1994 [1989].
— 'Equal to Whom?', *The Postmodern God*, ed. Ward, tr. Robert L. Mazzola, 1997, pp. 198–213.
Ishaq, Ibn, *The Life of Muhammed*, tr. A. Guillaume, Oxford: Oxford University Press 1955.

Jantzen, Grace M., 'Luce Irigaray (b. 1930): Introduction', *Postmodern God*, ed. Ward, 1997, pp. 191–7.
— *Becoming Divine: Towards a Feminist Philosophy of Religion*, Manchester: Manchester University Press 1999.
Johnson, Elizabeth A., *She Who Is: The Mystery of God in Feminist Theological Discourse*, New York: Crossroad 1995.
— *Friends of God and Prophets: A Feminist Theological Reading of the Communion of Saints*, London: SCM Press 1998.
Johnston, George, *The Spirit-Paraclete in the Gospel of John*, Cambridge: Cambridge University Press 1970.
Jones, Ernst, *Sigmund Freud: Life and Works*, 3 vols, London/New York: Hogarth Press 1953–7.
Jones, L. Gregory and Stephen E. Fowl (eds), *Rethinking Metaphysics*, Oxford: Blackwell 1995.
Jones, R. A., 'Writing the Body: Towards an Understanding of Ecriture Feminine', *Feminist Studies* 7, 1, 1981, pp. 250–7.

Kallistos, Bishop of Diokleia, 'No New Dogmas, Please', *The Tablet* 17 January 1998, pp. 93–4.

Kasper, Walter, *The God of Jesus Christ*, tr. Matthew J. O'Connell, London: SCM Press 1984 [1982].

Kemp, Eric Waldron, *Canonization and Authority in the Western Church*, Oxford: Oxford University Press 1948.

Kierkegaard, Søren, *Fear and Trembling: A Dialectical Lyric*, tr. Robert Payne, London: Oxford University Press 1939.

Kim, Maggie C. W., Susan M. St Ville and Susan M. Simoniatis (eds), *Transfigurations: Theology and the French Feminists*, Minneapolis: Fortress Press 1993.

Kimel Jnr, Alvin (ed.), *Speaking the Christian God: The Holy Trinity and the Challenge of Feminism*, Grand Rapids, Michigan: Eerdmans 1992.

Kinsley, David, *The Sword and the Flute: Kālī and Krishna, Dark Visions of the Terrible and the Sublime in Hindu Mythology*, Berkley: University of California Press 1975.

Kirschner, Teresa J., 'Encounter and Assimilation of the Other in *Arauco domando* and *La Araucana* by Lope de Vega', *Historicizing Christian Encounters with the Other*, ed. Hawley, 1998, pp. 33–44.

Kopf, David, *The Brāhmo Samāj and the Shaping of the Modern Indian Mind*, Princeton: Princeton University Press 1979.

Kramrisch, Stella, *The Art of India*, London: Phaidon 1965.

Kristeva, Julia, *The Kristeva Reader*, ed. Toril Moi, Oxford: Blackwell 1986.

— *In the Beginning Was Love: Faith and Psychoanalysis*, tr. Arthur Goldhammer, New York: Columbia University Press 1987 [1985].

— *Tales of Love*, tr. Leon S. Roudiez, New York: Columbia University Press 1987 [1983].

— *Black Sun: Depression and Melancholia*, New York: Columbia University Press 1989 [1987].

— *Julia Kristeva Interviews*, ed. Ross Mitchell Guberman, New York: Columbia University Press 1996.

Kuschel, Karl-Josef, *Laughter: A Theological Essay*, tr. John Bowden, London: SCM Press 1994 [1993].

LaCugna, Catherine Mowry, *God for Us: The Trinity and Christian Life*, San Francisco: Harper/Collins 1991.

Langkammer, H., '"Christ's Last Will and Testament" (John 19: 26, 27) in the Interpretations of the Fathers of the Church and the Scholastics', *Antonianum* 43, 1968, pp. 99–109.

Lannoy, Richard, *The Speaking Tree*, Oxford: Oxford University Press 1974.

Lash, Nicholas, *The Beginning and the End of 'Religion'*, Cambridge: Cambridge University Press 1996.

Laurentin, René, 'Look before you sign', *The Tablet* 31 January 1998, pp. 153–4.

Lloyd, Genevieve, *Man of Reason: 'Male' and 'Female' in Western Philosophy*, London: Routledge 1993.

Lossky, Vladimir, *The Mystical Theology of the Eastern Church*, tr. Fellowship of St. Alban and St. Sergius, London: James Clarke 1968 [1944].

Loughlin, Gerard, *Telling God's Story: Bible, Church and Narrative Theology*, Cambridge: Cambridge University Press 1996.

— 'Sexing the Trinity', *New Blackfriars* 79, 998, 1998, pp. 18–25.

Louth, Andrew, *Discerning the Mystery*, Oxford: Clarendon Press 1983.

Lyotard, Jean-François, *The Postmodern Condition: A Report on Knowledge*, tr. Geoff Bennington and Brian Massami, Manchester: Manchester University Press 1984 [1979].

MacBeth, George (ed.), *Poetry 1900 to 1965*, London: Longman with Faber & Faber 1967.

McDonnel, Killian (ed.), *The Holy Spirit and Power*, New York: Doubleday 1975.

MacEoin, Denis and Ahmed al-Shahi (eds), *Islam in the Modern World*, New York: Croom Helm 1983.

Macquarrie, John, *Mary for All Christians*, London: Collins 1991.

Maitland, Sara, *Angel and Me: Short Stories for Holy Week*, London: Mowbray 1995.

Martin, Francis, *The Feminist Question: Feminist Theology in the Light of Christian Tradition*, Edinburgh: T&T Clark 1994.

Mathothu, Kurian, *The Development of the Concept of Trimūrti in Hinduism*, Palai, Kerala: Sebastian Vayalil 1974.

Mattam, J., *Land of the Trinity: A Study of Modern Christian Approaches*, Bangalore: Theological Publications of India 1975.

Mernissi, Fatima, *Beyond the Veil: Male-Female Dynamics in Modern Muslim Society*, Cambridge: Schenkman Pub. Co. 1975.

Metz, Johannes-Baptist and Edward Schillebeeckx, *God as Father?*, *Concilium*, 1981.

Milbank, John, 'The End of Dialogue', *Christian Uniqueness Reconsidered*, ed. D'Costa, 1990, pp. 174–91.

— *Theology and Social Theory*, Oxford: Blackwell 1990.

— 'Can a Gift Be Given? Prolegomena to a Future Trinitarian Metaphysic', *Rethinking Metaphysics*, eds Jones and Fowl, 1995, pp. 119–61.

— *The Word Made Strange: Theology, Language, Culture*, Oxford: Basil Blackwell, 1997.

— Catherine Pickstock and Graham Ward (eds), *Radical Orthodoxy*, London: Routledge 1999.

Moi, Toril, *Sexual/Textual Politics: Feminist Literary Theory*, London: Routledge 1991.

Molinari, Paul, *Saints: Their Place in the Church*, tr. Dominic Maruca SJ, New York: Sheed & Ward 1965 [1962].

Moltmann, Jürgen, 'The Motherly Father: Is Trinitarian Patripassianism Replacing Theological Patriarchalism?', *God as Father?*, eds Metz and Schillebeeckx, *Concilium*, 1981, pp. 51–6.

— *The Trinity and the Kingdom of God*, tr. Margaret Kohl, London: SCM Press 1981 [1980].

Mühlen, Heribert, 'The Person of the Holy Spirit', *The Holy Spirit and Power*, ed. Killian McDonnel, New York: Doubleday 1975, pp. 11–34.

Müller, Max (ed.), *The Śatapatha-Brāhamana* according to the text of the Madhandina School, Pt 5, Books 11–14, tr. Julius Eggeling, *Sacred Books of the East*, Oxford: Clarendon Press 1900.

Neal, Diana, 'Out of the Uterus of the Father: A Study in Patriarchy and the Symbolization of Christian Theology', *Feminist Theology* 13, 1996, pp. 8–30.

Needham, A. D., 'The Politics of Post-Colonial Identity in Salman Rushdie', *The Massachusetts Review* 29, 4, 1988/89, pp. 602–34.

Neill, Stephen, *A History of Christianity in India: The Beginnings to AD 1707*, Cambridge: Cambridge University Press 1984.

Nelson, James B., *The Intimate Connection: Male Sexuality, Masculine Spirituality*, London: SPCK 1992.

— 'On Doing Body Theology', *Theology and Sexuality* 2, 1995, pp. 49–53.

— and Sandra P. Longfellow (eds), *Sexuality and the Sacred: Sources for Theological Reflection*, Louisville, Kentucky: Westminster/John Knox Press 1994.

Netland, John T., 'Encountering Christ in Shusaku Endo's Mudswamp of Japan', *Historicizing Christian Encounters with the Other*, ed. Hawley, 1998, pp. 166–81.

O'Donnell, John, 'In Him and over Him: The Holy Spirit in the Life of Jesus', *Gregorianum* 70, 1989, pp. 25–45.

— 'Pannenberg's Doctrine of God', *Gregorianum* 72, 1991, pp. 73–97.

Oduyoye, Mercy Ambia, 'Reflections from a Third World Woman's Perspective: Women's Experience and Liberation Theologies', *Feminist Theology from the Third World*, ed. Ursula King, London: SPCK 1994, pp. 23–34.

O'Flaherty, W. D., *Asceticism and Eroticism in the Mythology of Śiva*, Oxford: Oxford University Press 1975.

Olson, Roger, 'Trinity and Eschatology: The Historical Being of God in Jürgen Moltmann and Wolfhart Pannenberg', *Scottish Journal of Theology* 36, 1983, pp. 213–27.

O'Neill, Maura, *Women Speaking–Women Listening: Women in Interreligious Dialogue*, New York: Orbis 1990.

Ouspensky, Leonid, *Theology of the Icon*, tr. Anthony Cythie, Vol. 2, New York: St Vladimir's Seminary Press 1992.

— and Vladmir Lossky, *The Meaning of Icons*, G. E. H. Palmer and E. Kadloubovsky, New York: St Vladimir's Seminary Press 1982 [1952].

Pagels, Elaine, *The Gnostic Gospels*, New York: Vintage 1981.

Pannenberg, Wolfhart, *Systematic Theology*, Vol. 1, tr. Geoffrey Bromiley, Edinburgh: T&T Clark 1991 [1988].

Pelican, Jaroslav, *Mary through the Centuries*, New Haven: Yale University Press 1996.

Pieris, Aloysius, *An Asian Theology of Liberation*, New York: Orbis 1988.

Pittinger, Norman, *Our Lady: The Mother of Jesus in Christian Faith*, London: SCM Press 1996.

Plaskow, Judith, *Sex, Sin and Grace: Women's Experience and the Theologies of Reinhold Niebuhr and Paul Tillich*, New York: University Press of America 1980.

Prestiege, G. L., *God in Patristic Thought*, London: SPCK 1964.

Radhakrishnan, Sarvapelli, *Indian Philosophy*, Vol. 2, London: George Allen & Unwin 1923.

Rahner, Karl, *The Trinity*, tr. Joseph Donceel, New York: Herder & Herder 1970 [1967].

— 'Women and the Priesthood', *Theological Investigations*, Vol. 20, London: Darton, Longman & Todd 1981, pp. 35–47.

Rasmusson, Arne, *The Church as Polis: From Political Theology to Theological Politics as Exemplified by Jürgen Moltmann and Stanley Hauerwas*, Sweden: Lund University Press 1994.

Ratzinger, Joseph, 'Concerning the Notion of Person in Theology', *Communio* 17, 1990, pp. 443–54.

Ricoeur, Paul, *The Conflict of Interpretations: Essays in Hermeneutics*, ed. Don Ihde, Evanston: Northwestern University Press 1974 [1964].

Rizutto, Ana-Marie, *The Birth of the Living God: A Psychoanalytical Study*, Chicago: University of Chicago Press 1979.

Roberts, Michèlle, *Daughters of the House*, London: Virago 1993.

— *Impossible Saints*, London: Virago 1998.

Rosales, G. and C. G. Arévalo (eds), *For All the Peoples of Asia: Federation of Asian Bishops' Conferences Documents from 1970 to 1991*, New York: Orbis 1992.

Ross, Susan A., 'The Bride of Christ and the Body Politic: Body and Gender in Pre-Vatican II Marriage Theology', *The Journal of Religion* 71, 1991, pp. 345–61.

Rowland, Benjamin, *The Art and Architecture of India*, Harmondsworth: Penguin 1953.

Rudinesco, Elizabeth, *Jacques Lacan & Co: A History of Psychoanalysis in France 1925–1985*, London: Free Association Books 1990.

Ruether, Rosemary, *Faith and Fratricide*, New York: Seabury Press 1974.

Rushdie, Salman, *Midnight's Children*, London: Jonathan Cape 1981.

— *Shame*, London: Jonathan Cape 1983.

— *The Satanic Verses*, London: Viking Penguin 1988.

— *Haroun and the Sea of Dreams*, London: Jonathan Cape 1990.

— *Imaginary Homelands*, London: Granta Books 1991.

— *East, West*, London: Jonathan Cape 1994.

— *The Moor's Last Sigh*, London: Jonathan Cape 1996.

— *The Ground beneath Her Feet*, London: Jonathan Cape 1999.

Ruthven, Malise, *A Satanic Affair*, London: Chatto & Windus 1990.

Sacred Congregation for the Doctrine of the Faith, *Declaration on the Admission of Women to the Ministerial Priesthood*, 1976.

Sahi, Jyoti, *The Child and the Serpent: Reflection on Popular Indian Symbols*, London: Routledge & Kegan Paul 1980.

— *Stepping Stones: Reflections on the Theology of Indian Christian Culture*, Bangalore: Asian Trading Corporation 1986.

Said, Edward, *Orientalism: Western Conceptions of the Orient*, London: Routledge & Kegan Paul 1978.

— *Covering Islam: How the Media and the Experts Determine How We See the Rest of the World*, London: Routledge & Kegan Paul 1981.

Saldhana, C., *Divine Pedagogy: A Patristic View of Non-Christian Religions*, Rome: Liberia Ateneo Salesiano 1984.

Sankar, Sen Gupta, *Tree Symbol Worship in India: A New Survey of a Pattern of Folk-Religion*, Calcutta: Indian Publishing House 1965.

Sanneh, Lamin, *Encountering the West: Christianity and the Global Cultural Process: The African Dimension*, London: Marshall Pickering 1993.

Sardar, Ziauddin and Merryl Wyn Davies, *Distorted Imaginations: Lessons from the Rushdie Affair*, London: Grey Seal 1990.

Savory, R. M. (ed.), *Introduction to Islamic Civilization*, Cambridge: Cambridge University Press 1976.

Schüeller, S., *Angelo de Fonseca: India's Catholic Artist*, Aachen: Missio 1938.

Schüssler Fiorenza, Elizabeth, *In Memory of Her: A Feminist Reconstruction of Christian Origins*, New York: Crossroad 1983.

— *Jesus: Miriam's Child, Sophia's Prophet*, London: SCM Press 1994.

Schwab, Raymond, *The Oriental Renaissance*, tr. Gene Patterson-Black and Victor Reinking, New York: Columbia University Press 1984.

Segal, J. B., *Edessa: The Blessed City*, Oxford: Clarendon Press 1970.

Segundo, Jon Luis, 'Capitalism Versus Socialism: Crux Theologica', *Frontiers of Theology in Latin America*, ed. Rosino Gibellini, London: SCM Press 1980, pp. 240–59.

Sinkinson, Christopher, 'Scripture and Scriptures: The Problems of Hermeneutics in Inter-Religious Dialogue', *Discernment* 1/2, 1994, pp. 12–23.

Singer, Milton, *When a Great Tradition Modernizes*, Mount View, California: Pacific Press Publications Association 1980.

Sivan, Emmanuel, *Interpretations of Islam Past and Present*, Princeton: Darwin Press 1985.

Smail, Thomas A., *The Forgotten Father*, London: Hodder & Stoughton 1980.

Smith, Timothy L., 'Review of Weinandy, *The Father's Spirit of Sonship*', *Fellowship of Catholic Scholars Quarterly* 21, i, 1997, pp. 30–2.

Smith, Wilfred Cantwell, *The Meaning and End of Religion*, New York: Macmillan 1962.

— *Understanding Islam*, The Hague, Paris: Mouton Publishers 1981.

— *What Is Scripture?*, London: SCM Press 1993.

Sölle, Dorothee, 'Paternalistic Religion as Experienced by Woman', *God as Father?*, eds Metz and Schillebeeckx, *Concilium*, 1981, pp. 69–74.

Soskice, Janet Martin (ed.), *After Eve*, London: Marshall Pickering 1990.

— 'Can a Feminist Call God "Father"?', *Speaking the Christian God: The Holy Trinity and the Challenge of Feminism*, ed. Alvin F. Kimel Jnr, Grand Rapids, Michigan: Eerdmans 1992, pp. 81–94.

— 'Trinity and the Feminine Other', *New Blackfriars*, 1994, pp. 2–17.

Spivak, Gaytri Chakravorty, *In Other Worlds: Essays in Cultural Politics*, New York: Methuen 1987.

Stein, Dominique, 'The Murder of the Father and God the Father in the Work of Freud', *God as Father?*, eds. Metz and Schillebeeckx, *Concilium*, 1981, pp. 11–18.

Steinberg, Leo, *The Sexuality of Christ in Renaissance Art and in Modern Oblivion*, New York: Pantheon 1983.

Stuart, Elizabeth, *Spitting at Dragons: Towards a Feminist Theology of Sainthood*, London: Mowbray 1996.

Stutley, Margaret and James, *A Dictionary of Hinduism*, London: Routledge & Kegan Paul 1977.

Sullivan, Francis A., *Salvation outside the Church?*, London: Geoffrey Chapman 1992.

Surin, Kenneth, 'A Certain "Politics of Speech": Towards an Understanding of the Relationships between the Religions in the Age of the McDonald's Hamburger', *Christian Uniqueness Reconsidered*, ed. D'Costa, 1990, pp. 192–212.

Sutherland, Steward, Leslie Houlden, Peter Clarke and Friedhelm Hardy (eds), *The World Religions*, London: Routledge 1998.

Sykes, Stephen and Derek Holmes (eds), *New Studies in Theology*, London: Duckworth 1980.

Tagore, Rabindranāth, *Collected Poems*, London: Macmillan 1936.
Takenaka, Masao, *Christian Art in Asia*, Kyoto: Kyo Bun Kwan 1975.
Tamez, E. (ed.), *Through Her Eyes: Women's Theology from Latin America*, New York: Orbis 1989.
Taylor, Charles, *Sources of the Self: The Making of Modern Identity*, Cambridge: Cambridge University Press 1989.
Taylor, Richard, *Some Interpretations of Jesus in Indian Painting*, Religion and Society 17, 3, 1970, entire number.
Tewari, Nareen, *The Mother Goddess Vaiṣhna Devi*, New Delh: Lanner Institute 1988.
Thatcher, Adrian and Elizabeth Stuart (eds), *Christian Perspectives on Sexuality and Gender*, Leominster: Gracewing 1996.
Thiselton, Anthony, *New Horizons in Hermeneutics: The Theory and Practice of Transforming Biblical Reading*, London: HarperCollins 1992.
Thistlethwaite, Susan Brooks, *Sex, Race and God*, New York: Crossroad 1989.
Thurian, Max, *Mary, Mother of All Christians*, New York: Herder & Herder 1963.
Torrance, Alan, *Persons in Communion: An Essay on Trinitarian Description and Human Participation*, Edinburgh: T&T Clark 1996.
Torrance, T. F., *The Trinitarian Faith*, Edinburgh: T&T Clark 1988.
— *The Ministry of Women*, Edinburgh: Handsel Press 1992.

Vandana, Sr, *Ashrams and Social Justice*, Bangalore: Asian Trading Corporation 1981.
Vawter, B., 'Commentary on Genesis', *A New Catholic Commentary on Holy Scripture*, eds Johnstone and Kearns, 1969, pp. 166–205.
Volf, Miroslav, *After Our Likeness: The Church as the Image of the Trinity*, Grand Rapids, Michigan: W. B. Eerdmans 1998.
von Rad, Gerhard, *Genesis: A Commentary*, 3rd edn, London, SCM Press 1972.
Vorgrimler, Herbert (ed.), *Commentary on the Documents of Vatican II*, 5 vols, London: Burns & Oates 1967.

Wainwright, Arthur, *The Trinity in the New Testament*, London: SPCK 1962.
Ward, Graham, 'In the Name of the Father and of the Mother', *Literature and Theology* 8, 3, 1994, pp. 311–27.
— *Barth, Derrida and the Language of Theology*, Cambridge: Cambridge University Press 1995.
— 'Divinity and Sexuality: Luce Irigaray and Christology', *Modern Theology* 12, 1996, pp. 221–37.

— (ed.), *The Postmodern God*, Oxford: Blackwell 1997.

— 'The Displaced Body of Jesus Christ', *Radical Orthodoxy*, eds Milbank, Pickstock and Ward, 1999, pp. 163–81.

Warner, Marina, *Alone of All Her Sex: The Myth and the Cult of the Virgin Mary*, 2nd edn, London: Picador Books 1990.

Watson, Arthur, *The Early Iconography of the Tree of Jesse*, Oxford: Oxford University Press 1934.

Watson, Francis (ed.), *The Open Text: New Directions for Biblical Studies*, London: SCM Press 1993.

Weinandy, Thomas, *The Father's Spirit of Sonship: Reconceiving the Trinity*, Edinburgh: T&T Clark 1995.

Wessley, Stephen E., 'The Thirteenth-Century Guglielmites: Salvation through Women', *Medieval Women*, ed. Derek Baker, Oxford: Blackwell 1978, pp. 289–303.

Westermann, Claus, *Genesis 12–36: A Commentary*, re. John J. Scullen, London: SPCK 1986.

Wheeler, Mortimer, *The Indus Civilization*, Cambridge: Cambridge University Press 1953.

Whitford, Margaret (ed.), *The Irigaray Reader*, Oxford: Blackwell 1991.

— *Luce Irigaray: Philosophy in the Feminine*, New York: Routledge 1991.

Wilfred, Felix, *Sunset in the East: Asian Challenges and Christian Involvement*, Madras: University of Madras Press 1991.

— 'Some Tentative Reflections on the Language of Christian Uniqueness: An Indian Perspective', *Bulletin* 85/86, 1, 1994, pp. 40–57.

Williams, Rowan, 'The Via Negativa and the Foundations of Theology: An Introduction to the Thought of V. N. Lossky', *New Studies in Theology*, ed. Stephen Sykes and Derek Holmes, London: Duckworth 1980, pp. 95–118.

— *After Silent Centuries*, Oxford: The Perpetua Press 1994.

— 'Between the Cherubim: The Empty Tomb and the Empty Throne', *Resurrection Reconsidered*, ed. D'Costa, 1996, pp. 87–101.

Woodward, Kenneth L., *Making Saints: How the Catholic Church Determines Who Becomes a Saint, Who Doesn't, and Why?*, New York: Simon & Schuster 1996.

Zaehner, R. C., *Hinduism*, Oxford: Oxford University Press 1962.

— *Hindu Scriptures*, London: Dent 1966.

— *Our Savage God*, London: Collins 1974.

Zimmer, Heinrich, *Philosophies of India*, London: Routledge & Kegan Paul 1951.

— *Myths and Symbols in Indian Art and Civilization*, Princeton: Princeton University Press 1963.

Zizioulas, John, *Being as Communion: Studies in Personhood and the Church*, New York: St Vladimir's Seminary 1985.

Notes

1. The Holy Spirit within a hommosexuate trinity?

1. 'Equal to Whom?' *The Postmodern God*, ed. Graham Ward, (subsequently EW), p. 198. The quotation cited is in fact Irigaray's description of Elisabeth Schüssler Fiorenza's feminist critical approach, and, as noted by Grace Jantzen, reflects 'the sort of tactics Irigaray has used to such effect with the writings of Freud and the Western philosophical tradition'. Grace M. Jantzen, 'Luce Irigaray (b. 1930): Introduction', ibid, p. 194.

2. See *This Sex Shich is Not One* subsequently *This Sex*), pp. 119–69.

3. The following secondary critical material is helpful for an overall sense of Irigaray's project: Jane Gallop, *Feminism and Psychoanalysis: The Daughter's Seduction*; Elizabeth Grosz, *Sexual Subversions: Three French Feminists*; and Margaret Whitford, *Luce Irigaray: Philosophy in the Feminine*.

4. See esp. *Totem and Taboo* and *Moses and Monotheism*. All references to Freud are taken from the *Standard Edition of the Complete Psychological Works of Sigmund Freud*, unless otherwise stated. My criticisms of Freud will be developed in Chapter 3. One of the most creative theological rehabilitations of Freud is to be found in the work of René Girard. For Irigaray's criticisms of Girard, see 'Women, the Sacred and Money', *Sexes and Genealogies* (subsequently *Sexes*), pp. 75–88. Freud, like Girard, perpetuates the view of men as a universal, so that Girard's view of the necessary sacrifice that stabilizes society 'seems [to Irigaray] to correspond to the masculine model of sexuality described by Freud: tension, discharge, return to homostasis' (p. 76).

5. See Elizabeth Rudinesco, *Jacques Lacan & Co: A History of Psychoanalysis in France 1925–1985*, and Elizabeth Grosz, *Jacques Lacan: A Feminist Introduction*.

6. Julia Kristeva is more appreciative than Irigaray of the positive semiotic role that is enacted in the 'father' of prehistory, who, according to Freud, possessed the sexual characteristics and functions of both parents – see Sigmund Freud, *The Ego and the Id*. Kristeva sees that in the child's relation with a figure

who is 'love' this 'helps to bring about primary stabilization of the subject through its enduring character; because it is a gift of the self, it both encourages and hinders the desintergrative and aggressive agitation of the instincts'. See Julia Kristeva, *The Kristeva Reader* (subsequently: *Kristeva Reader*), p. 244. However, Kristeva nevertheless argues, like Irigaray, that: 'Because of its insistence on the paternal function, Christianity shapes the preconscious formulation of the basic fantasies characteristic of male desires.' From *In the Beginning Was Love: Faith and Psychoanalysis* (subsequently *Beginning*), p. 40.

7. For the 'enlightenment self' see Genevieve Lloyd, *Man of Reason: 'Male' and 'Female' in Western Philosophy*, and Sarah Coakley's development of Lloyd's argument in a theological key, in 'Gender and Knowledge in Western Philosophy: The "Man of Reason" and the "Feminine Other" in Enlightenment Thought'. For a wider survey of self-construction see Charles Taylor, *Sources of the Self: The Making of Modern Identity*. Phillip Blond perhaps too quickly assimilates Irigaray within enlightenment categories: see his comments in Phillip Blond (ed.), *Post-Secular Philosophy: Between Philosophy and Theology*, pp. 45–9.

8. On this point, see *Speculum of the Other Woman* (subsequently *Speculum*), ch. 1. See also 'Psychoanalytic Theory: Another Look', pp. 34–68, 'The Power of Discourse and the Subordination of the Feminine', pp. 68–85, and, for the politics of such staging, 'Women on the Market', pp. 170–92, all in *This Sex*. See also 'The Three Genders', *Sexes*, pp. 151–66.

9. Kristeva, given her historical assumption that Christianity is dying, thinks analysis the *only* cultural substitute for Christianity. In the transferential relationship of the analyst and the analysand, a person can find the love that can help them love – *Beginning*, pp. 25–6. She does not of course discount the *potential* transformative power of Christianity, were it not dying. Significantly, Kristeva also sees the reimagined trinity as the major resource for Christianity: 'The trinity itself, that crown jewel of theological sophistication, evokes, beyond its specific content and by virtue of the very logic of its articulation, the intricate intertwining of the three aspects of psychic life: the symbolic, the imaginary, and the real' (*Beginning*, p. 43). I only engage with Irigaray in this chapter, although Kristeva's focus on abjection and the importance of 'separation', remaining within the 'chora', facilitates a far greater attention to the narratives of the passion, the site of the revelation of the trinity, than does Irigaray's work. See Kristeva, *Beginning*, pp. 31–2; *Kristeva Reader*, pp. 93–8, on the 'chora'; and 'Stabat Mater', *Tales of Love*, pp. 234–63. See Phillipa Berry's extremely perceptive and helpful essay on Kristeva: 'Kristeva's feminist refiguring of the gift', *Post-Secular Philosophy*, ed. Blond, pp. 318–33.

10. *Ethics*, p. 104.

11. Fiorenza's book, *In Memory of Her* (1983). EW; see also 'Equal or Different?', *Je, Tu, Nous – Towards a Culture of Difference* (subsequently *Je*,

Tu, Nous), for an elaboration of her critique of the goal of 'equality' viz. Simone de Beauvoir's ground breaking *The Second Sex*. See also Schüssler Fiorenza's subsequent and important study: *Jesus: Miriam's Child, Sophia's Prophet*, which takes most seriously women's genealogies and especially Mary's, see pp. 33–66. I do not think Irigaray's rendering of Schüssler Fiorenza entirely convincing, but that is not relevant to the exposition. For an interesting comparison between Schüssler Fiorenza's tradition of American feminism and that of Irigaray's see Rebecca Chopp, 'From Patriarchy into Freedom: A Conversation between American Feminist Theology and French Feminism', *Transfigurations: Theology and the French Feminists*, eds Kim, St Ville and Simoniatis.

12. EW, p. 198.

13. EW, p. 202.

14. EW, p. 201.

15. EW, p. 208. In effect 'the whole of our western culture is based upon the murder of the mother. The man-god-father killed the mother in order to take power.' From 'Woman-Mothers, the Silent Substratum of the Social order', *The Irigaray Reader* (subsequently *Reader*), ed. Whitford, pp. 47–53, p. 46. Irigaray's critique of Schüssler Fiorenza would apply to many Anglo-Saxon feminist theologians. See, for example, Elizabeth A. Johnson, *She Who Is: The Mystery of God in Feminist Theological Discourse*. The exclusion of this problematic from Rebecca Chopp's discussion of differences between American and French feminists is curious – see Chopp, 'From Patriarchy'.

16. See Daphne Hampson, *Theology and Feminism*, and Mary Daly, *Beyond God the Father*.

17. See Tina Beattie in regard to John Paul II, 'Carnal Love and Spiritual Imagination: Can Luce Irigaray and John Paul II Come Together?', *Sex These Days: Essays on Theology, Sexuality and Society*, eds Davies and Loughlin, and, with regard to von Balthasar, 'A Man and Three Women – Hans, Adrienne, Mary and Luce'; and further on von Balthasar, see Gerard Loughlin, 'Sexing the Trinity'.

18. EW, p. 212.

19. EW, p. 207.

20. EW, p. 207.

21. EW, p. 207, referring to Schüssler Fiorenza, p. 147.

22. EW, p. 208.

23. EW, p. 209.

24. EW, p. 202, my emphasis, the French is *sont virtuellement dieux*.

25. EW, p. 208.

26. *Reader*, pp. 45–6. This is a different unmasking of things hidden since the foundation of the world (Girard), and one which Girard fails to see. See note 4.

27. *Reader*, pp. 213–18.

28. *Sexes*, p. 62.

29. *An Ethics of Sexual Difference* (subsequently *Ethics*), p. 124. Secular feminists like Margaret Whitford and Elizabeth Gross tend to interpret religious imagery in Irigaray exclusively in terms of 'strategic' employment (e.g. *Reader*, p. 164; Whitford, *Luce Irigaray*, p. 146; and Grosz, *Sexual Subversions*, p. 155). This is despite such explicit work as found in *Marine Lover of Friedrich Nietzche* (subsequently: *Marine*), pp. 123–90. Joachim of Fiore fused two different versions of traditional Christian eschatology. See Jürgen Moltmann, *The Trinity and the Kingdom of God*, pp. 203–9.

30. *Marine*, p. 166.

31. *Sexes*, p. 18. Kristeva, a mother herself, places a far stronger emphasis on the importance of motherhood. See Kristeva, 'Women's Time', *Kristeva Reader*, esp. pp. 205–8, and 'Stabat Mater', *History of Love*. See also Kristeva's 'controversial' comments about Nancy Chodorow's *The Reproduction of Mothering* and Dorothy Dinnerstein's *The Mermaid and the Minotaur* regarding the importance of 'difference' in the parenting of children, in Ross Mitchell Guberman (ed.), *Julia Kristeva Interviews*, pp. 113–21, esp. pp. 118–19.

32. *Marine*, p. 171.

33. *Speculum*, p. 27.

34. See, for example, Heribert Mühlen's comment that when we speak of God, the Holy Spirit is like an 'edifying appendage'; or Walter Kasper's comment that the Holy Spirit is 'faceless'; or Congar's claims that the Spirit is the 'half known God'. References: Heribert Mühlen, 'The Person of the Holy Spirit', p. 12; Walter Kasper, *The God of Jesus Christ*, p. 198; Yves Congar, *I Believe in the Holy Spirit*, Vol. 3, p. 6. None of these three writers is concerned with gender issues. See Elizabeth Johnson's documentation on this point, in *She Who Is*, pp. 128–31, and her marginal association between patriarchy and the neglect of the Spirit: pp. 129–30. Janet Martin Soskice also suggests a connection viz. female denigration and the neglect of the Holy Spirit in 'Trinity and the Feminine Other', p. 12.

35. EW, p. 202.

36. Thomas Weinandy, *The Father's Spirit of Sonship: Reconceiving the Trinity*, p. 10. Along with those unbaptized philosophical elements, there also entered the subordination of women within Aristotelian philosophy that affected Augustine, Aquinas, St Albert and the western tradition in differing degrees. This denigration also entered Jewish philosophy through Avicebron and Maimonides' appropriation of Aristotle, and likewise in Islam through Avicenna and Averroes. See the masterly study of the Aristotelian triumph in the west: Sr Prudence Allen RSM, *The Concept of Woman: The Aristotelian Revolution 750 BC–AD 1250*. Rather than generalize about the Aristotelian heritage, one would need to look at its effect upon specific writers. See also

Kari Elisabeth Børresen, *Subordination and Equivalence: The Nature and Role of Women in Augustine and Thomas Aquinas*, who confirms Allen's thesis.

37. Luke 1.26–56.

38. *Reconceiving*, p. 8, my emphases.

39. *Reconceiving*, p. 8, my changes.

40. See Stephen E. Wessley, 'The Thirteenth-Century Guglielmites: Salvation through Women'.

41. See for example, Colin Gunton, *The One, the Three and the Many: God, Creation and the Culture of Modernity*; Catherine Mowry LaCugna, *God for Us: The Trinity and Christian Life*; John Zizioulas, *Being as Communion: Studies in Personhood and the Church*.

42. *Reconceiving*, p. 10. See also T. F. Torrance, *The Trinitarian Faith*, pp. 236–42, for a similar incisive critique of the Cappadocians on this point.

43. Janet Martin Soskice (in 'Trinity and the Feminine Other') very pointedly calls into question the neo-Platonic and the Stoic underpinnings of male 'generation' in trinitarian language, focussing instead on the relations of difference. I do not think that Diana Neal does justice to the subtle *feminine* Other that is generated in Soskice's argument. See Diana Neal, 'Out of the Uterus of the Father: A Study in Patriarchy and the Symbolization of Christian Theology', p. 24.

44. *Reconceiving*, p. 9.

45. Alan Torrance, *Persons in Communion: An Essay on Trinitarian Description and Human Participation*, p. 289.

46. Zizioulas, *Being*, pp. 17–18.

47. Weinandy, *Father's Spirit*, p. 9.

48. Torrance, *Persons*, p. 293.

49. For a fuller account in this manner, see John Milbank, *Theology and Social Theory*, esp. chs 4 and 6. See also note 7.

50. Graham Ward, 'Divinity and Sexuality: Luce Irigaray and Christology'. Phillipa Berry helpfully explores this epistemological challenge to western philosophy and its positioning of the 'divine', and opens up quite radically the challenges that Irigaray (and Kristeva) pose to Christian theology: see especially her 'Woman and Space according to Kristeva and Irigaray', *Shadow of Spirit: Postmodernism and Religion*, eds Phillipa Berry and Andrew Wernick, pp. 250–64, and her piece, 'The Burning Glass: Paradoxes of Feminist Revelation in Speculum', *Engaging with Irigaray*, eds Burke et al, pp. 229–46.

51. Leonardo Boff, *Trinity and Society*. Latin American liberation theologians use the doctrine of the trinity very differently. I have chosen Boff because of his responsiveness to the feminist debate.

52. *Reconceiving*, p. 14.

53. David Cunningham in *These Three Are One: The Practice of Trinitarian Theology*, p. 28, suggests that Weinandy has not really transcended the notion

of person as 'three people', or not quite. He cites a rather poorly phrased passage in Weinandy, *Father's Spirit*, pp. 119–20. I do not think this is the real problem with Weinandy's thesis, but rather his failure to think through the significance of co-constitutive relationality. While Cunningham is full of creative ideas in his rethinking of relationality, because of his understandable reservations regarding 'person' (*These Three*, pp. 166–76, 186–95), he nevertheless tends towards depersonalizing the trinity in choosing and developing *prime* metaphors from nature (the spring) and culture (music), which are only extremely helpful *alongside* personal metaphors.

54. *Reconceiving*, p. 15, note 28.

55. *Reconceiving*, p. 9.

56. See John Milbank's attempt to deconstruct causality in terms of the Gift of the Holy Spirit in 'Can a Gift be Given? Prolegomena to a Future Trinitarian Metaphysic', *Rethinking Metaphysics*, eds L. Gregory Jones and Stephen E. Fowl. Milbank employs both the association of the Spirit with the Bride, and the Church with Mary: see, for example, pp. 136, 149–50.

57. Boff, *Trinity*, p. 142. Boff's resort to silence (which may reflect the imposition of silence upon him during the writing of the book) is nicely contrasted with the closing words (hence, ironic?) of Alan Torrance's book, *Persons*: 'Theological description, therefore, as it stems from our human participation in the triune life, remains *sola gratia*. Far from suggesting, however, that this means we dare not speak of God, it means that we dare not keep silent, that we ought not to keep silent and that we should not wish to keep silent' (p. 371).

58. *Reconceiving*, pp. 80–1, my emphases.

59. See, for example, in *Trinity*, pp. 160, 172.

60. *Trinity*, p. 210.

61. *Trinity*, pp. 210–11.

62. *Trinity*, pp. 210–11.

63. See Bertrand Buby, *Mary of Galilee*, Vol. 3, *The Marian Heritage of the Early Church*, pp. 37–52, for a translation of the *Protoevangelium of James*. Mary is barren in the technical sense of being a 'virgin'. The *Catechism of the Catholic Church* strongly stresses Mary's female genealogical line – see para. 489.

64. *Trinity*, p. 210.

65. See Herbert Vorgrimler (ed.), *Commentary on the Documents of Vatican II*, Vol. 1, pp. 285–96, and *Catechism*, paras 963–72, 489, 968–70. The passage in *Lumen Gentium* is listing titles employed by various fathers of the church, and the entire context of paras 55–69 mitigates against Boff's reading, especially 66b which specifically counters Boff's exegesis.

66. From Walter M. Abbott SJ (ed.), *The Documents of Vatican II*.

67. Otto Semmolroth in Vorgrimler, *Commentary*, p. 294, comments that

Mary's preeminent place 'does not mean that Mary takes the place of Christ as the model of Christian life, any more than Paul does so when he tells his churches to imitate his example (1 Cor 4:16; 11:1, Phil 3:17, I Thess 1:6).'

68. John 2.1–11.

69. Kristeva returns to the Genesis account for the productive difference that is creation – see *Beginning*, p. 31.

70. In this sense, Blond is correct in his criticism of Irigaray, but *only* in this limited sense; see note 7.

71. See the discussion of this term in G. L. Prestiege, *God in Patristic Thought*, ch. 14, and Hamson's discussion of Stead and others on perichoresis: Verna Hamson, 'Perichoresis in the Greek Fathers'.

72. See Aquinas, on the nature of God as pure activity, *Summa Theologiae*, 1a 41, 3–6; 1a 25, 1–3. See Michel de Certeau's arguments regarding the 'dethroning of the verb' in the fifteenth century: *The Mystic Fable*, Vol. 1: *The Sixteenth and Seventeenth Centuries*, p. 125.

73. Bishop Kallistos of Diokleia, 'No new dogmas, please', p. 93. See also Jerome Murphy O'Connor OP, in *A New Catholic Commentary on Holy Scripture*, Fuller, Johnstone and Kearns (eds), p. 1202, who sees this as an ecclesiological statement, such that 'Christ, then is not the historical Jesus but the Lord of the living in his members'.

74. The way in which women's bodies and stories form an integral part of the story of redemption is movingly depicted in Sara Maitland's collection, *Angel and Me: Short Stories for Holy Week*, and more darkly and ambiguously in Michèlle Roberts, *Daughters of the House*, and *Impossible Saints*.

75. René Laurentin, 'Look before you sign', p. 153. The full verse (1 Cor. 3.9), with its significant two remaining metaphors, reads 'For we are God's fellow workers; you are God's field, God's building.'

76. Janette Gray RSM, 'Celibacy These Days', p. 155. See also Elizabeth A. Johnson, *Friends of God and Prophets: A Feminist Theological Reading of the Communion of Saints*, and Elizabeth Stuart, *Spitting at Dragons: Towards a Feminist Theology of Sainthood*.

77. See Kristeva, 'Holbein's Dead Christ', *Black Sun: Depression and Melancholia*, pp. 105–38.

78. *She Who Is*, pp. 129–30. Johnson seems to have moved on in *Friends*, pp. 206–13.

79. Johnson, *She Who Is*, p. 293, cites Yves Congar, *I Believe in the Holy Spirit*, Vol. 1, pp. 159–66, esp. ch. 3, note 17.

80. Johnson, *She Who Is*, p. 130.

81. This is one of the arguments presented in the Sacred Congregation for the Doctrine of the Faith's (CDF) document, *Declaration on the Admission of Women to the Priesthood* (*Inter Insigniores*), para. 5. See Karl Rahner's extremely insightful commentary on this document: 'Women and the Priesthood', pp. 35–

47. The biblical arguments forwarded by the CDF had previously been seen as lacking definitive authority by the International Biblical Commission appointed by the Pope to examine this question. See also T. F. Torrance, *The Ministry of Women*, who deals with the biblical, symbolical and historical arguments on this question with special sensitivity, and concludes that the ordination of women to the priesthood is entirely admissible on purely theological grounds.

82. See Whitford's remarks on the earlier optimism in Irigaray's writings (1970s) about the possibility of *parler-femme*, and Irigaray's later recognition that such possibilities require gigantic shifts in society and culture (*Reader*, p. 4; and also *Irigaray*, pp. 39–42).

83. *Trinity*, p. 171.

84. Cunningham, *These Three*, pp. 49–50.

85. *Trinity*, p. 182.

86. *Trinity*, p. 211.

87. *Trinity*, pp. 230–1.

88. *Trinity*, p. 185.

89. For example: 'In the great Oriental traditions, a female trilogy exists alongside the male and, in their movements and their stability, neither one exists without the other' (EW, p. 209); and see also *Thinking*, pp. 12–13, 102–5. Admittedly on p. 12 Irigaray speaks of 'the myth of earthly paradise', thereby suggesting that she is critically aware of the social conditions within which such stories originate.

90. Caroline Walker Bynum, 'Introduction: The Complexity of Symbols', *Gender and Religion: On the Complexity of Symbols*, Caroline Walker Bynum, Stevan Harrell and Paula Richman (eds), pp. 1–22, pp. 3–4.

91. See her 'Feminine Imagery for the Divine: The Holy Spirit, the Odes of Solomon and Early Syriac Tradition'; *Asceticism and Society in Crisis: John of Ephesus and the 'Lives of the Eastern Saints'*; and with Sebastian P. Brock, *Holy Women of the Syrian Orient*. Sebastian Brock's linguistic analysis of early Syriac texts is also most helpful: 'The Holy Spirit as Feminine in Early Syriac Literature'.

92. Harvey, 'Feminine', p. 121.

93. Harvey's translation, 'Feminine', pp. 125–6. Harvey's translation is more dramatic in consistently rendering the object of the sentence *after* the gendering verbs. For example, James Hamilton Charlesworth's translation, *The Odes of Solomon*, has 'And the Father is He who was milked' (p. 82) rather than Harvey's 'And He who was milked is the Father', likewise with the Holy Spirit in the next line, Stanza 2.

94. For example, see J. R. Harris and A. Mingana, *The Odes and Psalms of Solomon*, Vol. 2, pp. 298–302.

95. Admittedly, Harris and Mingana translate Stanza 2 as 'the Holy Spirit

is He who milked him', but Charlesworth notes both ancient manuscripts read otherwise (*Odes*, p. 83).

96. Harvey, 'Feminine', p. 115. See also J. B. Segal, *Edessa: The Blessed City*, pp. 43–61, for family trinities of mother, father, son. This observation of Harvey's undermines Charlesworth's rather quick equation of the *Odes* feminization with that of the Jewish-Christian apocryphal literature where, for example, in the so-called *Gospel of the Hebrews* we find: 'Even so did my mother, the Holy Spirit, take me by one of my hairs and carry me away on the great mountain Tabor' (Charlesworth, *Odes*, p. 83).

97. Harvey, 'Feminine', p. 128; and for women saints see Harvey and Brock, *Holy Women*.

98. Harvey, 'Feminine', p. 131.

99. 'Feminine', p. 132.

100. Cited by Harvey, 'Feminine', p. 134. The author to Hebrews starts his letter with a not dissimilar destabilization: 'In many and various ways God spoke of old to our fathers by the prophets; but in these last days he has spoken to us by a Son, whom he appointed heir of all things [heirs are those who *succeed after*], through whom also he created the world,' (Heb. 1.1–2; see also John 1.1–18 and Paul's Col. 1.15–19).

101. See Elaine Pagels, *The Gnostic Gospels*, pp. 57–83, for a more positive reading of these texts as opposed to the critique of their static representations in J. J. Buckley, *Female Fault and Fulfilment in Gnosticism*. See also Segal, *Edessa*, pp. 43–61.

102. *Trinity*, p. 171.

103. See for example Elizabeth Achteimeier, 'Exchanging God for "No Gods": A Discussion of Female Language for God', and Roland M. Frye, 'Language for God and Feminist Language: Problems and Principles'; and Wolfhart Pannenberg, *Systematic Theology*, Vol. 1, p. 262.

104. EW, p. 209.

105. Harvey and Brock, *Holy Women*, pp. 25–6. See also especially ch. 2 on Pelagia, a woman prostitute who dresses herself as a monk to indicate her new-found sanctity; and this topos is also true of Anastasia (ch. 6).

106. Harvey, *Ascetism and Society*, pp. 132–3. The lives of Sosiana or Euphemia illustrate the point.

2. *Jesus' womb and the birth of the Father*

1. EW, p. 208.

2. Jantzen, 'Irigaray', p. 196. And see further her *Becoming Divine: Towards a Feminist Philosophy of Religion*, to see the Fuerbachian deconstructive direction in which Jantzen develops Irigaray.

3. Cited in Judith Butler, *Gender Trouble*, p. 157, note 54. Monique Plaza

and Christine Delphy also make similar criticisms of Irigaray, as does R. A. Jones, 'Writing the Body: Towards an Understanding of Ecriture Feminine', p. 253. In contrast Grosz defends Irigaray against such charges: *Sexual Subversions*, pp. 113–16, as does Whitford, *Irigaray*, ch. 4, and also p. 220, note 4. One of the most nuanced discussions of Irigaray's movement between essentialism and constructivism is to be found in Tina Chanter, *Ethics of Eros: Irigaray's Rewriting of the Philosophers*, ch. 1.

4. Ana-Marie Rizutto, *The Birth of the Living God: A Psychoanalytical Study*, pp. 206–7.

5. Rizutto, *Birth*, p. 206.

6. Rizutto, *Birth*, p. 206.

7. *This Sex*, p. 24.

8. This is *also* suggested by male theologians concerned with the body and sexuality. See James B. Nelson's *The Intimate Connection: Male Sexuality, Masculine Spirituality*, which, while extremely helpful, tends to finally render God within an encoding of 'liberal' Christianity.

9. Gallop is referring to *Et l'une ne bourge pas sans l'autre*, 1979, pp. 9–10, cited in Gallop, *Feminism*, p. 114.

10. Gallop, *Feminism*, p. 116.

11. *Feminism*, p. 117.

12. Toril Moi criticizes passages in Irigaray where she seems to affirm stereotypes of hysterical adolescent women: see Moi, *Sexual/Textual Politics: Feminist Literary Theory*, pp. 143–7. Again, I would emphasize that this criticism of Irigaray should not be pushed too far. The point is that Irigaray seems to deny sin to women, not withstanding the different senses in which sin for men and women might be understood: See Judith Plaskow's influential essay in which she argues that male and female 'sin' are different: *Sex, Sin and Grace: Women's Experience and the Theologies of Reinhold Niebuhr and Paul Tillich*.

13. *Feminism*, p. 118.

14. If Irigaray's autoerotic metaphor is *entirely* strategic, then the gravity of my criticisms (and that of Wittig's and Gallop's) are somewhat deflated. Margaret Whitford claims that the notion of 'unmediated relations', which indeed dominates the metaphor just quoted, does not imply 'direct unmediated relation between woman's language and woman's bodies' (and therefore equally woman's gods). Instead, she claims that 'for Irigaray, *un*mediated relations are a source of pathology and dereliction'. Whitford, *Reader*, p. 77. I am in agreement with Whitford regarding the pathological implications, but I do not think that Whitford successfully establishes her case from Irigaray's texts. See also note 2 above.

15. Beattie, 'Sexuality', p. 139.

16. 'Sexuality', p. 140.

17. My one reservation is that Beattie ends up possibly making women the *passive victim* of male sin, the one moment where passivity is allowed into such feminist discourse. For example, she says (not without truth): 'Feminist analysis has revealed the extent to which women (and, I would add, "womanly" men) have suffered and continue to suffer under phallic domination, to such an extent that the original goodness of sexual difference might seem irreparably damaged, and maleness eternally blighted in its potential to represent love and gentleness.' 'Sexuality', p. 141, Beattie's bracket. There is an assumption that 'macho' men do not suffer under such idolatrous conditions. This is not to say that all these groups 'suffer' in the same way, but surely all these groups are in need of redemption from the *different* disfigurements that such symbolic figurations generate? Furthermore, women within Beattie's taxonomy do not seem in danger of being 'eternally blighted' in any way, only men. This replicates the symbolic phallus being identified exclusively with men, so that Gallop's phallic mother is occluded. Furthermore, women who become part of the phallocratic order seem to escape comment, although admittedly Beattie redefines this on p. 142 – cited in the main body of the text, Chapter 2. While a phallocratic order may generate some distinctively male sins, there is an odd lacuna regarding women's disfigurement, again portrayed only passively in terms of having pain inflicted at childbirth. I completed my book before being able to read Beattie's *God's Mother, Eve's Advocate: A Gynocentric Refiguration of Marian Symbolism in Engagement with Luce Irigaray*, which substantially develops and nuances Beattie's position. Beattie develops the theme of female genealogies via Mary, rather than the saints, although there is room within her project for the latter.

18. Beattie is citing James Nelson's criticism of the metaphysics of male erection: big, hard, up = 'sovereign in power, righteous in judgement, the transcendent Wholly Other' – from Nelson's, 'On Doing Body Theology' p. 51.

19. 'Sexuality', p. 142.

20. 'Sexuality', p. 142, my brackets.

21. 'Sexuality', p. 143. See further Beattie, *Rediscovering Mary: Insights from the Gospel*. See also the recent political and feminist recoveries of Mary in Roman Catholicism: Ivone Gebara and Maria Clara Bingemer, *Mary: Mother of God, Mother of the Poor*; and Tissa Balasurıya, *Mary and Human Liberation: The Story and the Text*.

22. 'Sexuality', p. 146, my brackets.

23. See Janette Gray, 'Celibacy', p. 155, on this point concerning women's genealogies, and see also note 43, ch. 1.

24. 'Sexuality', p. 143.

25. For patriarchal sadomasochism in Christian spirituality and theology see Beverly Wildung Harrison and Carter Heyward, 'Pain and Pleasure: Avoiding the Confusions of Christian Tradition', and the useful survey of eroticizing

the divine in Sandra Friedman and Alexander Irwin, 'Christian Feminism, Eros and Power in Right Relation'.

26. See note 17 above and section 2 of this chapter.

27. See Argyle speaking about this work in 'Interview with Margaret Argyle'.

28. See Rowan Williams, 'Between the Cherubim: The Empty Tomb and the Empty Throne', and Kristeva's meditation on 'Holbein's Dead Christ'.

29. *Speculum*, pp. 199–200.

30. Graham Ward, 'Divinity and Sexuality', p. 228. See also Ward's ingenious development of this theme, in ways that complement my own: 'The Displaced Body of Jesus Christ'.

31. Steinberg, *Sexuality*, pp. 3–12.

32. See Caroline Walker Bynum, *The Resurrection of the Body in Western Christianity, 200–1336*, pp. 318–43.

33. Bynum, *Fragmentation*, p. 186, my bracket. Bynum carefully questions the modern erotic reading of these and other anatomical images.

34. Samuel Beckett depicts the erect phallus as the failed order of meaning in identifying the desire for death (hanging/suicide) as the means to sexual pleasure (Vladimir's way of getting an erection is to hang himself) in *Waiting for Godot* (1956).

35. *Reader*, p. 42. The employment of reciprocity at the end of this quotation admittedly deflates my suspicion of Irigaray's anatomical narcissism. Interestingly, the quotation transgresses Irigaray's rule that each sex must be allowed to speak its own language, to generate its own forms of representation. Here, *she speaks* for redeemed men's subjectivities.

36. I am well aware that here, as well as in the rest of the essay, the question of encoding homosexual and lesbian relations within the economy of signification *tends* towards the Freudian view of regression: that such relations are fixated on the refusal of otherness. Of course, within patriarchy, heterosexual relations can also reflect primary narcissism with equal, if not more, ease, as can celibacy.

37. See H. Langkammer, ' "Christ's Last Will and Testament" ' (John 19.26, 27) in the Interpretations of the Fathers of the Church and the Scholastics'.

38. E W, p. 208.

39. Raymond E. Brown, *The Gospel according to John. XIII–XXI*, p. 924.

40. Cited in Brown, *XIII–XXI*, p. 924, from Origen's commentary *In Jo*. 1 4(b); GCS 10:9.

41. Raymond E. Brown, *The Gospel according to John. I–XII*, p. 109. In *Lumen Gentium* 56a this parallelism is carefully noted. For the Genesis background to John, see Edward Hoskyns, 'Genesis 1–3 and St John's Gospel'.

42. Rudolf Bultmann rather stubbornly refuses that this was indeed a significant 'hour'. See Bultmann, *The Gospel of John: A Commentary*, p. 100.

43. Brown, *XIII–XXI*, p. 927.

44. See, for example, the important Protestant exegete, Max Thurian, *Mary, Mother of All Christians*. See also Norman Pittinger, *Our Lady: The Mother of Jesus in Christian Faith*, and John MacQuarrie, *Mary for all Christians*.

45. One might add that on this count Irigaray seems to have misunderstood Schüssler Fiorenza's argument. Admittedly, the patriarchal readings of Mary are legion: see Marina Warner, *Alone of All Her Sex – the Myth and the Cult of the Virgin Mary*. See also Warner's recognition of gender-different appropriations of the Marian tradition in the second edition: pp. 340–4.

46. Representation signifies the entire cultural order of production. In this book I look at philosophical-theological texts, literary texts and works of art. There remains, I think, to be carried out a sexuate analysis of religious music. Catherine Clément has begun with her analysis of opera in sexuate terms, under the metaphor of *Opera, or the Undoing of Women*. However, Clément's challenging book tends to treat opera as a text put to music rather than a mutual interaction by each on the other. Ironically, this prioritizes language and logos, rather than interpretation and Spirit. See for example her ideological reading of Mozart, where in performance the music often deconstructs the sung words. See especially her treatment of *Così fan tutte*, *The Marriage of Figaro* and *Don Giovanni*.

47. For example in her own outline of Steinberg's thesis she notes that he is concerned to focus on the penis primarily as evidence that 'humanation' meant 'enfleshing' (Bynum, *Fragmentation*, p. 84), but then she criticizes him for reading the penis as being *primarily* sexual to Renaissance audiences (pp. 88–92). Bynum actually offers very little analysis of Renaissance texts or art in her criticisms of Steinberg, despite her strong claims against his alleged readings: p. 92.

48. Bynum, *Fragmentation*, p. 85.

49. *Fragmentation*, p. 92.

50. See also on this point, Francis Martin, *The Feminist Question: Feminist Theology in the Light of Christian Tradition*, pp. 241–8. It is not clear to me that Martin's conclusion regarding the tradition's use of feminine terms within the context of speaking of God as 'he' shows that God is best called 'he' (p. 248) or that the term is gender neutral. Both arguments cannot be sustained, for, in the first instance, the accepted 'exceptions' (p. 248) permit a tradition-specific precedence. In the second instance, one could equally argue, as I have done, that the use of 'she' does not predicate gender *per se* to the divine.

51. The demise of allegorical reading of the bible, such as Frei charts in *The Eclipse of Biblical Narrative: A Study in Eighteenth and Nineteenth Century Hermeneutics* also finds a parallel in art: see Johan Huizinga, *The Waning of the Middle Ages: A Study of the Forms of Life, Thought and Art in France and the Netherlands in the XIVth and XVth Centuries*.

52. *Fragmentation*, p. 110.

53. *Fragmentation* p. 99.

54. See especially her provocative and helpful conclusions: Bynum, *Fragmentation*, pp. 178–9.

55. *Fragmentation*, p. 117.

56. *Speculum*, p. 16.

57. *Reader*, p. 14.

58. EW, p. 208.

59. Timothy L. Smith's review in *Fellowship of Catholic Scholars Quarterly*, 21, 1, 1997, pp. 30–2, p. 31.

60. See *Summa*, 1a. 28, and appendix 6 on 'Divine Relations' (pp. 141–4); 1a. 40; and 1a. 41, art. 5.

61. In what follows I rely heavily upon Robert Hamerton-Kelly, *God the Father: Theology and Patriarchy in the Teaching of Jesus*; and also Francis Martin, *Feminist Question*, pp. 265–92. The one instance, at the conclusion of this chapter, when Martin attributes the meaning of unique 'Unoriginate Source' to 'Father' (p. 289), he does so despite his technical exegesis which nowhere substantiates such an attribution.

62. Paul Ricoeur, 'Fatherhood: From Phantasm to Symbol', *The Conflict of Interpretations: Essays in Hermeneutics*, pp. 468–97.

63. 'Fatherhood', p. 468.

64. 'Fatherhood', p. 468.

65. 'Fatherhood', p. 469.

66. 'Fatherhood', p. 469, my brackets.

67. 'Fatherhood', p. 482.

68. 'Fatherhood', p. 486.

69. 'Fatherhood', p. 486.

70. 'Fatherhood', p. 487.

71. This lacuna is also true of Ricoeur's treatment of Genesis 1–2, where woman is invisible in his concentration on the creation of 'man' – see 'Fatherhood', p. 486. Hamerton-Kelly is more sensitive to Jewish patriarchal patterns shaping the expectation of responsibility regarding 'father', see Hamerton-Kelly, *God the Father*, pp. 55–7.

72. 'Sexuality', p. 146.

73. 'Fatherhood', p. 489.

74. 'Fatherhood', p. 490.

75. 'Fatherhood', p. 490–1.

76. 'Fatherhood', p. 493.

77. 'Fatherhood', p. 493.

78. 'Fatherhood', p. 493.

79. See, for example, Elizabeth Achtiemer, 'Exchanging God', and Roland M. Frye, 'Language for God'. See also Thomas A. Smail, *The Forgotten Father*, pp. 58–60.

80. See Dorothee Sölle, 'Paternalistic Religion as Experienced by Woman',

and Susan Brooks Thistlethwaite, *Sex, Race and God*. However, one should also see Irene de Bourbon-Parma-van Oranje Nassau, 'What Do I Think of When I Say the "Our Father"?', for a very positive reading. See the extremely nuanced reading provided in Janet Martin Soskice, 'Can a Feminist Call God "Father"?'.

81. Aquinas, *Summa Theologiae*, 1a. 33, arts. 1–4, esp. art. 2. One must acknowledge that Aquinas' argument for not using mother as an analogical name is utterly related to his uncritical Aristotelianism on this point. Aquinas argues, following Aristotle, in the *Summa Contra Gentiles*, iv, ii, that even though 'Father' is not a proper name it cannot be replaced by mother, for 'God begets actively, and the role of the mother in procreation is, on the other hand, passive'. See Prudence Allen, *Concept of Woman*, pp. 385–407, on Aquinas' uncritical appropriation of Aristotle's gender assumptions.

82. Colin Gunton, 'Proetus and Procrustes: A Study in the Dialectic of Language in Disagreement with Sallie McFague'.

83. *Reconceiving*, p. 14.

84. *Reconceiving*, p. 15.

85. I am drawing entirely on Moltmann's *The Trinity* and 'The Motherly Father: Is Trinitarian Patripassianism Replacing Theological Patriarchalism?'.

86. Moltmann, *Kingdom*, pp. 162–70.

87. *Kingdom*, p. 166.

88. Roger Olson, 'Trinity and Eschatology: The Historical Being of God in Jürgen Moltmann and Wolfhart Pannenberg'.

89. Olson, 'Trinity and Eschatology', p. 226.

90. Olson, 'Trinity and Eschatology', p. 226.

91. Miroslav Volf, *After our Likeness: The Church as the Image of the Trinity*, p. 217, note 110.

92. Cited by Moltmann, 'Motherly Father', p. 53; Moltmann, *Trinity*, p. 165; and see Boff, *Trinity*, p. 170; DZ 526. This is also the basic position of Maria Clara Bingemer, 'Reflections on the Trinity'. See how the questions posed to Toledo are interpreted properly by Diana Neal, 'Out of the Uterus of the Father'.

93. See Graham Ward, 'In the Name of the Father and of the Mother', who makes an analogous point about liturgical inclusivism which always threatens to obscure the realities of sexual difference.

94. Moltmann, 'Motherly Father', p. 53.

95. See also Moltmann, *Trinity*, pp. 182–5.

96. I must acknowledge that I am relying on the *Concilium* English translation of Moltmann's text, but the same language is used in the English translation of Moltmann's *Trinity*, pp. 162–6.

97. *Speculum*, p. 16.

98. *Reader*, p. 41.

99. *Reader*, p. 40. Moltmann's tendency to theorizing in an ahistorical 'lib-

eral' manner is thoughtfully isolated and criticized in Arne Rasmusson, *The Church as Polis: From Political Theology to Theological Politics as Exemplified by Jürgen Moltmann and Stanley Hauerwas*. Rasmusson's study is not concerned with gender issues, but his critique supports my reading of Moltmann in this instance.

100. *Systematic*, pp. 325, 334.

101. *Systematic*, p. 262.

102. *Systematic*, p. 319.

103. *Systematic*, p. 319.

104. *Systematic*, pp. 304ff.

105. See Weinandy, *Reconceiving*, pp. 25–52, and the bibliography therein; John O'Donnell's helpful article, 'In Him and over Him: The Holy Spirit in the Life of Jesus'; and J. D. G. Dunn, *Jesus and the Spirit*. All relentlessly show that the entire life of Jesus is 'inconceivable' without the Spirit.

106. *Systematic*, p. 312.

107. *Systematic*, p. 320.

108. John O'Donnell, 'Pannenberg's Doctrine of God', p. 96.

109. See Karl Rahner, *The Trinity*, pp. 21–38, 101–3. Catholic theologians like Kasper also express reservations about Rahner's vice versa, while nevertheless agreeing, like me, that the economic is the immanent trinity: Kasper, *God of Jesus Christ*, pp. 299–303. For an outright Roman Catholic departure from Rahner, so as to question the conceptual distinction between immanent and economic trinity, see Catherine Mowry LaCugna, *God for Us*, pp. 211–12. For two most incisive criticisms of the danger of LaCugna's move at this point see Weinandy, *Reconceiving*, pp. 123–36, and Joe DiNoia, Review of LaCugna.

110. *Systematic*, p. 262.

111. *Systematic*, p. 262.

112. Elizabeth Achtiemer, 'Exchanging God'.

113. See John Milbank, 'The Name of Jesus', *The Word Made Strange: Theology, Language, Culture*, pp. 145–6.

114. See my *The Trinity and the Meeting of Religions*, ch. 4.

3. Gendered divinity and Satanic fiction

I am using the first, London: Viking Penguin 1988, edition of *The Satanic Verses. The Ground beneath Her Feet*, London: Jonathan Cape 1999, was published after this MS was completed, but Rushdie's concerns continue to develop in this new book.

1. See Gavin D'Costa, 'Satanic Discourse and the Clash of Faiths: "The Satanic Verses" in British Society'. See also the bibliography in the notes there for secondary literature (including Said). Since then, see especially Ziaud-

din Sardar and Merryl Wyn Davies, *Distorted Imaginations: Lessons from the Rushdie Affair*; Dan Cohn-Sherbok (ed.), *The Salman Rushdie Controversy in Interreligious Perspective*; and most importantly Talal Asad, *Genealogies of Religion: Discipline and Reasons of Power in Christianity and Islam*.

2. Edward Said, *Orientalism: Western Conceptions of the Orient*; and see also *Covering Islam: How the Media and the Experts Determine How We See the Rest of the World*.

3. These two texts can be said to represent important aspects of postmodernism. See Jean-François Lyotard, *The Postmodern Condition: A Report on Knowledge*, and Jacques Derrida, *Of Grammatology*. Rushdie refers to both in various essays.

4. *Sexes*, p. v.

5. *Satanic Verses*, p. 95.

6. See Hassan Ibrahim Hassan, *Islam: A Religious, Political, Social and Economic Study*, pp. 24–6. See also Sara Maitland's retelling of the Abraham story which refuses to allow Abraham to be the unsullied 'hero': *Angel and Me*, pp. 3–35.

7. Rushdie, *Shame*, p. 38.

8. See Peter Harrison, *'Religion' and the Religions in the English Enlightenment*; see also Wilfred Cantwell Smith, *The Meaning and End of Religion*; and Nicholas Lash, *The Beginning and the End of 'Religion'*.

9. Lisa Appignanesi and Sara Maitland (eds), *The Rushdie File*, p. 39: from *India Today*, 15 August 1988.

10. Malise Ruthven, *A Satanic Affair*, p. 15; given without reference. The *fatwā* is reason enough for Rushdie's inconsistency.

11. Timothy Brennan, *Salman Rushdie and the Third World*, p. 101.

12. 'The Courter', *East, West*, pp. 173–211, closely and clearly overlaps with *The Satanic Verses*.

13. *Moor's Last Sigh*, p. 226.

14. *Moor's Last Sigh*, p. 218.

15. *Satanic Verses*, p. 43.

16. See Brennan, *Third World*, ch. 1, and also Gaytri Chakravorty Spivak, *In Other Worlds: Essays in Cultural Politics*, and Said, *Orientalism*. Of course these self-appointed spokespersons also represent their own interests. See for example the interesting criticisms of Said by Arab reviewers in Emmanuel Sivan, 'Edward Said and His Arab Reviewers', *Interpretations of Islam Past and Present*, pp. 133–54.

17. *Satanic Verses*, p. 370.

18. *Satanic Verses*, p. 4.

19. Arthur J. Arberry (translator), *The Koran Interpreted*, p. xi.

20. Arberry, *Koran*, p. ix.

21. Arberry, *Koran*, p. x.

22. Ibn Ishaq, *The Life of Muhammed*, pp. 95, 452 and esp. 95–8 tell the story of how Salman the Persian became a Muslim.

23. *Satanic Verses*, p. 102.

24. Ishaq, *Life*, p. 166.

25. A. Guillaume, *Islam*, p. 187.

26. Guillaume, *Islam*, p. 186.

27. *Satanic Verses*, p. 107.

28. Guillaume notes that the names and the phrase 'exalted maidens' are especially significant as they constituted 'the chant of the Quraysh as they processed around the Ka'ba'. Guillaume, *Islam*, p. 186.

29. *Satanic Verses*, p. 124.

30. This is Rushdie's interpretation. Muhammad Asad's commentary on these verses suggests that in fact they work only when understood as a critique of pagan Arabs who while worshipping female deities nevertheless treated their female offspring with contempt. Hence 'quite apart from the blasphemous belief in God's having "offspring" of any kind, their ascribing to Him what they themselves despised gave the lie to their alleged "reverence" for Him whom they, too, regarded as the Supreme Being'. From, *The Message of the Qur'an*, p. 814.

31. *Satanic Verses*, p. 363.

32. *Satanic Verses*, p. 364. Traditionally Muslims have seen the Koran as a very limited source of rules, with a common tradition that there are only about five hundred verses in the Koran which refer to legal matters. The most productive source in the construction of Islamic law is the Sunna of the Prophets. See Wilfred Cantwell Smith, *Understanding Islam*, pp. 78–109; and R. M. Savory (ed.), *Introduction to Islamic Civilization*, pp. 54–60.

33. See Rushdie's essays, 'The New Empire within Britain', *Imaginary Homelands*, pp. 129–38, and 'Outside the Whale', *Imaginary*, pp. 87–101.

34. *Satanic Verses*, p. 168.

35. See his interesting discussion of 'Palestinianess' with Edward Said in *Imaginary*, pp. 166–84, where Rushdie refuses to side uncritically with 'victims', in this case the Palestinians.

36. *Satanic Verses*, p. 340.

37. *Satanic Verses*, p. 392.

38. *Satanic Verses*, p. 3.

39. *Satanic Verses*, p. 44.

40. *Satanic Verses*, p. 43.

41. *Satanic Verses*, p. 370.

42. *Satanic Verses*, p. 285.

43. *Satanic Verses*, p. 413.

44. *Satanic Verses*, p. 415.

45. *Satanic Verses*, p. 52.

46. *Satanic Verses*, p. 52.

47. *Satanic Verses*, p. 52.

48. *Satanic Verses*, p. 54.

49. *Satanic Verses*, p. 16.

50. *Satanic Verses*, p. 17.

51. *Satanic Verses*, pp. 29f.

52. *Satanic Verses*, p. 206.

53. *Satanic Verses*, p. 209.

54. *Satanic Verses*, p. 209.

55. *Satanic Verses*, p. 30.

56. *Satanic Verses*, p. 211.

57. *Satanic Verses*, p. 210.

58. *Satanic Verses*, p. 211, my brackets.

59. *Satanic Verses*, p. 75ff.

60. *Satanic Verses*, p. 292.

61. This is an interesting reversal of colonial strategies. Rushdie is drawing from Eliot's use of eastern wisdom in *The Wasteland* with the voice of thunder over 'Himavant' deriving from Sanskrit Upanishadic words: da-datta-da-dayadhvam-da-damyata. 'Tat' is Sanskrit from the Upanishadic saying 'tat tvam asi', that art thou, and in co-joining it to taa he turns high classic into low doggerel: ta-ta, goodbye. T. S. Eliot, *The Wasteland*, *Collected Poems 1909–62*, Book V: 'What the Thunder Said', lines 397–420, pp. 78–9. Brennan is unnecessarily sanctimonious concerning Rushdie's use of dub/rap (Brennan, *Salman Rushdie and the Third World*, p. 164), reading intentional parody as Rushdie's bad political faith.

62. *Satanic Verses*, p. 3.

63. *Satanic Verses*, p. 455.

64. *Satanic Verses*, p. 297.

65. *Satanic Verses*, p. 297.

66. *Satanic Verses*, p. 298.

67. *Satanic Verses*, p. 4.

68. *Satanic Verses*, p. 45.

69. *Satanic Verses*, p. 217.

70. *Satanic Verses*, p. 81.

71. *Satanic Verses*, p. 78.

72. *Satanic Verses*, p. 95.

73. Freud, *Totem and Taboo*, Penguin Freud Library, Vol. 13, London: Penguin 1985, p. 51. Freud's texts will be subsequently referred to as *Moses* and *Totem* and both are taken from the Penguin edition. Other texts by Freud in this chapter are also from the Penguin edition. Most of my biographical comments on Freud are based on Ernst Jones, *Sigmund Freud: Life and Works*, and, for Rushdie: Appiganesi and Maitland, *Rushdie File*, and Ruthven, *Satanic Affair*.

74. *Moses*, p. 243. See also the interesting account of Freud's murdered Father God by Dominique Stein, 'The Murder of the Father and God the Father in the Work of Freud'.

75. See editor's note to *Moses*, p. 241.

76. *Satanic Verses*, p. 467.

77. *Satanic Verses*, p. 367.

78. *Satanic Verses*, p. 368.

79. R. W. J. Austen, 'Islam and the Feminine', p. 37.

80. *Satanic Verses*, p. 374.

81. Rushdie's previous novels, *Midnights Children* (1981) and *Shame* (1983) were both banned in a number of Muslim countries or countries with sizable populations of Muslims.

82. *Moses*, p. 283.

83. *Satanic Verses*, pp. 118, 366, 369, 374.

84. This severe judgment is found in Guillaume, *Islam*, pp. 71–2, who ironically, in the light of my own argument about Christian patriarchy, states: 'In this matter of the status of women lies the greatest difference between the Muslim and Christian world.' Wickens is slightly less presumptious about Christian/European practices, but makes a similar judgment to Guillaume. He says of women in Islam, with exceptions, 'there was a sense in which they had no identity outside the family, belonging (so to speak) to some male or other, father, husband, brother, uncle or whatever', in R. M. Savory, 'Islam in the Middle East', *Introduction to Islamic Civilization*, pp. 7–13, p. 7.

85. In *Totem*, despite Freud's disowning foundational status for his readings (pp. 159 and 220, note 2), it is present in the text, and even more strongly five years earlier in 'Obsessive Actions and Religious Practices' (1907), Vol. 13, p. 40. By the time of *Moses* (1934–8) there is no ambiguity in his foundational reading strategy – e.g. pp. 326–34. Since the completion of this MS, James J. DiCenso, *The Other Freud: Religion, Culture and Psychoanalysis*, has caused me to reconsider the position I advance here.

86. *Satanic Verses*, p. 110.

87. See 'Dreams', *Introductory Lectures on Psychoanalysis*, pp. 111–280.

88. *Satanic Verses*, p. 19

89. *Satanic Verses*, p. 19.

90. *Satanic Verses*, p. 19.

91. *Satanic Verses*, pp. 544–6.

92. *Totem*, p. 123.

93. Prefatory Note I to Part III of *Moses*, p. 295.

94. *Satanic Verses*, p. 468.

95. Freud, *Introductory Lectures*, Vol. 1, pp. 50–110.

96. *Totem*, p. 146.

97. *Totem*, p. 148.

98. *Totem*, p. 192.
99. *Totem*, p. 203.
100. *Moses*, p. 337.
101. *Moses*, p. 337.
102. As an aside, Freud's view of eastern religions is that they have 'come to a halt' for at their core they are 'ancestor worship'. *Moses*, p. 337.
103. *Satanic Verses*, p. 19.
104. *Satanic Verses*, p. 118.
105. *Satanic Verses*, p. 121.
106. *Satanic Verses*, p. 118.
107. *Satanic Verses*, p. 114.
108. *Satanic Verses*, p. 117.
109. *Satanic Verses*, p. 115.
110. *Satanic Verses*, p. 121.
111. *Satanic Verses*, p. 124.
112. *Satanic Verses*, p. 382.
113. *Satanic Verses*, p. 125.
114. *Satanic Verses*, p. 118.
115. See Ishaq, *Life*, on Khadija, pp. 82–3, 106–13, 191, 313. There is no account of why she died (191), but historically her death is correctly positioned in the novel.
116. *Satanic Verses*, p. 125.
117. I am especially indebted to Dr Robert Gleave, my Islamicist colleague at Bristol, for his linguistic help with these words.
118. *Satanic Verses*, p. 126.
119. *Satanic Verses*, p. 8.
120. *Satanic Verses*, p. 364.
121. Ruthven, *Satanic Affair*, p. 7.
122. Austen, 'Feminine', p. 43.
123. See Maura O'Neill, *Women Speaking–Women Listening: Women in Inter-religious Dialogue*, pp. 53–65, and also Diana Eck and Devalai Jain (eds), *Speaking of Faith: Global Perspectives on Women, Religions and Social Change*. The important Muslim woman writer Nadia Hijab makes some interesting comments in 'Nadia Hijab Speaks on Women in the Arab World'. Perhaps one of the best explorations of Islamic women is found in Fatima Mernissi, *Beyond the Veil: Male-Female Dynamics in Modern Muslim Society*.
124. *Satanic Verses*, pp. 366–7.
125. This is true at least of: Shabbir Akhtar, *Be Careful with Muhammad! The Salman Rushdie Affair*; Muhammad Mashuq ibn Ally, 'Stranger Exiled from Home'; Ruthven, *Satanic Affair*; Sardar and Davies, *Distorted Imaginations*; and the various Muslims cited in Appignanesi and Maitland, *Rushdie File*.
126. *Satanic Verses*, p. 374.

127. *Satanic Verses*, p. 374.

128. *Satanic Verses*, p. 374.

129. *Satanic Verses*, p. 394.

130. *Satanic Verses*, p. 394, my emphasis.

131. See Ishaq, *Life*, pp. 679–83, for this incident and fn. 36. There Muhammad is with Ayesha alone at his death and makes a choice for death with his last words being: 'Nay, rather the Exalted Companions of Paradise' (p. 681). Rushdie picks up on the title 'Exalted' which was also used with reference to the 'exalted maidens', Lat, Uzza and Manat. Technically, it should have been Manat, the goddess of fate and death at Mahound's bedside, but Rushdie, it would seem, has chosen to overthrow such realistic identification and implicitly goes for a perichoretic view of the divine.

132. *Satanic Verses*, p. 19.

133. *Satanic Verses*, p. 22.

134. *Satanic Verses*, p. 22.

135. *Satanic Verses*, p. 23.

136. *Satanic Verses*, p. 24.

137. *Satanic Verses*, pp. 40, 44.

138. *Satanic Verses*, p. 49.

139. *Satanic Verses*, p. 53.

140. Augustine, *Confessions*, 1.1, and *The Trinity*, 1.2.

141. See *Moses*, pp. 339–46; and Ernst Jones's discussion of this concept in his biography, *Sigmund Freud*, Vol. 3, ch. 10.

142. The one theologian he comments on favourably is Don Cupitt, although I would read Cupitt as proposing a form of constructive nihilism rather than expressing an apophatic Christian faith. See Rushdie's mention of Cupitt, in 'Is Nothing Sacred', *Imaginary*, p. 423. For a good theological reading of Cupitt, see Gerard Loughlin, *Telling God's Story: Bible, Church and Narrative Theology*, pp. 10–17.

143. See Gavin D'Costa, 'Secular Discourse', pp. 425–9.

144. *Satanic Verses*, p. 95.

145. *Summa Theologiae*, 1a. 2–11. I am indebted to David Burrell in reading Aquinas on this matter: see Burrell, *Aquinas: God and Action*. Burrell also deals with the Muslim and Jewish parallels to this doctrine in *Knowing the Unknowable God: Ibn-Sina, Maimonides, Aquinas*. Where postmodernity turns into religious sensibility rather than nihilism see, for example, John Caputo, *The Prayers and Tears of Jacques Derrida: Religion without Religion*, and especially his comments on Rushdie and the problem of 'determinable' religions in Section 4. It is worth pursuing the allusions to Moses on Sinai, in his being encountered by the unnameable ineffable 'God', and Allie Cone's experience at the top of Everest where she faces death 'because it is not permitted to mortals to look more than once upon the face of the divine' – *Satanic Verses*, p. 303. For an

illuminating discussion of different forms of postmodernist 'religion' see Gerard Loughlin, *Telling God's Story*, pp. 3–26.

146. *Satanic Verses*, p. 318.

147. *Satanic Verses*, p. 318.

148. *Satanic Verses*, p. 409.

149. See for example: Brennan, *Third World*; Wimal Dissanayake, 'Towards a Decolonized English: South Asian Creativity in Fiction'; A. D. Needham, 'The Politics of Post-Colonial Identity in Salman Rushdie'.

150. *Satanic Verses*, p. 537.

151. Admittedly, immediately after the incident Swatilekha's point of view is undermined by herself: 'Too much college education' she apologizes to Bhupen (*Satanic Verses*, p. 537).

152. *Satanic Verses*, p. 321.

153. *Satanic Verses*, p. 353.

154. Translated by Muhammad Asad, *Message*, pp. 446–7, his brackets. See also pp. 994–5 where Asad indicates the different senses the word jinn has within the Quran.

155. *Satanic Verses*, p. 323.

156. *Satanic Verses*, p. 323.

157. *Satanic Verses*, p. 353.

158. *Satanic Verses*, p. 37.

159. *Satanic Verses*, p. 43, my brackets.

160. *Satanic Verses*, p. 49.

161. *Satanic Verses*, p. 51.

162. *Satanic Verses*, pp. 50–1.

163. *Satanic Verses*, p. 49.

164. *Satanic Verses*, p. 26.

165. *Satanic Verses*, p. 427.

166. *Satanic Verses*, p. 427.

167. *Satanic Verses*, p. 294.

168. *Satanic Verses*, p. 526.

169. *Satanic Verses*, p. 530.

170. *Satanic Verses*, p. 540. Brennan misreads the entire book on the basis of excluding a vital part of a quotation to support his own conclusion regarding the book's 'triumphant conclusion' (Brennan, *Third World*, p. 154) that 'evil is never total, that its victory, no matter how overwhelming, is never absolute' (p. 154, citing *The Satanic Verses*, p. 467). The proper context of the quote (including an omitted question mark) means that there is a lot more ambivalence than Brennan allows for: '*Is it possible* that evil is never total, that its victory, no matter how overwhelming, is never absolute?' (p. 467, my emphasis).

171. *Satanic Verses*, p. 547.

172. Joseph Ratzinger mounts a similar argument against the western trinit-

arian tradition, mainly Augustine, for not applying the insights regarding 'relations' in God to that of the human person. See his 'Concerning the Notion of Person in Theology'.

4. Icons and idols

1. Graham Ward, *Barth, Derrida and the Language of Theology*, p. 174; see also John Milbank's reflections on the liberal pluralist undergirdings of the term 'dialogue' in John Milbank, 'The End of Dialogue'. Kenneth Surin also supports the point: 'A "Politics of Speech": Towards an Understanding of the Relationships between the Religions in the Age of the McDonald's Hamburger'. Talal Asad, *Genealogies of Religion*, also makes clear (from a Muslim point of view?) that dialogue is too uncritical a term in view of the politics of encounter.

2. See Leonid Ouspensky, *Theology of the Icon*, Vol. 2, esp. pp. 262–73, 399–403. See also Leonid Ouspensky and Vladimir Lossky, *The Meaning of Icons*, which contains more colour plates, and specifically on Rublev's trinity see pp. 200–5. See also *Contemplating Icons: An Introduction to Icons and Prayer*, a video based on Viktor Bakchine's work, *Introduction à la Connaissance des Iconês*.

3. Gen. 18.1–18.

4. See the commentaries by Claus Westermann, *Genesis 12–36: A Commentary*; Gerhard von Rad, *Genesis: A Commentary*; St Augustine, *The Trinity*, 2.11–12. It is also worth comparing the startling commentary on Abraham and Isaac provided by Søren Kierkegaard, *Fear and Trembling: A Dialectic Lyric*, and Erich Auerbach, *Mimesis: The Representation of Reality in Western Literature*, ch. 1; and the feminist rereading provided by Sarah Maitland (from Sarah's point of view) in *Angel and Me*, pp. 3–35, and Rushdie's reading (from Hagar's point of view) in *The Satanic Verses*, pp. 78, 95–9. Engaging with these multiple readings constantly brings us back to the scriptural texts afresh.

5. See Westermann, *Genesis*, p. 275.

6. Gen. 17.5, 15. Von Rad, *Genesis*, p. 204, while still constrained by the historical-critical method, is more open to such rereadings than Westermann. Nevertheless, he says, 'The interpretation given by the early church that the trinity of visitors is a reference to the Trinity has been universally abandoned by recent exegesis' (p. 206). But 'recent' exegesis has moved on considerably; see for example Francis Watson (ed.), *The Open Text: New Directions for Biblical Studies*, and Anthony Thiselton, *New Horizons in Hermeneutics: The Theory and Practice of Transforming Biblical Reading*.

7. See Ouspensky, *Icon*, p. 263. I say Marcionite because such rereadings of extinction are rightly deemed heretical. Rosemary Ruether prioritizes Jewish reading strategies and simply reverses the univocal control over the texts. See

Faith and Fratricide and my critical engagement with her in 'One Covenant or Many Covenants? Towards a Theology of Christian-Jewish Relations'.

8. Compare the inclusion of the cluttered table and Abraham and Sarah in a number of icons of this incident. For example, see the *Old Testament Trinity*, Novogorod School, *c.* 1400, Russian Museum, Leningrad.

9. Ouspensky and Lossky, *Icons*, p. 202; see also Ouspensky, *Icon*, ch. 14, regarding the edicts of the Great Moscow Council of 1667 on the iconic rather than idolatrous representation of God. In the Orthodox tradition, represented by Lossky, following Gregory Palamas, the Godhead in itself is the darkness of unknowing; the 'energies' mediate Father, Son and Spirit. See Vladimir Lossky, *The Mystical Theology of the Eastern Church*, esp. ch. 2, 'The Divine Darkness', and ch. 5, 'Uncreated Energies'. One of the best introductions to Lossky is Rowan Williams, 'The Via Negativa and the Foundations of Theology: An Introduction to the Thought of V. N. Lossky'.

10. See Andrew Louth's *Discerning the Mystery* for the early church's methods of exegesis; and Hans Frei, *Eclipse of Biblical Narrative*, for an analysis of the 'eclipse' of this manner of reading.

11. Westermann, *Genesis*, p. 277. The cargo cults also worked on this principle, but with very different results!

12. Freud's view of laughter can be tellingly employed here regarding the linguistic dissonance in the Hebrew word 'yishaq'. See Sigmund Freud, *Jokes and the Relationship to the Unconscious*, 1905; Penguin Freud Library, Vol. 6, Harmondsworth: Penguin 1976. On Aristotle, see Karl-Josef Kuschel, *Laughter: A Theological Essay*, pp. 16–31.

13. Rom. 4.19–21. See also Karl-Josef Kuschel's discussion of the Pauline repression, in *Laughter*, pp. 49–53.

14. See B. Vawter's commentary on Genesis in *A New Catholic Commentary on Holy Scripture*, ed. Fuller, Johnston and Kearns, pp. 166–205, p. 194.

15. For an interesting analysis of 'gift' within postmodern philosophy, see John Milbank, 'Can a Gift be Given?', esp. pp. 144–61, where he argues against Derrida and Bourdieu, who question the very possibility of 'gift'. Milbank firmly locates the possibility of gift within trinitarian relationships.

16. This is an initial argument in Wilfred Cantwell Smith, *What Is Scripture?*, who seeks to show that no one owns different scriptures. However, Cantwell Smith does not take seriously the claims made within any interpretative community in deference to an allegedly general descriptive theory that he *imposes* upon all 'scriptures' without theological warrant. His warrant is that of the positivist historian. See Christopher Sinkinson, review in 'Scripture and Scriptures: The Problems of Hermeneutics in Inter-Religious Dialogue'.

17. See Robert Hughes, *The Shock of the New: Art and the Century of Change*, pp. 348–53, Plate 230.

18. Admittedly, there is considerable controversy regarding the status of the trinity within the New Testament communities. But see Arthur Wainwright, *The Trinity in the New Testament*, the interesting study by A. T. Hanson, *Jesus Christ in the Old Testament*, and Wolfhart Pannenberg, *Systematic Theology*, Vol. 1, pp. 259–79.

19. See: Paul Hacker, *Theological Foundations of Evangelization*, ch. 2; Henri de Lubac, *The Church: Paradox and Mystery*, ch. 4; and the very helpful monograph by C. Saldhana, *Divine Pedagogy: A Patristic View of Non-Christian Religions*. For an excellent overview see Francis A. Sullivan, *Salvation outside the Church?*

20. To see these questions being posed by the Roman Catholic Indian hierarchy, see G. Rosales and C. G. Arévalo (eds), *For All the Peoples of Asia: Federation of Asian Bishops' Conferences Documents from 1970 to 1991*.

21. For an excellent history of Christianity in India see Stephen Neill, *A History of Christianity in India: The Beginnings to AD 1707*. For the complex and pluralist state of theological reflection today see M. Amaladoss, T. T. John and G. Gispert-Sauch (eds), *Theologizing in India*.

22. See especially Richard Taylor, *Some Interpretations of Jesus in Indian Painting*, John F. Butler, *Christian Art in India*, and the study of Angelo de Fonseca by S. Schüeller, *Angelo de Fonseca: India's Catholic Artist*. There is a brief section on India in Masao Takenaka, *Christian Art in Asia*.

23. See Jyoti Sahi, *The Child and the Serpent: Reflection on Popular Indian Symbols* and *Stepping Stones: Reflections on the Theology of Indian Christian Culture*. Both contain illustrations by Sahi, and *Stepping* contains many fine colour and black and white reproductions of a wide range of his works offering something of an artistic autobiography. For helpful background on Indian art and symbolism, see also: Heinrich Zimmer, *Myths and Symbols in Indian Art and Civilization*; Stella Kramrisch, *The Art of India*; W. D. O'Flaherty, *Asceticism and Eroticism in the Mythology of Śiva*; and, for a concise overview, Roy C. Craven, *A Concise History of Indian Art*.

24. Some of the information on Sahi is derived from my long interview with the artists for 'How Far Can an Artist Go?'

25. See my article on Griffith's ashram and its architectural and cultic ethos in 'A Hindu Christianity', and the subsequent two numbers in the letter pages regarding these issues.

26. Regarding the ashram movement, see Sr. Vandana, *Ashrams and Social Justice*, and Catherine Cornille, *The Guru in Indian Catholicism*.

27. *Stepping*, pp. 73–4. See also the similar criticisms of Asian theologians well summarized in George Gispert-Sauch, 'Asian Theology'.

28. *Stepping*, pp. 74–5, my bracket.

29. *Stepping*, pp. 74, 8–27; see also Lamin Sanneh on translation: *Encountering the West. Christianity and the Global Cultural Process: The African Dimension*,

pp. 73–116. Fiction is a helpful medium in which these issues are explored: see the problem of inculturation explored in the fiction of Chinua Achebe (of Nigeria) in *Things Fall Apart*, in an African Trilogy, and Shusaku Endo (in Japan), *Silence*.

30. Salman Rushdie, *Shame*, p. 71.

31. *Stepping*, p. 75, my bracket. For the notion of non-identical repetition see John Milbank, *Word Made Strange*, pp. 145–70.

32. Many western depictions of Mary and the angel pay marvellous attention to the hands. See the illustrations and discussion in Jaroslav Pelican, *Mary through the Centuries*, esp. pp. 81–96.

33. For example see Felix Wilfred, *Sunset in the East: Asian Challenges and Christian Involvement*, pp. 212ff.; and 'Some Tentative Reflections on the Language of Christian Uniqueness: An Indian Perspective'; and Aloysius Pieris, *An Asian Theology of Liberation*, pp. 47, 59–65.

34. See J. Gray, 'Legacy of Canaan'.

35. *Stepping*, p. 24.

36. See the analysis of modernity on Hinduism offered by: Paul Hacker, in various essays in his *Kleine Schriften*; David Kopf, *The Brāhmo Samāj and the Shaping of the Modern Indian Mind*; Milton Singer, *When a Great Tradition Modernizes*.

37. Richard Lannoy, *The Speaking Tree*, pp. 36–9. Of course, the Jesse tree has a long iconographical and genealogical history within Christianity: see Arthur Watson, *The Early Iconography of the Tree of Jesse*.

38. See 1 Cor. 13–12; Rev. 22.4. It is worth recalling Rushdie's focus on the great walnut tree in Saladin's childhood garden, his naming of the plants and trees as a sign of his loss of innocence, and his father's eventual transformation of the tree at the end of the novel, bringing together father and son. See *Satanic Verses*, pp. 44–5, 515, 520–2.

39. See Lannoy, *Speaking Tree*; Sen Gupta Sankar, *Tree Symbol Worship in India: A New Survey of a Pattern of Folk-Religion*; James Fergusson, *Tree and Serpent Worship or Illustrations of Mythology and Art in India in the First to Fourth Centuries after Christ*.

40. Max Müller (ed.), *The Śatapatha-Brāhamana, Sacred Books of the East*.

41. Benjamin Rowland, *The Art and Architecture of India*, p. 38. See also Mortimer Wheeler's discussion of the yakshī in *The Indus Civilization*, plus Sahi, *Child*, p. 157 with its eyewitness account of the religious practice around a tree in Gwalior Fort, and Lawrence A. Babb, *The Divine Hierarchy: Popular Hinduism in Central India*.

42. Sahi, *Child*, pp. 151–2. The quote importantly continues, 'Thus soma, the Vedic offering of intoxicating drink, and coefficient with Agni in the Vedic *yajna* or sacrifice, is represented as a plant. From the distilled liquor of the tree of life, man is brought into the ecstatic kingdom of the gods.'

43. See Sahi's entrance porch to Bede Griffith's ashram, where Jesus is central, and also the window grill for the NBCLC, and the trinity for the Missio Calendar, 1975 – with the former two illustrated in *Stepping*, p. 154 and Fig. 12 for the latter on an unnumbered page.

44. Friedhelm Hardy is critical of the easy assimilation of 'trinity' to *trimūrti*, especially because of the tradition of the fourth head, which, as we shall see, Sahi takes most seriously. See Steward Sutherland et al. (eds), *The World Religions*, p. 610. This assimilation has a long artistic and conceptual pedigree. See J. Mattam, *Land of the Trinity: A Study of Modern Christian Approaches*, who examines a number of key figures in this assimilative tradition.

45. Margaret and James Stutley, *A Dictionary of Hinduism*, p. 304.

46. *Stepping*, p. 189. Īshwara is the term used for 'Lord' and comes from the Sanskrit root 'is': to have power. See also E. B. Havell, *Indian Sculpture and Painting*.

47. See David Kinsley, *The Sword and the Flute: Kālī and Krishna, Dark Visions of the Terrible and the Sublime in Hindu Mythology*; Wendell Charles Beane, *Myth, Cult, Symbols in Śākta Hinduism: A Study of the Indian Mother Goddess*; and Nareen Tewari (on Durga): *The Mother Goddess Vaiṣhna Devi*.

48. R. C. Zaehner most clearly saw this in Christianity and Hinduism in his marvellous study, *Our Savage God*, which raises important critical questions for Hinduism.

49. See *Child*, pp. 153–4.

50. See Endo, *Silence*, and the analysis of Endo by John T. Netland, 'Encountering Christ in Shusaku Endo's Mudswamp of Japan'.

51. See the exploration of this question in: David Bosch, *Transforming Mission: Paradigm Shifts in Theology of Mission*, esp. pt II; Netland, 'Mudswamp'; and the essays by Teresa J. Kirschner, 'Encounter and Assimilation of the Other in *Arauco domando* and *La Araucana* by Lope de Vega', and Andrew Fleck, 'Crusoe's Shadow: Christianity, Colonization and the Other', *Historicizing*, ed. Hawley, pp. 33–44 and 74–89 respectively.

52. See *Stepping*, pp. 155–7; and the seminar publication with a contribution from Sahi in Cecil Hargreaves and Christopher Duraising (eds), *India's Search for Reality and the Relevance of the Gospel of John*.

53. For materials on the connection between John's prologue and Genesis see note 41, Chapter 2.

54. See also Sahi, *Child*, pp. 8–11.

55. *Guha* means 'secret one' and is an epithet applied to Skanda, Shiva and Vishnu.

56. Sahi, *Child*, p. 106.

57. R. C. Zaehner, *Hinduism*, p. 69. For a detailed exposition of the place

of the *guṇas* within Sāmkhya metaphysics, see Sarvapelli Radhakrishnan, *Indian Philosophy*, Vol. 2, pp. 248–335.

58. See *Reader*, pp. 45–6.

59. See Mortimer Wheeler, *Indus Civilization*, on the *trimūrti* and the meditating yogi, and Kurian Mathothu, *The Development of the Concept of Trimūrti in Hinduism*.

60. See O'Flaherty, *Asceticism and Eroticism*, which explores these themes in considerable detail.

61. Sahi, *Child*, p. 113.

62. See Bharat Dogaria, *Towards a Liberation Theology of Hinduism*, which reads the *Rāmāyana* in terms of liberation, including feminist liberation in Dalit theology. Of course, feminists within the west have also raised similar issues, but the differences here should not be minimized, especially because of the different dynamics inherent within the cultural symbolic traditions. See also Sahi, *Child*, chs 3, 9 and 10, which in turn are also heavily dependent on Jung. Sahi is uncritical of Jung's equating the feminine with the intuitive, dark and irrational forces – which tends to mimic the female hysteric.

63. See Heinrich Zimmer, *Philosophies of India*, pp. 372–8. There is a considerable difference in the understanding and use of *Aum* within the Hindu tradition. The Christian interpolation enters yet one more, but related, reading.

64. Sahi, *Child*, pp. 95–6. The *liṅga* represents the male phallus and is joined to the *yoni*, female genitals, in the sacred altar of Shivite and other temples.

65. Caroline Walker Bynum, *Fragmentation and Redemption*, esp. chs 6 and 3.

66. Sahi, *Child*, p. 114.

67. See R. C. Zaehner (ed.), *Hindu Scriptures*, pp. 48–50.

68. Sahi, *Child*, p. 38. But see Bynum, *Fragmentation and Redemption*, pp. 139–42, 186–8; and on the religious significance of food and its lack of consumption, see Rudolph Bell (and the epilogue by William N. Davis), *Holy Anorexia*, esp. pp. 1–21, 180–90 (by Davis).

69. See his own comments on this: 'all concepts of this child god flow in and out of each other' (*Child*, p. 3).

70. R. Tagore, from the collection, *The Crescent Moon*, entitled 'The Beginning', *Collected Poems*.

5. *Postscript: A never-ending vigilance*

1. Julia Kristeva, *In the Beginning Was Love: Psychoanalysis and Faith*, p. 43.

2. From 'Not Waving but Drowning', *Poetry 1900 to 1965*, George MacBeth (ed.), p. 216.

3. DZ 3807.

4. See Tina Beattie, *God's Mother, Eve's Advocate*, for a searching Marian development providing women's genealogies: both in relation to Anne and her daughter, Mary, and Mary and her forebear, Eve. See also Elizabeth Stuart, *Spitting at Dragons*, who reinterprets women saints to recover the genealogical relations within the symbolic tradition.

5. DZ 3808.

6. St Thomas, *Comm. in Ep. ad Eph.*, Cap. 1, lect. 8. DZ 3809, my emphasis.

7. Paul Molinari, *Saints: Their Place in the Church*, pp. 57–8.

8. See Aquinas, *Summa Theologia*, 1a. 40, esp. art. 2.

9. Interestingly John Milbank makes this precise *theoretical* point: that Christology is always ecclesiology, and that Jesus' person 'can only be finally specified as the entire content and process of every human life, in so far as it *is* genuinely human life, according to the formal specifications of the gospel narratives and metaphors. If Christ is the total "context" for our lives, then he is both already and not yet' (*Word Made Strange*, p. 156). However, Milbank fails to name this as the doctrine of saints.

10. Molinari, *Saints*, pp. 64–5, my emphasis added.

11. Molinari, *Saints*, p. 70, my emphasis added.

12. Especially in regard to saints, see Stuart, *Splitting at Dragons*, pp. 11–28, Elizabeth A. Johnson, *Friends*, pp. 141–62.

13. Molinari, *Saints*, p. 73.

14. See Kenneth L. Woodward, *Making Saints: How the Catholic Church Determines Who Becomes a Saint, Who Doesn't, and Why?*, who gives a very accessible and critically interesting account of the process. The standard work for the history of canonization is Eric Waldron Kemp, *Canonization and Authority in the Western Church*.

15. See Susan A. Ross's close reading of pre-Vatican II marriage manuals for the interrelation between marriage symbolics, the church and the role of the male Christ: 'The Bride of Christ and the Body Politic: Body and Gender in Pre-Vatican II Marriage Theology'. I have critically examined various feminist writers on sacraments in 'Church and Sacraments', *Blackwell Companion to Theology*, Gareth Jones (ed.).

16. The process has been temporarily reversed in the questionable standard of argumentation, biblical and symbolic, presented in the CDF's *Declaration on the Admission of Women to the Priesthood* (1976), whereby certain images of the church are essentialized and given rigid ontological status.

17. Kristeva, *Beginning*, p. 39.

18. Irigaray, *Sexes*, p. 62.

19. Irigaray, *Sexes*, p. 62; even if she sees this as a provisional strategy in typically Freudian manner: 'No human subjectivity, no human society has ever been established without the help of the divine. There comes a time for

destruction. But, before destruction is possible, God or the gods must exist'
(p. 62).

20. 'Rublev', quoted with kind permission from Rt Revd Rowan Williams,
After Silent Centuries, p. 33.

Index

An 'n' after the page number indicates that the entry is to be found in the notes at the end of the book.

Scripture references